Exploring Grammar in Context

*upper-intermediate
and advanced*

Ronald Carter, Rebecca Hughes
and Michael McCarthy

CAMBRIDGE
UNIVERSITY PRESS

PUBLISHED BY THE PRESS SYNDICATE OF THE UNIVERSITY OF CAMBRIDGE
The Pitt Building, Trumpington Street, Cambridge, United Kingdom

CAMBRIDGE UNIVERSITY PRESS
The Edinburgh Building, Cambridge CB2 2RU, UK   www.cup.cam.ac.uk
40 West 20th Street, New York, NY 10011–4211, USA   www.cup.org
10 Stamford Road, Oakleigh, Melbourne 3166, Australia
Ruiz de Alarcón 13, 28014 Madrid, Spain

First published 2000

Printed in the United Kingdom at the University Press, Cambridge

Typeface Garamond 10.5/13pt   *System QuarkXPress (Apple Macintosh)*

A catalogue record for this book is available from the British Library

ISBN 0 521 568447 paperback

Contents

Acknowledgements

This book has had quite a long genesis, and many people deserve thanks for its publication. We thank Jeanne McCarten of CUP, who originally commissioned the book, Alison Sharpe, who saw it through to completion and encouraged us when spirits flagged, Jane Cordell and Barbara Thomas, whose editorial advice has been invaluable, and all at CUP who have contributed to its design, production and marketing. We also thank Colin Hayes, Jean Hudson and Patrick Gillard of CUP who have made it possible for us to access the spoken and written corpora that are the bedrock of the book, and for providing the resources and technical support such an enterprise requires.

Amongst our colleagues and academic friends, Margaret Berry, Almut Koester, John McRae, Norbert Schmitt and Anoma Siriwardena have always lent a sympathetic ear to our puzzlings over discourse grammar, and have offered examples and the benefit of their own experience as grammar teachers in our department. Particular thanks also to our teaching colleagues at the Centre for English Language Education (CELE), University of Nottingham, and the various cohorts of students who have used and helped us with the materials during their development – especial thanks to the 1996 group of Monbusho-sponsored Japanese teachers for their patient and helpful feedback. Others who have contributed indirectly include Mike Baynham, Doug Biber, David Bowen, Joan Cutting, Bill Dunn, Tony Fitzpatrick, Julia Harrison, San San Hnin Tun, Jim Lantolf, Aaron Lawson, Tessa Moore, David Nunan, John Sinclair, Diana Slade, Jeff Stranks, John Swales, Hongyin Tao, Scott Thornbury, Geoff Tranter, and Linda Waugh.

Thanks must also go to the reviewers and piloters who worked with earlier drafts of the material and whose advice has been extremely valuable. Especial thanks go to Keith Mitchell, of Edinburgh University, whose patient work on the manuscript has improved the grammatical statements immeasurably. There are few better or more perceptive grammarians in Great Britain. Whatever faults remain in the book are, of course, entirely our own responsibility.

The author and publishers are grateful to the following copyright holders for permission to reproduce copyright material. While every endeavour has been made, it has not been possible to identify the sources of all material used and in such cases the publishers would welcome information from copyright sources. Apologies are expressed for any omissions.

p. 7: *Treoir Journal* for 'A World Stage for Bru Boru'; pp. 17, 24, 36, 42, 73, 84, 90, 104, 133, 140: Randy Glasbergen for cartoon illustrations, © Randy Glasbergen. Reprinted with special permission from www.glasbergen.com; p. 27: *The Observer* for 'New head set to take charge'; p. 94: Erin Pizzey for extracts from *For the Love of a Stranger*; p. 108: Rand McNally for extracts from *The World: Afghanistan to Zimbabwe*; p. 116: Extract from *Big Two-Hearted River* © Hemingway Foreign Rights Trust; p. 119: *Australian Cosmopolitan* 1993 for Fact File on Arnold Schwarzenegger; p. 128 *International Herald Tribune* for the article 'A Doctor at 17...'; p. 167: Advertisement from *The Independent* © Vauxhall Motors; p. 177: Subaru advertisement text provided with the permission of Subaru (UK) Limited.

Many thanks also to the following teachers, students and institutions from all over the world who reviewed and pilot tested material from *Exploring Grammar in Context*:

Margaret Bell, UK; Sarah Fitt, APU, UK; Dr Susan H. Foster-Cohen, Wendy Gibbons, APU, UK; The British Institute in Paris, France; John Palfrey, Edinburgh; Paul Roberts, UK; Anila Scott-Monkhouse, Parma, Italy; Elzbieta Sielanko, Poland; Jesus Romero Trillo, Universidad Autonoma, Madrid, Spain; Elizabeth Wall, Buenos Aires, Argentina.

To the student

Exploring Grammar in Context (upper-intermediate and advanced) is designed for self-study use by a student working alone or for class use with a teacher.

This book:

- distinguishes, where relevant, between written and spoken English.
- uses real spoken and written texts, wherever it is instructive to do so. Many of the examples used are drawn from the 100 million word Cambridge International Corpus. A corpus is a collection of authentic examples of language stored in very powerful computers and used to exemplify the language as it is actually spoken and written.
- offers grammatical description and texts at upper-intermediate to advanced level, assuming as a starting point at least an intermediate level of knowledge. Some features of grammar will already be known but will be explored in greater depth.
- has a full **Answer key**, and explanations in the **Observations** sections.
- has **Reference notes** giving you further detailed information and real examples of the most important features of English grammar.
- emphasises the element of **choice** in grammar as well as **rules** for correct structures. For example there is an emphasis in many places on learning how to choose the appropriate grammar according to how informal or formal a context is.
- gives you opportunities to work out rules for yourself and to work out what is the most probable choice in particular contexts. This is called inductive learning.
- gives you opportunities to do further work by encouraging greater language awareness and by developing the ability to observe closely language form and language in use.

To the teacher

What does this book do?

Exploring Grammar in Context (upper-intermediate and advanced) does two things. It focuses on core areas of grammar, such as tenses and articles and gives the learner the opportunity to work in depth with these topics through a series of exercises. Secondly, it offers detailed Reference notes which give authentic examples of a wide range of uses of the core features.

What is grammar in context?

Exploring Grammar in Context is a guide to some key features of English grammar. *Exploring Grammar in Context* is different from traditional grammar books because many of the examples are taken from real contexts of grammar in use. These authentic examples show speakers and writers using the language to communicate in a wide variety of contexts.

Like most grammar books, which often illustrate grammatical forms by means of single sentences, several of the examples in this book involve single sentences. But in this book the emphasis on grammar **in context** means that the examples also frequently contain several sentences or short conversational extracts and show grammar at work across the boundaries of the sentence or the individual speaking turn. The book regularly draws attention to **grammar as choice** and gives the learner opportunities to exercise grammatical choice in relation to particular contexts in which the language is used.

What is a grammar of choice?

Exploring Grammar in Context makes a distinction between **grammar as structure** and **grammar as choice. Grammar as structure** means: what rules does the learner need to know in order to use this form effectively? An example of a structural rule would be, for example, that in ellipsis a modal verb normally attracts the repeated verb *have*, as in:

A: Has she taken it with her?
B: She <u>may have</u>, I'm not sure.

In such a case as this, **grammar as choice** means: when is it normal to use ellipsis? Are some forms of ellipsis more likely to be used in spoken than in written modes? Are the forms linked to greater or lesser degrees of intimacy and informality? For example subject ellipsis in expressions such as 'Looking forward to seeing you', 'Don't know' and 'Think so' is largely the speaker's/writer's choice.

In this book both **grammar as structure** *and* **grammar as choice** will be treated. But the grammar of choice will be as important as the grammar of structure.

What do we mean by corpus?

Many of the examples in the book are taken from a multi-million word computerised corpus of spoken and written English called the Cambridge International Corpus (CIC). This corpus has been put together over many years and is based on real examples of everyday English, written and spoken. At the time of writing the corpus contained over 100 million words of English.

A unique feature of CIC is a special corpus of spoken English – the CANCODE corpus. CANCODE stands for Cambridge and Nottingham Corpus of Discourse in English and is a unique collection of five million words of naturally-occurring, mainly British, spoken English, recorded in everyday situations. The CANCODE corpus has been collected throughout the past six years in a project involving Cambridge University Press and the Department of English Studies at the University of Nottingham. The CANCODE corpus is part of CIC. Dialogues and spoken examples are laid out as they actually occur in CANCODE recordings. Except where there may be misunderstandings, interruptions, overlaps, pauses and hesitations are indicated.

The existence of a spoken corpus means that several of the examples in this book can enable us to describe differences between spoken and written grammar and to highlight differences between grammar in informal and formal contexts of use. The CIC corpus contains a wide variety of different texts. Examples in this book are therefore drawn from contexts as varied as: newspapers, popular journalism, advertising, letters, literary texts, debates and discussions, service encounters, formal speeches and friends talking in a restaurant.

Corpus examples also help with illustrations of authentic everyday vocabulary in use. Less common words are explained in special footnotes.

What is an inductive approach to learning grammar?

Exploring Grammar in Context encourages an inductive approach to grammatical rules and principles, rather than relying exclusively on the presentation–practice–production approach of many traditional grammar books.

Grammatical rules can sometimes be best explained by means of a single sentence and a rule which can then be applied to other examples. Sometimes it is helpful to learners for the sentence to be invented or for the authentic language to be modified in order to illustrate the rule. This practice is found in *Exploring Grammar in Context*. However, the main focus in the book is on helping learners to work out grammatical rules for themselves. This inductive approach to learning grammar often involves providing lots of examples so that patterns of usage can be seen. Of course, within such patterns certain forms are either right or wrong and rules have to be learned. However, the examples can also show that some forms are more probably used in one context rather than another, or that there are choices which depend on whether you are writing or speaking or whether you want to sound more or less formal. *Exploring Grammar in Context* helps learners of English to make their own choices and to understand what those choices mean.

The approach in the book therefore helps learners to learn more inductively, to notice more and to be more aware of the uses of language. It fosters learner autonomy, encouraging learners to be more independent and to develop some of the skills they need beyond the classroom when they work on their own and when the teacher isn't present. An upper-intermediate level of English is assumed throughout.

Are there new types of tasks for inductive learning and for a grammar of choice?

In *Exploring Grammar in Context* teachers and students will find a variety of traditional exercise types (for example: gap-filling, rewriting, cloze, multiple choice) alongside tasks and activities which involve problem-solving, observation, awareness-raising and more inductive and text-manipulating activities. In general, tasks and exercises are chosen to suit the activity, though in those parts of the book which are particularly concerned with a grammar of choice there is more emphasis on awareness-raising and on helping learners notice and to work out what the choices help them to express.

Towards a discourse grammar of English

This book combines traditional and innovative approaches to English grammar. It is traditional in its attention to correct forms and structures and innovative in its attention to appropriate choices and to the illustration of such choices through a wide variety of different texts.

However, several grammars make use of texts for illustration. What is different about *Exploring Grammar in Context*? In this book the idea is not to take a text and then extract atomised, grammatical points from it. Rather, the texts in *Exploring Grammar in Context* serve a steady, inductive unfolding of core grammatical features in use. The place, distribution and sequencing of the grammatical feature in its text is as important as its actual occurrence. This book is innovative, therefore, in bringing in insights from the fields of text and discourse analysis, rather than merely using texts for exemplification. Where appropriate, and by no means throughout the whole book, our emphasis is on the relationship between formal choice and contextual factors. In parts the book represents a first step towards a context-based or 'discourse' grammar of English.

In what ways is this book an advanced grammar?

Exploring Grammar in Context is not a survey of all the more advanced or problematic uses of English. Even in a book of this length it is not possible to cover all the aspects of advanced uses of grammar. The focus in the book is on core grammatical features. Sometimes this means that learners will meet uses of grammar with which they are unfamiliar; sometimes it means that they will revisit familiar ground.

The features covered in the 25 units are all core in that they are particularly sensitive to spoken and written contexts and because they can exhibit differences between speech and writing and between formal and informal usage. They are core because such sensitivity to context is especially apparent when real examples are explored in texts which go beyond a single sentence or a single utterance.

Some topics in *Exploring Grammar in Context* such as articles and modals or noun phrases will have been studied already by most upper-intermediate learners. In addition to introducing new grammatical areas, this book encourages learners to go more deeply into a topic and to explore a wide range of uses and functions of particular points of grammar in extended texts. It helps learners to recycle material and to come to know it better. Looking at grammar in context gets us to look at familiar topics in new ways.

Introduction

The structure of the book

The book is divided into five parts.

Part A: Tenses in context

The units in this section cover a wide range of uses of core tenses in a variety of spoken and written contexts.

Part B: Modals in context

The units in this section cover a wide range of modal forms in a variety of different spoken and written contexts. The units also explore some forms which are not conventionally considered under the heading of modals.

Part C: Choosing structures in context

In this section a range of grammatical structures which contrast in use and function, are explored. The units explore the meanings and effects open to users when one structure rather than another is chosen.

Part D: Around the noun in context

In this section a further range of structures, some familiar and some less familiar, are examined with a focus on differences and contrasts in the ways they are used.

Part E: Exploring spoken grammar in context

The units in this section explore aspects of grammar which are likely to be found in contexts of naturally-occurring speech. The emphasis is on raising awareness as much as it is on practising and using forms. Some learners may choose not to, or not have an opportunity to use some of the forms of spoken grammar which are explored but it is important that the effects and functions of the choices are understood.

Organisation of the units

Each unit of the book is designed with the following main structure:

A Introduction

One or two exercises based, where possible, on examples which are designed to orient you to the unit as a whole. Some exercises are more information-based and some are more task-based. The examples generally contain authentic data. For some students the material may be new; for others the material will provide opportunities for revision.

B Discovering patterns of use

The topics and tasks in this section look at typical patterns of grammar in context. An **Observations** section helps you to understand rules and exceptions, ordering of elements and similar features which relate to the examples.

C Grammar in action

This contains topics and tasks which are more based on data and which explore more fully grammar patterns in use and in context. Attention is also given to idiomatic patterns and uses in everyday language. Where appropriate, a further **Observations** section, which focuses on speaker/writer choices, is included.

D Follow-up

This consists of tasks which are more open-ended, some of which may involve mini-projects, exploring further data for more extensive study in class or outside the classroom or alone. The section ends with a **Summary** which draws together the main points of the whole unit.

Further exercises

At the end of each unit there are further exercises which give more extensive practice in using or showing awareness of the aspects of grammar covered in the unit. Answers to these exercises are given at the back of the book but wherever relevant, explanations are also given alongside answers.

Answer key

Answers to tasks and exercises in each section of the unit are given in the key in the back of the book. Some of the tasks are open-ended and do not have answers which are either correct or incorrect. The key therefore offers suggested answers in these cases. The **Observations** section of the book also gives fuller explanations, where appropriate. A key symbol (☞)indicates places where the answer key needs to be consulted. Where this is not used, the Observations section should be consulted.

Other features

Reference notes

Reference notes give further detail and examples for the topics covered in each unit. They have the following main purposes:

- to extend observations and descriptions made in the relevant unit.
- to offer further examples, where possible, from the CIC/CANCODE corpora.
- reference, that is, for reading in class or for self-study, or for referring to when you have a question about usage.

There are no accompanying exercises in the Reference notes section.

Glossary

A glossary provides guidance and definitions of grammatical terms which are likely to be less familiar to you.

Using the book

Exploring Grammar in Context can be used either in class or for self-study. The book is designed to be worked through from beginning to end but you may follow individual units in any order. Exercises can be done separately and answers and suggested answers checked at the back of the book. The reference notes can also be read and used independently, although they do assume knowledge of the topics covered in the individual unit to which they refer.

When working through each unit different routes are available:

- If the **Introduction** section is found to involve mainly revision, then it is possible to go straight to the **Grammar in action** section.
- It is also possible to work through **Discovering patterns of use** and then to go straight to the exercises; or to concentrate on the **Grammar in action** section before moving on to work through the **Reference notes.**
- **Follow-up** tasks are more likely to be carried out outside the classroom but the ground can be laid by doing the exercises in the unit first.
- The book is organised so that there is a steady progression from **Introduction** to **Discovering patterns of use** to **Grammar in action** to **Follow-up** to **Exercises** to **Reference notes.** But there is no pre-determined direction and you can **choose your own route** through the material.

About the authors

Ronald Carter is Professor of Modern English Language at the University of Nottingham. He has published extensively and internationally in the fields of educational, literary and applied linguistics.

Rebecca Hughes is Senior Lecturer, Deputy Director of the Centre for English Language Education and Vice-Dean of the Faculty of Arts at the University of Nottingham. She has published widely and presented internationally in the field of English language teaching and has researched extensively in the field of spoken and written English.

Michael McCarthy is Professor of Applied Linguistics at the University of Nottingham and is widely known internationally for his work on discourse analysis, vocabulary and English language teaching.

All three authors of *Exploring Grammar in Context (upper-intermediate and advanced)* share extensive experience of teaching English in schools, colleges and universities at all levels and in many different parts of the world.

Tenses in context

A Introduction

1 These two news stories use **different tenses**. Text (a) uses present perfect (e.g. *have spoken, have looked*); text (b) uses mostly past simple (e.g. *spoke, looked*). The important verbs are marked in bold.

■ Why do you think the tenses are different in the two texts?

a)
> Unemployed Terry Fitton **has applied** for an amazing 2,350 jobs … and he's still out of work. Terry, 50, **has posted** applications at the rate of nearly four a day for the past two years.

b)
> Superstar Paul McCartney last night **watched** a heart-stopping sea search for his 15-year-old son James. The ex-Beatle and his wife Linda **stood** ashen-faced on a beach after the youngster **was** swept out of sight while surfing. But thirty minutes later they were joyfully hugging James as he **stepped** unharmed from the waves.

Observations

● Text (a) has a time phrase: *for the past two years*, which sets the time as time coming up to now. Text (b) has the time phrase *last night*, which sets the time as time finished, separated from now. These can be shown as diagrams:

Time coming up to now:

has applied / has posted —→ NOW

Time finished, separated from now:

watched/ stood/ was/ stepped	NOW

2 Organise these phrases into three columns headed *used with past simple, used with present perfect* and *used with either.* ☞

up to now   in the last century   during President Kennedy's lifetime

over the last hundred years or so   for three months   three months ago

since three months ago   recently   this is the first time I   lately

throughout the 17th century   since the Vietnam War   today

within the last three months   after the Second World War

B Discovering patterns of use

1 Present perfect in spoken language

In these pieces of real spoken English, the tenses change.

- In (a), when Pat comments, the tense changes to present perfect and in (b), when Mary talks about finding the bottle-opener, she also changes tense. Why? ⊙━

a) [Roger is a guest at Pat's house. He is just finishing a personal ghost story, which he has told all in the **past simple** tense, which is normal for stories.]
Roger: It was definitely there, some figure there, definitely a figure there …
Pat: Well, as long as you haven't brought it down here with you. This is a friendly house, we don't have any ghosts here.

b) [Mary and Peter are in the kitchen. They are trying to open a bottle of wine.]
Mary: What have we done with the bottle-opener? We found one, didn't we?
Peter: Yeah.

- Below are some rules for the use of the present perfect and the past simple when *no* explicit time phrases are used. Tick which one you think sounds most useful, based on the ghost story and the woman in the kitchen. ⊙━

Possible rules:
i) Present perfect is for things that are very **recent**; past simple is for things that happened **a long time ago**.
ii) It doesn't matter which tense you choose when there is no time phrase. Both are always possible.
iii) Present perfect is used for things the speaker considers important in relation to **now**; past simple is used for things the speaker considers as **separated** in his/her mind from now.

2 Past simple and present perfect in news stories

If you read English language newspapers, it is useful to observe how the two tense-forms are used in news stories. Look at this newspaper story.

- What tense should the first sentence be in?
- Does it change for the same reasons as in the spoken extracts you have just studied?
- Does it make you want to add anything to the rule you chose for the use of the two tenses?

OUR ROADS THE SHAME OF EUROPE

Britain's motorways [**vote**] the second worst in Europe, according to a new survey. They are plagued by poor facilities, roadworks and bad signposting, say continental motorists.

Only Portugal's motorways were rated worse than ours. The survey, by rental giant Eurocar, put Germany way out in front, then France miles ahead of the rest – Belgium, Switzerland, Italy, Holland, Spain, Britain and Portugal.

Observations

- The examples we have looked at so far point to a difference between (a) things that we want to bring to the foreground and say 'This is new or important or relevant or connected in some way in my mind to **now**' and (b) things that we want to report/narrate or simply to say 'This is not important any more, or not relevant to **now**, or I have chosen to separate it **in my mind** from **now**'.

- Newspaper language is often distinctive. A typical pattern in a news story is for the opening sentence to be in the present perfect, and the details of the story to be in the past simple. In the text above, about roads, the verb in brackets was *have been voted*.

C Grammar in action

1 Deciding to use the present perfect

Look at these examples of spoken language.

- **Why do you think the speakers chose the particular tense of each verb in bold?** 🔑

a) [Clare and Sam are brother and sister.]
   Clare: I think I'**ve broken** Mum's hair-dryer.
   Sam: How?
   Clare: Don't know. It doesn't work any more.

b) [A teacher is talking about her class that day.]
   Teacher: I **had** a bit of a row today and I **practised** my shouting in the classroom and Liz reckons my lesson **went** really really well.

c) [Faye has a problem with her camera and Dave is helping her. The film is stuck; they discuss whether to take it out.]
   Faye: I can't take it out half way through and …
   Dave: Well, **have you started** it?

2 Switching between present perfect and past simple

■ **In this example, why do you think the speaker changes the tense? (The important verbs are in bold.) See 'Observations' below for answer.**

I've been going to the weightwatchers, but **I went** the first time and I'd lost three and a half pound, and I went last week and I'd lost half a pound, so I went down to the fish shop and got fish and chips, I was so disgusted.

■ **What do you think they said? Here are some mini-extracts from real conversations. See if you can guess which answer B gave in the original tape-recording.** ☞

(Remember this may not be a question of right or wrong answers, but what B might have been likely to say, given the context. The key tells you which one B did in fact say.)

a) A: I live in Exeter. D'you know it?
   Did B say:
       Yes, I was there. I've stayed there a couple of days.
   or: Yes, I've been there. I stayed there a couple of days.
   or: some other combination of the two tenses? If so, write what you think it was.

b) A: I've been to Barcelona for a few conferences, I don't know if you've ever been?
   Did B say:
       Yeah, I went to one, yeah.
   or: Yeah, I've gone to one, yeah.
   or: Yeah, I've been to one, yeah.

c) A: We make our own pasta.
   Did B say:
       Yeah, we did that, we started off using recipes, and then we soon discovered it was easier to make it our own way.
   or: Yeah, we've done that, we've started off using recipes, and then we've soon discovered it's been easier to make it our own way.
   or: Yeah, we've done that, we started off using recipes, and then we soon discovered it was easier to make it our own way.

Observations

● Speakers use present perfect to indicate that a topic is still happening, or is still relevant within the conversation:
   'I've been going to the weightwatchers.' (She is still going every week.)
● Speakers use past simple to indicate that an event is completed. For example, the woman who went to weightwatchers changed to the past simple to talk about the separate past events which depressed her.

D Follow-up

- If you can buy an English language newspaper or if you can get English language news on radio or TV, make a note of how news stories are reported. Do the reports use present perfect at the beginning, followed by past tenses for the details, as we have seen in this unit, in the written and spoken news?
- If you want more practice exercises, do the Further exercises at the end of this unit.
- If you want further details of points relating to this unit, go to the Reference notes section on pages 185–7.

Summary

- Past simple is used by speakers to talk about past events which are, or which they regard as, finalised, or over and done with.
- Present perfect is used by speakers to talk about events which are still current, or which they want to highlight as being incomplete or still relevant.
- Do not use time expressions which suit completed events (e.g. *two months ago*) with the present perfect tense.
- Do not use time expressions which suit current events (e.g. *lately*) with the simple past tense.
- Some time expressions (e.g. *today, this morning*) can be used with either tense depending on the attitude of the speaker:

  'I've seen him this morning.' (The morning is not finished, and the speaker saw him at some point in it. Note that you could not say 'I've seen him this morning' in the afternoon or evening, and be correct.)

  'I saw him this morning.' (If the morning is not yet finished, then the speaker is looking back at an earlier part of the morning as if it is completely separate from the time of speaking, for example, before coming to work.)

Further exercises ☞

1 Match each question on the left with a suitable answer from the right.

Have you ever* been to Moscow?	I studied there, actually.
How long have you been at college?	I've studied a lot.
What did you do in Oxford last year?	I've been there three weeks.
How many weeks were you in Paris?	I've studied there, actually.
What have you done at college?	I was there three weeks.

---

* *Ever* is similar in meaning to 'up to now'.

2 Somewhere in these texts, the tense changed from present perfect to past simple. Where?

- Put the verbs in brackets in the tense you think the writer used.

a)

SAM DIES AT 109

The oldest man in Britain [**die**] aged 109 – six weeks after taking the title. Sam Crabbe, from Cadgwith, Cornwall, [**not give up**] smoking until he was 98 and [**enjoy**] a nightly tot* of whisky. He [**be**] taken ill just hours before his death.

b)

A WORLD STAGE FOR BRU BORU
(an Irish music/dance group)

The Bru Boru group [**return**] from a most successful engagement at Expo '92 in Seville. They [**be**] there at the invitation of the Irish Government. In addition to performing at the many Irish events at Expo, they also [**give**] an unprecedented performance at the American Pavilion.

3 Now imagine how you might report a news event you have just heard on the radio to a friend who hasn't heard it. If you are in class, do this with a partner. Here are some events to help you. What tenses will you use?

You begin: 'Have you heard? …'

a) Woman in Madrid wins five million dollars in lottery. Only buys one ticket. Loses ticket. Finds it in rubbish bin. Claims prize.
b) President has heart attack. Collapses during a debate in Parliament. Rushed to hospital.
c) Canadian woman becomes first person to cross the Pacific Ocean solo on a raft. Only one small sail. Built it herself. Journey six months.

4 Choose between the present perfect and past simple tenses for the verbs in brackets. If you think both are equally possible, write both forms.

a) Nowadays I take a vitamin C tablet every day. I [**do**] so ever since a friend [**tell**] me it was good for you.
b) I [**buy**] a computer with a DVD/drive. You must come round and have a go on it. It [**teach**] me a lot in the few weeks I [**have**] it.
c) I [**buy**] a personal stereo but I [**sell**] it to my teenage daughter as it [**look**] silly on me at my age.
d) The other night I [**hear**] a noise coming from the garden. I [**not hear**] anything since, but it [**worry**] me at the time. There [**be**] a few burglaries round here lately.
e) I [**notice**] I was having trouble reading small print so I [**go**] to the optician's and I [**have**] my eyes tested. She [**say**] I need reading glasses. I know my eyes [**get**] worse. I think it's working with computers that [**cause**] it. I wish I didn't have to use them so much.
f) He always manages to look so neat, doesn't he, as if he [**just come**] from his tailor's.

*A *tot* is a small amount.

5 Complete these sentences in any way you like, taking care to choose appropriately between the present perfect and past simple tenses.

a) Ever since I was a child I …
b) Lately the weather …
c) During the 1980s, the economy in my country …
d) A: Do you still have your school books from when you were a kid?
   B: No, my parents …
e) Over the last six months I …
f) This is the first time I …

6 What do you think the speaker would be most likely to say in these mini-conversations? Choose the most likely tense for the verb in brackets. If you think past simple and present perfect are both equally possible, write both forms.

a) A: A letter, for me?
   B: Yes.
   [A opens letter.]
   A: Oh! I [**win**] two tickets for the U2 concert in London next month!

b) A: Where's that thing you used to have for slicing tomatoes?
   B: Oh, that stupid thing. I [**throw**] it away. It was useless. I've got a new one now.

c) A: Isn't she married to a Scandinavian or something?
   B: Yes, she [**marry**] to a Swede, but she's married to a New Zealander now.

d) A: Who [**write**] *A Tale of Two Cities*?
   B: Charles Dickens, I think.

e) A: Who [**eat**] my sandwich?
   B: Oh, I'm sorry. I thought you didn't want it.

f) A: I see they [**dig**] another hole in the road. I wonder what the problem is?
   B: Where? Oh yes, I see it. No, no idea.

g) A: Who [**be**] the first to get to the top of Everest, Hillary or Tensing?
   B: Don't know.

A Introduction

1 **In this extract, a woman describes being invited into the pilot's cabin on an aeroplane she was travelling on:**

> The pilot said, 'You can go in the cabin,' you see. Well, my mouth dropped open … you see … Oh, I'd had a joke with one of the girls, you know, the stewardess girls, and, maybe it was her. Or there was a young man with us who had been in our hotel, maybe he'd said something. Somebody had, anyway. So they took me right into where the two pilots were. It was absolutely fantastic.

- How did the woman react when the pilot told her she could visit the cabin?
- The woman says 'Somebody had, anyway'. Can you expand her sentence to help you explain the story?
- Underline the verbs which are in the past simple tense.
- Use a different colour to underline the verbs which are in the past perfect tense.
- Which tense is used to try to explain why she was invited to see the pilots' cabin? ⊙━

2 **In the following extract another woman describes an accident in her car, when she hit a tramp.**

- Work out which tense the woman used for the verbs which are in brackets. They are either in the past simple or the past perfect. (Although other tenses might be **possible**, we are interested in what the speaker actually used.) ⊙━

> Woman: I wasn't going very fast, you see, I (only just) [**turn**] the corner … and there [**be**] a bit of a line of traffic, and then …
> Friend: So it was a bit of a miracle he wasn't hurt, wasn't it?
> Woman: Apparently, it [**be**] his party-piece*, because the police told me that he [**do**] it very often, this, 'cos it [**get**] him a bed for the night, you know, it got him in hospital. And they were getting a bit fed up. He already [**have**] them there that morning apparently, saying someone [**put**] a bomb under his bed. But then he picked on me, and it got him a bed for the night in hospital.
> Friend: Good grief!

---

*The expression *party-piece* means that the tramp regularly did this in order to gain attention.

- You have probably learned that the past perfect tense is used in English to describe events which happened before other events in the past (i.e. that it is primarily to do with time and sequences of events). This is a fundamental part of learning about the past perfect. However, in this unit you can learn about how speakers use the past perfect, and the typical clause patterns it is found in.

B Discovering patterns of use

1 Past perfect and explanations

In the extract where the woman describes her visit to the pilots' cabin, we saw that she used the past perfect tense quite a lot when trying to explain something.

Main events of the story	Possible cause of main events	Tense
The pilot said, 'You can ...'		past simple
my mouth dropped open		past simple
	I'd had a joke with one of ... the stewardess girls ...	past perfect
	young man ... maybe he'd said something.	past perfect
	Somebody had (said something)	past perfect
So, they took me right into (the cabin)		past simple

- Add any rules which you can think of for the uses of the past perfect tense.

i) Past perfect is used to describe events which happened before other events in the past.

ii) ...

iii) ...

2 Past perfect and clause construction

- If you wanted to join the following sentences together, which conjunctions would you use? ☞

but   because   when   as

a) I wasn't going very fast. I had only just turned the corner.
b) John came round on Sunday. He only stayed about ten minutes.
c) John came round on Sunday. I had promised to lend him a video.
d) I was out celebrating last night. I'd had my exam results.

- The past perfect tense is used to describe events which happened before other events in the past.
- Because the past perfect describes events which happened before other events, it is very useful for giving clear **explanations**, or the **background** to a past situation.
- When a main clause is a past event, and a subordinate clause is the explanation of the past event, the following tense pattern is often seen:
    main clause – past simple tense
    subordinate clause – past perfect tense
- Note that the past perfect will never be found in conjunction with any present tenses, for example in the same sentence, or even the same paragraph.

- Sometimes, especially in written English, the past perfect is used with more of an emphasis on the timing of events than on explanation or giving background events:

    'Ancient woodland once covered Britain, but by 1100 AD most of it **had been cleared** to make farmland.'

    In these cases, past perfect can be regarded as an equivalent to the present perfect tense but in the context of past events. Such use is usually marked by a time adverbial phrase, such as *by 1100 AD*. Again, the context is frequently that of background information which is introducing a main idea.

c Grammar in action

Further contexts for the past perfect

The past perfect is frequently used to give explanations of why past events happened. We can think of the past perfect as giving useful background information to events in the past.

Because of this, there are three important ways in which the past perfect is often used:

i)   In a clause after a verb reporting speech or thought, e.g. 'She said that she hadn't seen him.' (See also Unit 20)
ii) In a relative clause to give more background information about a noun, e.g. '... the house, which had been sold three times in five years, was now worth £200,000.'
iii) In a clause giving details of background information to a past event. These clauses often begin with a conjunction or adverbial phrase of time (Note: this is more common in writing than in speech), e.g. 'When they had finished eating, they cleared the table and played cards'.

- **Underline the examples of the past perfect in the following extracts.**
- **Decide which type of context the tense appears in, and mark the example (i), (ii) or (iii).** ⚷

a) [This is part of a newspaper article about brewing beer.]

> We never thought we'd be 'home brew' experts, but now we're really hooked. It all started when we moved house two years ago. Alan's father had put six great big brewing jars up in our attic, and we had forgotten all about them. We didn't like to throw them out, so we put them to good use immediately.

b) [Mary and Sally are discussing how they went home after a shopping trip.]

Mary: Oh I thought it was later. Oh, of course, you arrived about three, didn't you?

Sally: Mm. Oh yeah, we were … mm …

Mary: I thought I'd missed you. I thought, what's the betting we each go home in a taxi!

c) [In this conversation two people are discussing an outdoor concert.]

John: The best bit, they made a stage built up with scaffolding and things like that.

Peter: Very stylish.

John: And all the little tents round this little field … some bits were bits of ruins they'd added onto. And there was a beer tent and a very posh restaurant tent … there's something for everybody.

D Follow-up

■ Next time you read a book or magazine, look for the past perfect tense. Underline the places in the text where it is used. Is the context an explanation? Is the sentence giving background information about a main topic?

■ If you want more practice do the Further exercises at the end of this unit.

■ If you want further details of points relating to this unit, go to the Reference notes section on pages 188–9.

Summary

● The past perfect tense is used to give explanations about why past events happened in the context of a *because*-type clause.

● The past perfect tense is used to give background information including:
  — after a reporting/thought verb in a relative clause
  — after a noun in order to give information about a subject
  — in a main clause (often with an adverbial time phrase, e.g. *Last winter*)

● It is rare for past perfect to be the only tense in a prolonged section of discourse.

● The past perfect is never used close to any present tense forms.

Further exercises ⚬—

1 Look at the following examples of people using the past perfect tense.

- ▪ Find where the speakers use the past perfect. Do they fit the patterns you have learned?

a) [Speaker A is talking about rolling down a hill in big tractor tyres when he was a child, and one kid being injured.]

'…and this kid. I remember, he got into a big tyre and he, it went down, you must remember it it was a terrible, he just fell over on the side and the iron rings crushed his head and he went, he was taken away. I remember he was taken away, he was never, we were never told he was killed but I found out afterwards, John told me he'd actually died from his injuries you know.'

b) [Speaker B is talking about a power cut in London, and its effects on traders.]

'Well I mean the one chap in Covent Garden who I bought the fountain pen off erm, he was saying that he'd had a terrible day that it'd been so quiet all day.'

2 Decide which tense to put the verbs into in the following stories.

a) There was this guy who [**go**] to work on the South Coast and when he first [**arrive**] he [**stay**] in this hotel that [**be**] badly built and one day he [**turn**] on the tap and there was this terrible noise … he thought he [**start**] an earthquake.

b) Well, I got on better with David really. Last time we [**stay**] in London we [**share**] a flat, because Ben [**go**] to America.

3 Practise using the past perfect in the three ways defined.

a) Using the past perfect after reporting/thought verbs:

- ▪ Change the following examples using the verb indicated in the same way as the example. Imagine that the context is written English, not informal conversation.

Example:
'Mr Jones arranged a mortgage for me.'
He said Mr Jones had arranged a mortgage for him.

i) 'I don't believe that the tax loops* have been closed.'
She didn't believe ....

ii) 'They hired investigators to find the information.'
He claimed ....

iii) 'The design for the building was inspired by rock formations.'
She revealed ....

iv) 'The pay settlement was linked to the previous two years' productivity.'
It emerged ....

Tax loops are opportunities to avoid paying tax where the law is not completely clear and can be interpreted in different ways.

b) **Using the past perfect when adding to nouns:**

■ **Join the two pieces of information as in this example. Put the information from the second sentence into a relative clause following a noun.**

Example:
He returned to the lovely island. He lived there in the early 60s.
He returned to the lovely island where he had lived in the early 60s.

i)   The baby became ill again. The baby was ill from birth.
The baby, ..., became ill again.

ii) There were two accidents on the same corner. The accidents were not reported.
Two accidents, ..., were on the same corner.

iii) The tennis champion gave an interview. The tennis champion won three tournaments in successive years.
The tennis champion, ..., gave an interview.

iv) She bought a cheap house in the village. The village was divided by a motorway.
She bought a cheap house in the village, ...

c) **Using the past perfect in a background clause:**

■ **Join the two pieces of information as in the example. Put the background information into a subordinate clause, or a clause marked with an adverb of time.**

Example:
The bomb disposal team made the shop safe. The staff returned to work on Friday. (use *when* or *by Friday*)
The staff returned to work on Friday, when the bomb disposal team had made the shop safe.
or *By Friday*, the bomb disposal team had made the shop safe. The staff returned to work.

i)   I phoned you on Saturday. You were already out shopping. (one sentence; use *when* at the start of the sentence and *go* in your answer)
....

ii) The central defender was sent off towards the end of the match. He was previously given a yellow card. (two sentences; use *earlier*)
....

iii) The boy was questioned by police. Then he went home. (one sentence; use *after*)
....

iv) The restaurant was closed by the health inspectors. Health inspectors visited it. The restaurant was breaking food regulations. (two sentences; use *last week*)
....

A Introduction

Look at the extract below.

■ Where do you think this extract is from? (e.g. a book, newspaper, magazine, real people speaking)
■ Decide what tense is best for each of the verbs in brackets. In some cases, either tense is possible. Try to guess what was in the original. ☞

a)
> Nowadays people [**use / are using**] the Internet to do their shopping and banking. Roger Hawkins of Auctions On-line [**says / is saying**]. 'We [**find / are finding**] more and more people taking part each month. Some even [**enter / are entering**] their cars or houses at auction and [**sell / are selling**] them.'

b)
> I think it [**makes / is making**] me realise how much of the time that I spend with my family is spent doing, you know, chores where I [**don't have / 'm not having**] quality time with another person ... I [**do / 'm doing**] the washing, and I [**do / 'm doing**] the cooking, I [**tidy / 'm tidying**] up.

Observations

● You have probably learned that the present continuous is used for incomplete actions which are happening at the time of speaking. In this unit you can learn more about the choices which speakers and writers make, particularly between the simple and continuous present tenses.

● Although the present simple would be grammatically possible in the last three cases in **A(b)**, the speaker does not want to emphasise the fact that the actions are repeated, but that they cause a problem when they are occurring:

> 'I'm not having quality time with another person ... I'm doing the washing, and I'm doing the cooking, I'm tidying up.'

Compare:

> 'I don't have quality time with another person ... I do the washing, and I do the cooking. I tidy up.'

This second version sounds rather strange, as if doing these tasks affects your whole life, rather than the context of the situation she is describing.

B Discovering patterns of use

1 Talking about current events: present simple or continuous

Look at the following extracts. Some contain places where the tense has been changed from the original.

- Find the uses of the present simple or the present continuous and decide whether it has been changed.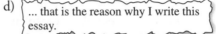

a) There's a lot of people ... who are earning a lot of money and they still think they aren't earning enough.

b) The raw material is becoming more refined at each stage of the process, until, finally, you have the white sugar you put in your tea or coffee.

c) Usually, I am driving to work.

d) ... that is the reason why I write this essay.

Observations

- The present continuous is used to talk about **current** events or states, often those which are in the process of happening at the time of writing or speaking, and may be unfinished.
- When a fact is presented as universal, rather than related to the current state of the world, the present simple tense is chosen:

  'People try to sell their cars for a profit, but generally this is not possible.' (always true)

  'People are trying to sell their cars for a profit these days.' (true at the moment)

- In section **A** the aim in **(a)** is to inform the reader about what is true now, rather than what is true in general. Equally, in **A(b)** although the tasks the woman talks about are habitual, she wants to focus on the activities as the cause of her problem (not having *quality time* with another person), and to put them into this limited context.
- Some verbs, for example *say*, are used in particular ways with the present continuous. These are discussed in more detail in **C2**.

2 Present continuous in conditional clauses

Look at the following extracts.

- Underline the examples of the present continuous.
- Decide whether they could be replaced with the present simple.

a) [This is part of a newspaper article about exercise.]

> If you feel tired, breathless or unable to hold a conversation, you are going too fast ... Take your pulse after 10 minutes, using a watch with a second hand. If your heart is beating beyond the high end of your aerobic rate, you are exercising too hard.

b) [A woman is talking about her relationship with her husband.]

If he's cooking for example a roast meal, or any kind of meal, curry or whatever, I can sometimes sort of do the typical, you know, wife bit of going in the kitchen and saying, 'Oh I'll take over.' You know, 'I can do this better than you,' and he quite rightly says, 'Shove off!*'

GLASBERGEN

"I'm learning how to relax, doctor – but I want to relax better and faster! I WANT TO BE ON THE CUTTING EDGE OF RELAXATION!"

Observations

- If you use the present continuous in a **conditional** sentence, you change the meaning so that it applies to a specific and limited context introduced in the *if* clause.
- Compare the examples above with a conditional sentence using the present simple:
  'If you walk quickly, your heartbeat increases.' and:
  'If he cooks, I always wash up.'
  The meaning here is general and universal, rather like 'If you heat metal, it expands'.
- Note also that the continuous form can only be used in this way if the context is specified first:
  'If you feel tired' (limiting context/situation) 'you are going too fast'
  (you go too fast (**x**))
  'Take your pulse' (limiting context/situation). 'If your heart is beating (beats (**x**))
  beyond the high end of your aerobic rate, you are exercising (exercise (**x**)) too hard.'
  See also Unit 11.

C Grammar in action

1 Present continuous and verbs of speaking

Compare the following examples. In each case (a)–(c), a similar idea is expressed differently.

- Analyse the structure of the three kinds of sentence.
- What is the different effect of the three kinds of sentence? When might a speaker choose one kind but not another? ☞

a) 'I need more time.'
   'I'm saying that I need more time.'

Shove off is an informal, sometimes rude expression meaning 'go away'.

b) 'The proposal is not practical.'
   'I'm suggesting that the proposal is not practical.'
   'What I'm suggesting is that the proposal is not practical.'
c) 'It's a great idea.'
   'I'm saying that it's a great idea.'
   'What I'm saying is that it's a great idea.'

Observations

- You can use the present continuous to:
  — focus on the point you want your listener to remember
  — 'soften' a negative comment
- You can make the effect stronger by using a *wh-* clause. Therefore, in each of the above examples **C1(a)**, **(b)**, **(c)**, the first of the three sentences is very direct, and the last (*What ...*) the most indirect.
- Speech verbs which can be used in this way include: *say, suggest, ask (for)*, and *talk (about)*, *propose, argue*.
- Some other verbs which you have probably learned should not be used in the continuous form (e.g. *think, hope*) can be used in a similar way if the speaker wants to highlight the fact that the idea is limited or temporary. The next section deals with some of these. See also Unit 20 **C1**.

---

2 Using verbs that are not usually in the present continuous

You have probably learned that some verbs are rarely used in the present continuous. These include opinion verbs such as *hate, like, love, want*, verbs of cognition such as *believe, know* or *mean*, and verbs of perception such as *hear, see, taste*.

Look at these examples in which such verbs are in bold.

- **Why do these speakers and writers use the continuous forms?**
- **Would the meaning be different if they used simple forms?** ⚷

a) [part of a letter from a woman to a friend, taking about her son who is doing voluntary work oveseas]

> He chose to take a year out* and is now in Northern Kenya at a remote Africa Inland Mission station teaching in their primary school. He is loving it. About 20 other young people left with him, all volunteers with AIM

b) [part of a e-mail from a student to a university library]

> I am thinking about going to Cambridge this Summer and would like to know if this training could be included in the programme ...

c) [Some people are talking about a sociological survey.]
   I would see that having a database of people who are wanting to be involved in the research in the future will be an important benefit of this first study.

d) [Jenny is on the telephone organising her charity social, which is next Friday night.]
   They are hoping to make a lot of money.

* *Take a year out* is something young people sometimes choose to do when they finish school. It means that they spend one year out of education before going to university.

D Follow-up

- Find some examples of the present continuous in your own reading. Do they follow the patterns you have learned about in this unit?
- Record a short item from the radio or television news in English. Listen for any uses of the present continuous. Can you replace the verbs with the present simple? If you can, does the meaning change?
- If you want more practice, do the Further exercises at the end of this unit.
- If you want further details of points relating to this unit, go to the Reference notes section on pages 189–92.

Summary

- The present continuous is used to talk about current events or states.
- Using the present continuous is like using the adverbs *now* or *nowadays*.
- Care is needed when choosing between the present simple and the present continuous forms of verbs. Remember, the present simple is used to make generalisations, or convey information that is universal:

  'Birds migrate south.' (general truth)

  'Birds are migrating south.' (focus on an event happening at the time of speaking)

- In conditional clauses additional care is needed. Using the present continuous limits the action/event, in contrast to the present simple which gives a general sense. Frequently, the particular limiting factor is given in the *if* clause, and then the present continuous is appropriate for the main clause. (See also Unit 11.)
- The present continuous can be used to 'soften' a negative comment with verbs of speech (*say, suggest, propose, argue, claim* and so on). This is especially true in the context of a *wh*-clause. Compare:

  'We need more time' and

  'What I'm saying is we need more time'.

- Some verbs are rarely used in the present continuous (for example, verbs to do with thinking, believing, or perceiving) or have a different meaning when they are put into this form. However, if a speaker or writer wants to highlight the temporary or very current nature of a state or event, these verbs can be used in the present continuous form. (See also Units 12 and 20 (**C1**).)

Further exercises ⌕

1 a) A student arrived in Britain to study for a degree. He was asked to write a journal of his experiences, in English, by his English tutor. Which of the following comes from his journal?

   i) It takes time for me to get used to British English.
   ii) It's taking time for me to get used to British English.

   b) Write a similar sentence to (i) above, but make it more general so that present simple is the appropriate tense.

2 This speaker is talking about the Health Service. Choose between present simple and present continuous for each verb.

a) People [**live**] longer, and treatment [**get**] more expensive.
b) It [**cost**] thousands of pounds to give people heart surgery.
c) More and more people [**buy**] private health insurance, because, if you [**suffer**], you can't wait even a short time.

3 Rewrite the following sentences, using the verb suggested.

Example:
This is a problem. [say]
What I'm saying is that this is a problem.

a) He's wrong. [**say**]
b) We need to discuss this further. [**suggest**]
c) He will pay for the meal. [**hope**]

4 Choose the correct verb form to complete the gaps.

a) If you don't have too much to do I [**think**] that Christmas can be quite magical. You know, especially if you [**spend**] it with children.

b) If you [**earn**] a hundred pound and your basic rate of tax is twenty three per cent and they put it up to twenty five you (still) [**pay**] two pence. The only thing is that the more you [**earn**] in the long run you'll pay a bigger slice because you're earning more. But you can afford to pay more.

c) Mary: Sometimes I think, 'Oh my goodness' when I talk to some of these other divisional managers they seem to know every single thing that [**go**] on in their divisions.'
Marianne: Yeah.
Mary: Er and when I [**feel**] particularly vulnerable it makes me [**feel**] uneasy.
Marianne: Yeah.

A Introduction

1 **Think about your plans for this weekend.**

- How would you answer if someone said: 'What are you doing this weekend?'
- Can you think of any other ways of saying your answer? Do they all have the same meaning? ☞

2 ■ **Which of B's answers seem most natural?** ☞

a) A: Do you want a sandwich?
   B: I'm going to have lunch in ten minutes. Thanks anyway.
   or: B: I'll have lunch in ten minutes. Thanks anyway.

b) A: I'm going to go home now.
   B: Okay. I'll see you on Saturday.
   or: B: Okay. I'm going to see you on Saturday.

3 **Look at the following text taken from a popular novel. For each verb in bold, decide which tense was used in the original: *will* or *be going to*. ☞**

[A child has hurt her ankle and is being helped by strangers who have found her.]

> What we **do** is take you back. Jake **have to** carry you because you can't walk. But what we **do** first is give you a nice drink, and we can have a little chat while you rest a bit. Your ankle **be** all right. It's only a sprain. It **hurt** a bit but soon it **be** well.

Observations

- You have probably already learned something about these two common future forms. However, the difficulty is knowing when to choose which form (or the other future forms dealt with in Unit 5). Our starting point in this unit is the following:
- *Will* seems to be best for situations when you are in the process of making a decision about the future.
- *Be going to* seems best for situations when you are informing someone about a plan you have already made.

B Discovering patterns of use

1 Linking predictions to present circumstances

Compare these two remarks.

■ **Why do you think the format of the verb *rain* is different in (a) and (b)?**

a) It'll rain tomorrow as soon as we get to the beach, I bet you ten pounds.

b) According to the weather forecast it's going to rain tomorrow. Maybe we shouldn't go to the beach.

> **Observations**
>
> ● If we make a general prediction about something, we can use *will*.
> ● If we link our prediction to the present in some way we can use *be going to*.
> ● In sentence **(b)** above, the speaker uses *be going to* because he/she wants to emphasise that the prediction is based on the present weather forecast. Here are some more examples of linking a prediction with the present:
>
> 'Look out! Your chair's going to collapse!' (I can see it starting to happen.)
>
> 'You're going to find it difficult to get a ticket; Mandy says they were sold out during the first week.' (There are already difficulties.)
>
> 'I've eaten too much. I think I'm going to be sick.' (I can feel it now.)

2 Making decisions versus telling people about them

Compare these two situations.

■ **In which one is the speaker *deciding* something with another person and in which one is the speaker *informing* the other person?**

a) [Jenny and Ronan are talking about a new job which Ronan has just obtained.]
Jenny: When will you get the contract then? When do you start?
Ronan: Helen's going to see Mary on Friday.
Jenny: Oh right.

b) [Sue and Clare are having lunch together; the waitress is showing them to their table.]
Waitress: Would you like smoking or non-smoking?
Clare: Smoking, please.
Sue: Non-smoking.
[both laugh]
Clare: Well you sit down there and I'll sit up here!

- When you are telling someone about an arrangement which has already been made, it is usually appropriate to use *be going to* (or one of the other forms which are dealt with in Unit 5).
- When you are in the process of making an arrangement, it is generally better to use *will*. If you use *be going to* while you are making decisions with someone, it may seem as if you are not allowing the other person to have an opinion:

   'I'm going to drive.' (The person you are speaking to has no choice.)
   'I'll drive.' (The person you are speaking to can respond to the suggestion.)

- In extract **B2(b)** above, the (joking) decision to sit in different parts of the restaurant is a reaction to something which has just happened. If Clare had said, 'You sit down there, but I'm going to sit up here,' it would seem as if she was serious and had decided to sit elsewhere and was informing her friend of her considered decision.
   These differences in meaning are due in part to the way in which the two forms behave in conditional contexts. This is dealt with in **C**.

C Grammar in action

Will and *be going to* in conditional circumstances

Look at the extracts below.

- **In extract (a) do you think Susan has:**
   already decided to *break* (i.e. start spending) her twenty-pound note?
   or: has not decided, and will only break it if someone wants a drink?
- **What would it have meant if she had used *will break*?**
- **In extract (b), why does Helen not say *she will eat them*?** ☞

a) [This is taken from a conversation between a group of friends who are just about to leave the house to go for a drink.]
   Susan: I'm going to break a twenty-pound note, if anyone wants a drink.

b) [Helen is talking about a friend who can't keep sweets for long without eating them.]
   Helen: If she's got sweets in the house it's because she's going to eat them straight away.

- *Will* and *be going to* behave rather differently from each other in the context of conditional clauses (or situations which imply conditions on future actions/events).
- In **C(a)** above Susan has **already decided** to break the twenty-pound note, and therefore the information in the *if* clause (*if anyone wants a drink*) cannot affect or alter the ideas of the main clause (*I'm going to break a twenty-pound note ...*).
- If Susan said *I'll break a twenty-pound note, if anyone wants a drink*, the meaning would be different. This would imply that the ideas in the *if* clause would **cause** her to break into the note (and that otherwise she would not spend it).

"I'm going to order a broiled skinless chicken breast, but I want you to bring me lasagna and garlic bread by mistake."

D Follow-up

■ If you can, before an important event such as an election, big legal trial or new budget, look out for articles in English language newspapers predicting what will happen. Note how often the forms *will*, *be going to* and *be to* (see also Unit 5) are used, then imagine how you would tell someone informally about the article.

■ If you want more practice, do the Further exercises at the end of this unit.

■ If you want further details of points relating to this unit, go to the Reference notes section on pages 190–1.

Summary

● Use *will* to make decisions about the future made at the time of speaking.

● Use *be going to* to talk about decisions you have already made.

● Use *be going to* to talk about things that are strongly connected to the present situation (for example, if they have already begun).

● You can use *be going to* to **remind** someone of something but be careful when you **arrange** something with them, they may think you are deciding for them! (See below.)

   Reminding:

   A: I've won a weekend trip to Paris for the 27th.

   B: We're going to be in Scotland then. Have you forgotten?

   Arranging:

   A: What do you want to do tonight?

   B: We're going to clean the living-room.

   A: Well, you might be, I'm not!

● *Will* and *be going to* behave differently from each other in the context of conditional clauses.

   Will +*if* clause = action in the *if*-clause is strongly dependent on action in main clause:

   'I'll water the plants, if they're dry'

   be going to + *if* clause = action in the main clause is already decided, and therefore less dependent on the action in the *if* clause:

   'I'm going to water the plants, if you want to help me'.

Further exercises ⌐

1 Here is a slightly edited real conversation between two young women having lunch together in a café in London.

■ Note what verb forms they use when they are talking to each other, and what forms they use when they talk to the waitress.

■ If you are in class, discuss with someone why you think the verb forms are the way they are. If you are working alone, make a few notes then compare them with the comments in the key to this unit.

A: I'm going to have an Old timer burger with cheese.

B: Right, I'm going to have, I think I'm going to have a vegetarian burger with barbecue sauce on it.

A: Mm. Are you going to have a starter? What are you going to have?

B: I'm either going to have nachos or potato skins.

A: I'm going to have deep fried mushrooms.

[The waitress, C, comes up to take their order.]

A: I'll have the deep fried mushrooms with an Old timer burger. Can I have cheese on it?

C: Yeah.

B: And I'll have a vegetarian burger with barbecue sauce.

C: Okay.

2 Imagine you have just read this news clip and you are telling someone informally what you have just read.

(Note: We do not normally use *is to* in informal spoken English. What would you say instead?)

KATE'S NEW MOVIE

Veteran film actress Katharine Hepburn is to make another film – at the age of 85. She will begin filming 'This Can't Be Love' in Vancouver, Canada, in October.

3 Think of situations when you might say the following.

a) I'm going to have a headache tomorrow morning.

b) You'll get about five thousand pounds for it, I should say.

c) You're going to get a letter tomorrow.

d) You'll get a letter, and they'll probably invite you for an interview.

4 In each of these sentences decide whether you think the speaker is arranging something with someone, deciding something or informing/reminding someone and then fill in *will* or *be going to*, as appropriate.

a) You .... ring Jo, and I'm supposed to organise the food, that's what we said; don't go changing everything now.

b) If you like, I .... see to the car hire if you get the plane tickets.

c) Right, if that's the case then I .... leave the letter with you and she can pick it up tomorrow.

d) The boss .... meet the visitors for coffee at 11.30. She wants to know if you'd like to come along.

Be + to *forms and other tenses with future reference*

A Introduction

Look at the newspaper headlines (a) and newspaper report (b).

- Underline all the future references. 🗝

a)

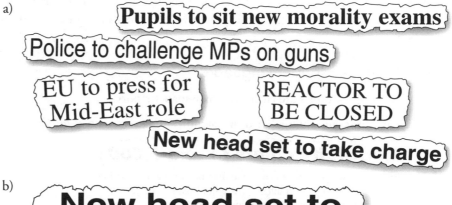

Pupils to sit new morality exams

Police to challenge MPs on guns

EU to press for Mid-East role

REACTOR TO BE CLOSED

New head set to take charge

b)

New head set to take charge

Government inspectors will be asked to draw up an emergency report on the troubled Halifax school where staff say 60 pupils are out of control, the Secretary of State for Education, Gillian Shepherd, is expected to announce today. Mrs Shepherd is due to make a statement on the school after consultation with senior officials from the schools' inspection body, OFSTED, who are preparing a report on an apparent breakdown of discipline.

For revision of *will* and *be going to* see Unit 4.

Observations

- The uses of *is to / are to* are quite formal and are usually used to communicate orders and to regulate behaviour, rather in the manner of modal verbs such as *must* and *should*. (See Units 8 and 9.)
- The person who uses *is to / are to* or *due to / set to* is often communicating orders and instructions in a formal way or is regulating behaviour in some way, rather in the manner of modal verbs such as *must* and *should*. (See Units 8 and 9.)

This unit looks at common patterns of verbs with these forms, and also at other ways of communicating about future events.

B Discovering patterns of use

1 Be + to – real future reference?

Here we shall look at some patterns which occur with the use of *be + to* for future reference.

- Underline the *be + to* forms in the following sentences.
- What types of clauses do these *be + to* forms occur in?
- Rewrite the parts of the clauses you have underlined, replacing them with other future forms. (Note that not all are possible.) ☞

a) If Tom's to go and live with his mother, then so should his sister.
b) If we're to get there by five, we'd better drive more quickly.
c) What's to happen to all of us, if they move the factory to the north of England?
d) They'll write if I'm on the shortlist. Otherwise, I'm to assume I haven't got the job.

2 Be + to in newspaper language

The following examples are taken from newspaper reports.

- What words and phrases occur in a significant pattern with *is to*? ☞

a)
Electricity chiefs to axe 5,000

Five thousand jobs are to be axed by electricity generating firm National Power, it was announced yesterday. Smaller power stations will close but bosses pledged no compulsory redundancies over the next five years.

b)
Just the job for Shilts

Peter Shilton is to continue his career with the England football team after all. The Derby keeper, who announced his international retirement after the World Cup, is to carry on in a new role as goalkeeping coach. Shilton will replace the existing goalkeeping coach Mike Kelly, but the move has not yet been made official.

Observations

- *be + to* forms are common in formal written English, especially in newspaper reports and to refer to events which will occur in the near future.
- *be + to* forms are regularly used to control behaviour in orders, commands and instructions.
- Alternatives to *is to / are to* include *be due to* and *be about to*. These are more formal and are more likely to be used in written rather than spoken English.
- *be + to* forms commonly occur with conditional *if*-clauses.
- When *be + to* occurs in the opening lines of a report, the reference to the future is frequently followed by the verb *will*.

C Grammar in action

1 *Be* + *to* in relation to past actions and events

Here are some examples of *be to* in the past tense.

- Underline the examples of *be* + *to*.
- Do they still refer to the future?
- Can you explain the difference between *he was about to leave* (a) and *I was to play* (d)? ☞

a) [extract from a report]

> He was about to leave for the airport when he found that he'd left his passport in the hotel safe.

b) [extract from a contemporary novel]

> June had been invited for tea at the hall of residence. If the weather was fine – and we were in the middle of a heat wave – it was to take place on the lawn in front of the college.

c) [extract from an academic history book]

> One of the great debates in the Holy Roman Empire in the early 1520s was about a deluge which astrologers prophesied for February 1524, when a major eclipse was to occur in the sign of Pisces, the fish.

d) [The speaker is talking about a tennis match.]

I was to play this boy and we hated each other. And he was … he'd been laughing at me, taking the mickey* out of me the whole week and being an idiot. I had to play him in the final. And I just really wanted to beat him. I went out and played really well, and I beat him two and love or something like that.

2 Present tenses and future reference

All the following sentences use a present tense to refer to the future.

- What do the situations here have in common? ☞

a) If she doesn't work harder, they'll ask her to leave the college.
b) The last bus leaves at 15.10 this afternoon.
c) Mary's arriving tonight. I tried to stop her but she wouldn't listen.

3 Future reference in speech and writing

- Which of the following sentences are more likely to occur in spoken rather than in written English? Give reasons. ☞

a) I was just about to get out of bed when …
b) They are to fly to Hong Kong at lunchtime today.
c) The grease spots are to be removed with a special solution.
d) I am being sent to Japan in the New Year.
e) They're leaving at midday.
f) He is to be promoted in August.

*The expression *take the mickey* means to tease or make fun of.

D Follow-up

- If possible, buy three English newspapers. Look for *be + to* constructions and underline them. What other ways of referring to the future can you find?
- If possible, find some horoscopes in English. What future forms are used in these?
- If you want more practice, do the Further exercises at the end of the unit.
- If you want further details of points relating to this unit go to the Reference notes section on page 192.

Summary

- In general, *be + to* forms and phrases such as *be + due to* are much more common in written than in spoken English.
- The present simple tense is used for future reference, often in conditional clauses or in a clause followed or preceded by a conditional clause. (See also Unit 11.)
- The present simple tense normally enables us to refer to events which are going to occur in the near future, or which are inevitable because they are part of some kind of schedule.
- When the present continuous is used to refer to future events, this signals that the speaker/writer feels that the event is already planned, or current in some way, but is not necessarily part of a bigger schedule.
- *Be + to* forms and related forms in the past tense help us to refer to events in the past which were definitely planned (as in the context of a sports tournament) or are being completed at the time.
- *Be + to* forms are normally associated with authoritative, factual statements or in situations where instructions or commands are issued. However, this does not apply in the context of newspaper language, or if combined with *about* in the *be + about to* construction.

Further exercises ⌐

1 Rewrite the following statements. Make them more formal by making use of structures with *be + to*.

a) What will happen to us now that the factory has closed?
b) The Foreign Minister will issue a statement later in the day.
c) What should we make of all the stories about aliens?
d) The company must deliver the goods by next month at the latest.

2 After matching the parts, put all the following sentences into the past simple tense.

a) The school is to
b) She is to
c) They are on the verge of

d) The minister is due to
e) They are all set to
f) If they're to
g) If Tom's to
h) The town is about to

i) be attacked.
ii) selling the house.
iii) go and live with his sister, then his family should be informed.
iv) start work on Tuesday
v) get there by five, they need to hurry.
vi) close.
vii) speak at the conference.
viii) be promoted.

3 Look at the following horoscopes. In which of the bold references to the future is it possible to substitute a *be + to* structure?

a) Early in 2001, **you'll be freed** from a burden that's been weighing you down for ages. You've no idea how joyous **it's going to** be to discover the new you.
b) The wolf may growl outside your door but he can't possibly pass the threshold. **You'll find** 2001 stable, profitable and extremely fulfilling.
c) **You'll be** so busy in 2001 that you'll hardly have time to notice whether you're happy or not. Slowly, though, **you'll realise** you are.

4 Look at the following extract of speech. What tense do you think the speakers used?

Susan: Do you think Claire will want to come next weekend 'cos Johnny will be here?
Helen: Of course she will. Yeah. Definitely.
Susan: I don't know what time Johnny [**get**] here but ...
Helen: ... He [**come**] down on Thursday.
Susan: I know ... Can't believe he [**come**] this week.
Helen: Still haven't asked Mum which bedroom he [**sleep**] in.
Susan: The thing is where's Dan gonna sleep?
Helen: Rob's room.
Susan: Yeah. Oh.

5 Write headlines, using *be* + *to* forms and the following information. (Note that headlines are usually short, and so often omit non-essential words.)

a) Hostages will be released tomorrow.
b) Strong winds will cause damage across the country.
c) Top band will release new album in the summer.
d) Six ministers will have resigned by the weekend.

Modals in context

6 Can *and* could

A Introduction

Look at the following examples of things people have actually said.

■ **Put each use of *could/can/can't* in bold in the extracts, against its function in the table.** ☞

	could	*can*	*can't*
possibility			
capacity or ability			
impossibility			
none of the above			

a) [This is part of a conversation between a father and son. There has been a telephone call for the father while he was out.]
Son: Did you see the note about the club, Dad, that I left?
Father: Yeah. Who phoned?
Son: **Can't** remember. Jack, **could** it have been?

b) [Tony is taking part in a discussion about healthcare.]
Tony: How would the doctor know what sort of arthritis it was? I mean, **could** he tell by just looking?

c) [Two friends are speaking about someone they know.]
Mary: Oh Ingrid Meadows has just got engaged.
Helena: Oh right. Who to? Not the chap that she was working for?
Mary: Well it **could** be, I don't know.

d) [A doctor speaking to a patient.]
Doctor: You **can** sometimes find, in the first few weeks, these give you side effects.

e) [Two friends are talking about someone they see in a restaurant.]
Sonia: That looks like Charlotte, but it **can't** be.
Natasha: Oh, yeah.

B Discovering patterns of use

1 Expressing ability or inability

Look at the extracts (a)–(d) from written advertisements using *can* or *could*.

- **The types of products are given after the extracts. Which one do you think is being advertised in (a)–(d): a bank (×2)/a website agency/a computer firm?**
- **Consider why the advertisement uses the modal verbs.** ☞

a) You can sail on a course to long-term prosperity with (name of company).
b) With a simple solution from (company name) you can actually shrink your communication and administration costs.
c) Can you imagine how much more effective, and cost effective your company could be?
d) Sometimes technology falls short of its promise. Maybe it's your first site. Or you've tried to build your brand on-line. Or you just can't get your sales-order application to connect with your manufacturing system.

> **Observations**
>
> - Both *can* and *could* are used to express ability:
>   'You can shrink your costs' (You are able to shrink your costs.)
> - *Can('t)* refers to present ability, *could(n't)* refers to ability in the past. When used to express ability, they are synonymous with *be able to*:
>   'Nowadays, you can buy most things via the Internet. In the early days you could only get computer software.'
> - Notice, however, that the use of *could* in **B1(c)** above is different. The next section helps you learn when to use *could* other than to express past ability.
> - If you are talking about being able to do something on **one** very limited occasion in the past you do not use *could*:
>   'The thieves escaped, but the police were able to arrest them eventually.' (✔)
>   'The thieves escaped, but the police ~~could~~ arrest them eventually.' (✗)
>   This contrast does not apply to the negative form:
>   'The thieves escaped, and the police couldn't find them.' (✔)

2 Expressing probability (including logical impossibility)

Read the following extracts.

- **Underline the examples of *could*. Is it possible to replace them with *can* without changing the meaning?** ☞

a) [This is part of an advertisement.]

> To find out what we could do for you,
> ring, fax or visit our website. It could
> change your life. Forever.

b) [A husband and wife are clearing up after a meal. The wife speaks to her son, who is eating.]

Wife: Finish it up. Then I'll wash the plate.

Husband: We could leave it all till later.

c) [Some friends are comparing the drive-on / drive-off train which goes through the tunnel between England and France.]

Brian: It was about three hours from Calais into Bournemouth.

Dave: Well there's no way you could achieve that on a normal train.

"In business, an intimidating facial expression can be a valuable asset."

Observations

- *Could* is used to express ability in the past (as in section **B1**) and the hypothetical future:
  'When I was a child, I could read by the time I was four.' (expression of past ability)
  'When you visit London, you could visit us, if you want to.' (hypothetical future)

- When the speaker or writer thinks that a future event is a real possibility, *can* is used in place of *could*:
  'When you visit London, you can visit us.' (real possibility)

- Using *could* to talk about future events, therefore, is like saying 'it is possible in the circumstances that you will be able to', whereas using *can* is equivalent to saying 'you will be able to'. Therefore, you can only replace the **first** could in extract **B2(a)** with *can*:
  'To find out what we can (✔) do for you, ring, fax or visit our website. It ~~can~~ change your life.' (✗)

- *Can* is never used to express a current possibility/probability:
  A: Where's Julia?
  B: She ~~can~~ be in the kitchen. (✗)
  B: She could be in the kitchen. (✔)

- Remember that the opposite of a positive modal verb isn't always the negative form:
  A: Where's Julia?
  B: She could be in the kitchen.
  A: No, she can't be there. I've just come from the kitchen.

So, although *can* is never used to express probability, *can't* is used to express a logical **impossibility**.

3 Using *can* to express facts

- Read these four extracts from written advertisements containing *can*. Do they all express ability? If you find this difficult, try to replace each one with *is / are able to*: 🔑

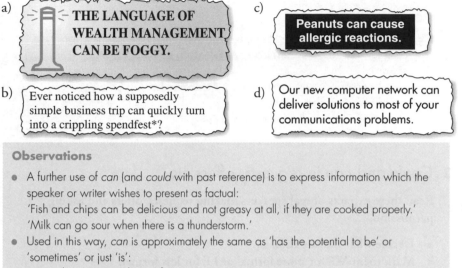

a) THE LANGUAGE OF WEALTH MANAGEMENT CAN BE FOGGY.

b) Ever noticed how a supposedly simple business trip can quickly turn into a crippling spendfest*?

c) Peanuts can cause allergic reactions.

d) Our new computer network can deliver solutions to most of your communications problems.

Observations

- A further use of *can* (and *could* with past reference) is to express information which the speaker or writer wishes to present as factual:
  'Fish and chips can be delicious and not greasy at all, if they are cooked properly.'
  'Milk can go sour when there is a thunderstorm.'
- Used in this way, *can* is approximately the same as 'has the potential to be' or 'sometimes' or just 'is':
  'Local accents **can** be confusing.'
  means: 'have the potential to be confusing'
     or: 'are often confusing'
     or: 'are sometimes confusing'
- To check on this use, try to replace *can* with *be able to*:
  'Peanuts ~~are able to~~ cause allergic reactions.' (✗)
  'Our new computer network is able to deliver solutions to most of your communication problems.' (✓)

C Grammar in action

1 Some fixed expressions using *can't*: *can't help, can't tell* etc.

- Match the following patterns using *can't* with a close paraphrase from the box.
- How would you form the past tense of the sentences? 🔑

> not possible to know
> not possible to prevent yourself from
> not able to come
> not able to be certain of

a) It's silly really, 'cos you can't help having feelings for someone you know.

b) Well, I suppose, I'm kind of cynical. You can't help wondering whether it isn't, you know, the media trying to influence things.

*A *spendfest* is an occasion where a lot of money is spent all at once.

c) You can't tell the condition of an old car just by looking, can you?

d) [doctor to patient]
   In fact, side effects are not very common but they're recorded, okay, and I can't say whether it'll happen to you or not.

e) I can't make it tonight.

> **Observations**
>
> - *Can't* is used in a number of fixed, or semi-fixed expressions including *can't help*, *can't say*, *can't tell* and *can't make*. All these form their past by changing the *can't* to *couldn't*.
> - Note that not all of them can be used in the positive form:
>   'I ~~can~~ help wondering.' (✗)
>   'I ~~can say~~' (✗) (when it means 'decide')

2 *Could* and *can* in requests, offers etc.

Read these extracts of real speakers making requests, offers and asking permission.

- Decide what the situation is.
- Mark them MF for more formal or LF for less formal. ☞

a) Could we have some ice at all?

b) You can stay if you want to.

c) Can I have that bag?

d) Can you open the roof, Bill?

e) Can I have roast duck, please?

f) Could you give me a call about nine o'clock tonight?

g) Could you give me a refund on that do you think?

h) Can I turn this radiator off now?

> **Observations**
>
> - *Can* and *could* are both used in requests. *Could* is used when the speaker either wants to be extra polite, or the request is for something beyond the expectations of the situation.
> - If we compare **C2(c)** and **(g)** above, the speaker expects the reply to be 'yes' when asking for a carrier bag, but there might be a difficulty in receiving a refund.

D Follow-up

- Find several written advertisements in English language magazines. Make a list of the uses of *can* and *could*. Categorise them according to whether they are expressing ability, probability or facts.
- If you want more practice exercises, do the Further exercises at the end of the unit.
- If you want further details of points relating to this unit, go to the Reference notes section on page 193.

Summary

- The problem in learning about modal verbs is that they have a variety of functions and meanings. Also, in terms of their meanings, they do not always behave like other verbs when past or negative forms are used.
- The most common use of *can* and *could* is to express ability:
  'I saw a nice car for sale this weekend, but I couldn't see the registration, so I don't know how old it was.' (I was not able to see it.)
  'I can't possibly find somewhere to live and move out in a week.' (I am not able to)
  When used in this way, the modal verbs are equivalent to 'be able to'; *can* refers to now and *could* refers to a past event.
- An exception to this rule is when a successfully completed action is referred to in the past:
  'The inspector could meet the head of the company' (✗) (does not mean 'was able to meet', because *could* is used for present/future probability).
  However, the negative form is not affected in this way:
  'The inspector couldn't meet the head of the company.'
- *Can't* also has a very specific use when referring to things which are logically impossible:
  [looking at a total on a calculator]
  'That can't be right. I think I multiplied when I should have divided!'
- *Could* is used to speculate about probability:
  'I could be entitled to a tax rebate.' (Maybe I'm entitled to a tax rebate.)
- *Can* is never used to speculate about probability unless there is an underlying question about ability:
  'How can they be so rich?' (How are they able to be so rich?)
- *Can't* occurs in a number of fixed or semi-fixed expressions (e.g. *can't help* = unable to prevent; *can't say/tell* = unable to decide or judge). The past of these is formed by *couldn't* and they do not have the same sense if they are used in the positive form.
- *Can* and *could* are both used in requests. *Could* is used for more tentative requests, and in rather more formal contexts than *can*.

Further exercises ⚯

1 Choose the form you think is best for each of the following and decide what the time reference is, and the meaning of the modal verb. The first one has been done for you.

a) The many delicate instruments on board the Mars space probe were miraculously untouched by their passage through the tail of debris from Halley's comet and the scientists on earth [**can/could**] bring it back on course without difficulty.

could ✓   time reference: past   meaning: were able to

b) Voice recognition systems used for security purposes have long been dogged* by problems of interference from background noise, or potential for imitation. AlphaBetter systems [**can/could**] adapt a solution to this problem from biological sciences. Specialist microphones used to analyse frequency modulations in Australian honey-bees are proving far more effective than standard technology.

c) By the time I left the island, we [**can/could**] talk enough to exchange that I was Irish and they were from Ethiopia.

2 Which modal verb do you think the speakers in the following extract used? (Sometimes more than one is possible, the answer key will tell you which the speakers used.)

a) Jane: I'm ever so thirsty.
Sarah: Are you?
Tony: Mm. Quite hot in here.
Sarah: [**Can/Could**] you open the roof Bob?

b) Ayumi: We're nearly there now anyway.
Bella: What time's it start? Three?
Henry: No half past.
Bella: Oh.
Ayumi: We [**can't/couldn't**] expect to be there on time though.

3 Choose the correct form to follow each of these expressions.

expression	*following construction*
can't help	who told me
can't tell	wondering if I made the right decision
can't say	the party
can't make	if the postmark is Nottingham or Northampton

* *Dogged* (v) means that it has regularly caused problems.

A Introduction

Look at the following extracts of people talking.

- **Can you guess what each speaker is talking about, or where they are speaking?**
- **Underline the use of *will* and *would*.**
- **Decide whether they refer to present, past or future events.** ⌐

a) I hope this film will come out well, because there should be some quite good photos of us.

b) So, as I say, in five years' time, I won't be there anyway.

c) I'm not a political kind of person. I won't even vote, I never have done. [Note: this speaker is speaking generally about his personality, and there is no election in the near future.]

d) Waiter: Would you like chips, jacket, or new potatoes, ladies?
   Customer: I'd like new potatoes and veg[1] please.

e) I wouldn't come back and live in a big town, not at all, they're dirty, they're noisy.

f) I spent the New Year pulling my hair out[2] because the baby wouldn't sleep.

B Discovering patterns of use

1 Conditional contexts and meanings

- **Decide whether the speakers used *will* or *would* in the following extracts.** ⌐

a) [Two speakers are speaking in front of a two-year-old child who is the daughter of their friend. They are trying to stop the child from taking plates out of a cupboard.]

   John: We can get the plates out when we're going to have our dinner, but if we get them out now we might break them, and where [**would/will**] we be then?

   Lucy: We [**wouldn't/won't**] be able to have our dinner.

   John: We [**'d/'ll**] have nothing to eat our dinner off. We [**'d/'ll**] have to eat our dinner off the floor then, and that [**would/will**] mean cleaning the floor first.

   Lucy: And that [**'d/'ll**] be a terrible thing to have to do!

---

[1] *Veg* is a common shortening of *vegetables* in spoken English.

[2] *Pulling / tearing one's hair out* is an expression used to convey irritation and inability to find a solution to a problem.

b) [Here John and Lucy are getting the table ready for dinner on a different day.]
John: I [**'ll/'d**] get the plates.
Lucy: Yeah, ok, but I [**'ll/'d**] need to warm them, so don't put them there.

2 Volition (wanting or desiring to do something)

■ Look at the following extracts. Decide which paraphrase is closest in meaning to the original phrase, in bold. ©━

a) [A woman is talking about her aunt who was in hospital.]
Obviously they tried to get fluids down her. **She wouldn't take anything**.

   i)   She was not able to take the fluids.
   ii) She did not want to take the fluids.
   iii) She did not want to take the fluids and she refused to take them.

b) [A woman is talking about a police interview.]
Obviously **they won't tell you** who he was.

   i)   They are not able to tell you.
   ii) They do not want to tell you.
   iii) They do not want to tell you and they will refuse to tell you.

c) [A man is talking about a new baby.]
I'd carry her or I'll wear one of those harnesses, but **I will not push a pram**.

   i)   I do not want to push a pram.
   ii) I do not want to push a pram and I will refuse to.
   iii) It is not probable that I will push a pram.

"I'd like to offer you a seven-figure salary — $13,525.95"

- A further important use of *will* is not primarily to express future time, or to form a hypothesis. Speakers use the modal verb *will* to express their **attitude** to something, and whether they agree to do an action. For example, in **A(c)**, the time reference is not future:

    'I'm not a political kind of person. I won't even vote, I never have done.'

    The speaker is talking about something that is true now (i.e. the fact that he **never** votes). Speakers can use *will* or *won't* to express their volition (or *will* (n.) as in the term *willpower*). When it is used in this way *will* can be replaced by present simple forms indicating habitual action (where the meaning is less emphatic):

    'I'm not a political kind of person. I won't even vote, I never have done.'

    means: 'I'm not a political kind of person. I **don't** even vote, I never have done.'

- *Would* can also be used to express opinion and volition in past situations:

    'I spent the New Year pulling my hair out because the baby wouldn't sleep.'

- In the past, it can be replaced by the past simple tense, but then it loses the idea of the subject of the clause willing or acting to cause the event:

    'I was tired for three months after Johnny was born because he didn't sleep much.'

- In the three examples in **B2**, the speaker has an element of choice. *Will/won't* (present) and *would/wouldn't* (past) are used to express the combination of not wanting to do something and using your strength of personality to refuse to do it.

C Grammar in action

1 Expressing opinions and preferences

Would is used in several fixed expressions to give your opinion about something:

I'd say ...
I wouldn't say ...
It wouldn't surprise me if ...
Wouldn't it be a good idea if ...

Look at the following topics.

- **Use some of the *would* constructions to write your opinion on each of the topics.**
- **Which of your answers can you make into questions and use to ask someone else's opinion?**
- **How would you form the past tense of your answers?** 🔑

    The environment: polluters pay?
    Education: standards?
    Newspapers and privacy: censorship?
    Transport: ban the car?

2 Understanding the different uses of *will* and *would*

It is sometimes difficult to understand whether a modal verb is referring to now, then, or the future. Here are some examples to show the difficulty:

'So who do you think will win the World Cup?' (future, hypothesising about a real situation)
'What would happen if they changed the offside rule in football?' ('unreal' future, hypothesising about something which has not yet begun, or will not happen)
'The baby won't sleep.' (present volition or the future, hypothesising about a real situation)
'I wouldn't pay that much, so the deal fell through.' (past 'volition')

It is also difficult to decide, without the context, whether a speaker means that they do/don't want to do something (volitional meaning), or whether they are hypothesising about a situation.

- ■ **Decide whether each of the following sentences refer to the past, present or future. How real are the situations the speakers are talking about?** ⌒

a) So what do you think would happen?
   So what do you think would have happened?
   So what do you think happened?
b) I wouldn't drive a Jeep – I don't like four-wheel drive cars.
   I wouldn't drive the Jeep – so Dave had to.
c) The baby wouldn't sleep.
   The baby wouldn't have slept.
   The baby didn't sleep.
d) The job will be difficult to get.
   The job would be difficult to get.
   The job would have been difficult to get.

Observations

- Modal verbs usually have something else in the context which points to the past time reference, such as an adverbial phrase:
  'The baby wouldn't sleep **at New Year**.'
- Additionally, when *will* or *would* have a volitional meaning, they are often negative:
  'I wouldn't ring him, he was quite rude last time we spoke.'
  You can check whether the meaning is volitional by trying to replace the modal with either *didn't/don't want* to or *refuse(d) to*:
  'I wouldn't ring him, he's probably out.' (✔) (*wouldn't* = hypothetical, offering advice)
  'I ~~don't want~~ to ring him, he's probably out.' (✗)
  'I wouldn't ring him, he was quite rude last time we spoke.' (*wouldn't* = past volition) (✔)
  'I didn't want to / refused to ring him, he was quite rude last time we spoke.' (✔) (*wouldn't* = volitional, expressing opinion)
- When a speaker wants to talk about a past event which did not happen (hypothesising about the past) he or she uses a perfect tense:
  'The guests wouldn't leave, so we had a late night.'
  'The guests wouldn't have left, even if we had asked them to!'

D Follow-up

- This unit has mainly discussed *will* and *would* in the context of speech. When you are next reading a text, make a note of the way these modal verbs are used. Are they used in ways that are similar to the ones discussed in this unit?
- If you want more practice exercises, do the Further exercises at the end of this unit.
- If you want further details of points relating to this unit, go to the Reference notes on pages 193–5.

Summary

- Two important contexts for *will* and *would* are conditional statements and questions, and expressions of volition.
- *Will* is used to make predictions, suggestions and offers (or decisions, see Unit 4) or to form questions about the future. In a conditional clause, *will* rarely comes in the *if*-clause. It is used in the main clause when the speaker is certain that the condition will be fulfilled:
  [Score Manchester United 0 Coventry City 3, in the 75th minute of the football match.]
    'I'll be surprised if United win this one!'
- In a conditional context such as following an *if* clause, the use of *would* allows speakers to talk hypothetically.
  Even if there is no *if* clause, the use of *would* suggests a situation that is hypothetical or unreal:
    'A pay rise would be nice (but I don't think I'm going to get one!)'
- This unit also dealt with what we termed 'volitional' meanings. If there is no *if* clause, and no underlying condition which makes a statement unreal, a speaker may be expressing how far they agreed to do something, or what their opinion is. Generally, this use is in the negative form. In this case it is equivalent to 'refuse to':
    'The postman wouldn't shut the gate. He said the catch was rusty.'
    'Jenny won't eat cabbage. She hates it.'
- *Would* is used in common expressions of opinion such as *I would(n't) say*, *would(n't) be surprised*. The past tense of these forms is created by using the auxiliary *have*:
    'I wouldn't have said.'
    'I wouldn't have been surprised.'

Further exercises ⚿

1 **Choose the form you think best for each of the following.**

a) If it had been serious he [**would/will**] have been in prison, [**wouldn't/won't**] he?
b) [A police officer is asking the victim of a crime about the criminal.]
   How [**would/will**] you describe him?
c) Working nights gave me a social life really that I probably [**wouldn't/won't**]
   have had otherwise.
d) What [**would/will**] your ideal Christmas be like?
e) If we don't do it now we never [**would/will**].

2 **Match the following bold examples with the function/meanings in the box below.**

a) Allow the subjects time to read the questionnaire, **just as they would be doing in a quantitative study.**
b) If I've got some spare money at the end of the month, **I'll buy those shoes.**
c) When you've visited Italy, **you'll want to go back there.**
d) I couldn't train to do first aid, because it was training one night a week, and **my mum wouldn't let me go out.**
e) Leave some for your dad, **will you**?
f) **Communicating the results of research will be** a very interesting opportunity for publishers.
g) In five years' time, **I won't be there**, anyway.

> future action, conditional on something else
> hypothetical situation
> volition
> prediction
> future action

3 **Choose an item from the right-hand column to match the items in the left-hand column.**

expression	*following construction*
I'd say	if he was older than he looks.
It wouldn't surprise me	to just ask him?
Wouldn't it be sensible	he was older than he looks.

May, might *and* must

A Introduction

■ Look at these sentences and decide which of the possible continuations sounds most suitable or most likely. In each case there are three possibilities. Circle YES if you think the continuation is suitable or likely. (In some cases you can circle YES more than once.) Circle NO if you think the continuation is impossible or not likely.

■ Where you have circled NO, why is it unlikely? ⌘

1 Maura: I'm trying to ring Alan but there's no answer.
a) Nick: He might be in the garden. You never know.   YES/NO
b) Nick: He may be in the garden. He often has lunch outside
          on sunny days.   YES/NO
c) Nick: He must be in the garden. You never know.   YES/NO

2 George: You might have told me you were going away for the
              weekend.
a) Fred: Sorry, I probably just forgot.   YES/NO
b) Fred: Yes, I can't remember now who I told and who I
          didn't.   YES/NO
c) Fred: Did I? How can you be so sure?   YES/NO

3 Sarah: She must be older than 70. She's been married 57 years.
a) John: Hmm, so it's just possible she is.   YES/NO
b) John: Yes, there's no way she can be less than that.   YES/NO
c) John: Oh, it's impossible to say.   YES/NO

B Discovering patterns of use

1 *May* versus *might*

May and *might* are often close in meaning, but there are cases where one is generally used rather than the other.

■ Look at these extracts and complete the guidelines after each one. (Cover the Observations section until you have finished.)

a) [encyclopaedia text about types of government]
A cabinet may also be found in a non-parliamentary system.
[encyclopaedia text about frogs and their breeding habits]
There may be 3,000 eggs in a large clump of frog-spawn.

May is preferred when ....

b) One person you might talk to is Roger Bird. He knows a lot about jazz.
   You might like to thank your uncle George for that lovely card he sent you.

   Might is preferred when ....

c) [Customer to waiter in a restaurant:] I think I might try the salmon, please.
   I might do some gardening after lunch if the weather stays fine.

   Might is preferred when ....

d) [Customer to waiter in a restaurant:] And, please, may I have a coffee?
   [On the telephone:] Oh, hello, may I speak to David please?

   May is preferred when ....

e) The police suspected that he might be an enemy agent.
   He brought some magazines because he thought I might get bored.

   Might is preferred when ....

f) He might have been killed, but he had survived.
   I'm glad you discovered that leak in the bathroom. We might have flooded the
   whole house.

   Might is preferred when ....

Observations

- *May* is preferred when statements about very probable facts are made, especially in scientific, academic and technical contexts, as in the encyclopaedia texts above.
- *Might* is preferred when the speaker is making a polite suggestion or giving polite advice:
   'One person you might talk to is Roger Bird. He knows a lot about jazz.'
   'You might like to thank your uncle George for that lovely card he sent you.'
- *Might* is preferred when announcing decisions. It softens the force of the statement.
- *May* is preferred when asking for permission. *Might* can be used in **B1(d)**, but is very polite and rather too formal.
- *Might* is preferred when a reporting clause is used with the reporting verb (*suspected* and *thought* in **B1(e)** above) in the past tense.
- *Might* (plus *have*) is preferred when we talk about something that was possible, but did not happen. *He **may** have been killed* would suggest the speaker did not know if he was killed or not.

---

2 Differences in meaning between *may* and *might*

Now here are some cases where *may* and *might* would be equally suitable, but sometimes there is still a slight difference in meaning.

■ What is the difference, if any, between *may* and *might* in the following? ☞

a) It takes so long by train. You *may/might* as well fly.
b) If you explain the problem, I *may/might* be able to help you.
c) They *may/might* be just jokes, but a lot of people take them seriously.
d) Don't do it. You *may/might* end up losing all your money.

3 Must

■ Sort these sentences into five types using the following descriptions:

Type 1: Talking about how certain/definite you feel something is.
Type 2: Giving yourself or someone else an order, instruction or advice.
Type 3: Saying how you think things should be.
Type 4: Imagining what a past event or situation was like.
Type 5: Saying what is forbidden. ☞

a) Do excuse me. I must be going back to Anne now.
b) A Muslim wedding, in the street? That must have been nice.
c) [Notice at a railway station] Passengers must not cross the line.
d) What's he going to do with all his money? He must be worth a couple of million.
e) There should be a free health service. Everybody must be treated equally.
f) I mustn't be selfish. I'll ask her if she wants to share it.
g) And the other thing you must do is have a meal in Joe's Restaurant. It's great.
h) Getting a letter like that must have been very upsetting for you.
i) The government must do something about all this traffic, it's crazy.
j) We must not be afraid to stand up for what we believe.
k) With music, you are allowed to photocopy the words, but legally we mustn't copy the music itself.

Observations

- *May* is used to talk about the typical characteristics of something. This is especially so in academic styles. It is also used to make polite requests. *Might* is possible in **B1(d)**, but would sound extremely formal.
- *Might* is often used for giving polite or indirect advice. It is also often used when the speaker is assessing an idea / thinking of what to do. It is also often used in past reported clauses after verbs such as *thought, said, knew, suspected, wondered* etc. *Might* is used when we are talking about something that was possible, but did not happen.
- *May* and *might* are close in meaning when they simply refer to the possibility of something happening. *May* tends to be preferred for slightly stronger possibilities.
- *Must* is used for saying that we feel something is sure to be true, or for how we imagine a situation was likely to have been in the past. It is also used for giving orders, advice and instructions, especially to yourself, and for saying what is the rule and what is forbidden.

C Grammar in action

1 May, might or must?

Here we are going to consider some uses of *may*, *might* and *must* that are characteristic of spoken or written English, and also some uses which are more fixed and idiomatic.

Look at these extracts from a brochure about camping holidays, produced by a travel company that can book camping places for people. The brochure explains the system.

■ Do you think the gaps should have *may*, *might* or *must*? ☞

> *information*
>
> - Camp site owners .... at times restrict the use of barbecues, especially if the weather is dry, when there .... be a fire risk.
> - Outdoor chairs and tables are available for hire on almost all sites. These .... be reserved in advance.
> - During winter months, the full range of facilities .... not be available on all sites.
> - Inevitably, some details in this brochure .... have changed since the information was printed. At the time of booking, customers will be informed of such changes.

Observations

- In formal written styles, especially in texts explaining systems or rules and regulations, *may* is preferred to *might* when referring to possible events.
- *Must* is used for referring to absolute obligations, rules and conditions.

2 May, might and must in fixed expressions

Now try to imagine situations in which you would use these expressions.

■ Write a sentence using each one. ☞

a) I might have guessed ...
b) (X) may arise from ...
c) If I may say so, ...
d) It's what you might call ...
e) I must admit, ...
f) I must say, ...
g) May I offer my ...

D Follow-up

- Collect more fixed expressions with *may*, *might* and *must*, especially those which are concerned with speaking, and making your point (e.g. *I might add ...*, *I must insist that you ...*, *I might have known ...*, *It may well be that ...* etc.).
- Look at signs and notices and see how many times *must (not)* and *may (not)* are used.
- Consider how *may* and *might* relate to *can* and *could*. If you find this difficult, look at Unit 6.
- If you want more practice exercises, do the Further exercises at the end of the unit.
- If you want further details of points relating to this unit, go to the Reference notes section on pages 195–7.

Summary

- *May* and *might* both express possibilities. *May* is for stronger possibilities than *might*.
- *May* is often used in formal, written styles to express what the characteristics of something are, or how systems generally work, or what the usual state of affairs is.
- *May* is used to make polite requests or to ask for permission. *Might* can be used in these situations, but it is extremely formal.
- *Might* is used for giving indirect advice.
- *Must* is used for orders and instructions, for saying what the rules are and what is forbidden. It is also used for saying how we think things should be.
- *Must* is used for saying that we are quite certain that something is true, or for imagining how a situation was most likely to have been in the past.
- There are several fixed expressions which use *may*, *might* or *must*. These are best learnt as whole phrases.

Further exercises ⚯

1 Which of the possible responses to these remarks sounds most suitable or most likely? In each case three possible responses are given.

- Circle YES if you think the continuation is the most suitable or likely or NO if you think the continuation is impossible or not likely.

(You can use YES and NO more than once for each set of three alternatives.)

a) Nancy: I've written to Sheila but she hasn't replied.
  - i) Bob: She might be away. You never know with her.   YES/NO
  - ii) Bob: She may be in Paris. She often goes there on business.   YES/NO
  - iii) Bob: She must be in Paris. You never know.   YES/NO

b) Alistair: You might have left some food for me.
  - i) Jo: I probably just thought you wouldn't want any.   YES/NO
  - ii) Jo: That's why I knew there'd be something to eat when I got home.   YES/NO
  - iii) Jo: I had to go out in the rain looking for a restaurant.   YES/NO

c) Sean: There must be more than 50 people here. There were 50 chairs and there are at least a dozen people standing.

    i)   Sue: So it's just possible there are more than 50.   YES/NO

    ii) Sue: So there's no way there can be less than that.   YES/NO

    iii) Sue: It's impossible to tell.   YES/NO

2 Fill the gaps with *may, might* or *must*. If more than one is possible, what is the difference in meaning?

    a) Do excuse me rushing off. I .... get back to the office.

    b) You idiot! Stop the car at once! We .... have been killed!

    c) Tickets can be reserved in advance but .... also be purchased at the door.

    d) Three weeks in the Bahamas? That .... have been nice. You lucky thing!

    e) I think I .... stay at home tomorrow and paint the kitchen.

    f) I know it .... not always be easy, but we .... all obey the law.

    g) .... you make so much noise? I'm trying to work in here!

    h) You .... have warned me you were bringing a friend. I've only booked for the two of us.

    i) I thought you .... like to see these photos of New York since you're going there.

    j) .... I ask what is in that bag?

3 How would you make the sentences with modals negative?

    ■ **If you simply make the modal form negative, have you changed the meaning? (The verbs to change are in bold.)**

    a) I **must hurry**. The train leaves at 6.30.

    b) I **might have guessed** that Ivor would end up marrying Nellie.

    c) I **may be** in the office tomorrow. I'll ring you and let you know.

    d) Visitors to the zoo **must feed** the animals.

    e) She **might be** his sister, you never know.

4 Join the following expressions with the best conclusion.

expression	*conclusion*
I must say/admit, ...	... you're wrong.
May I offer my ...	...'restructuring'.
I might have guessed ...	... sympathy.
If I may say so, ...	... you were right.
It's what you might call ...	... he would leave before the bill came!

Shall *and* should

A Introduction

- Guess whether these people used *shall* or *should*.
- Could you exchange *shall* and *should* in any of the extracts? Would this change the meaning, or would it be ungrammatical?
- Which of the two forms is used to refer to future events? ☞

a) [John and Alan are discussing the traffic plans for the city in which John lives.]
   John: There'll be a lot of through traffic.
   Alan: Mm.
   John: But if that bridge is built it'll take a lot off the London Road.
   Alan: Mm. Mm.
   John: 'Cos we have got a by-pass for the A52.
   Alan: Yeah. Mm.
   John: And I [**shall/should**] be able to get out of this cul-de-sac occasionally.
   Alan: [laughs] Do you find it hard?
   John: At times.

b) [Tessa, a young tennis player, is talking about her attitude when she plays for her country.]
   Tessa: I think when I play for Great Britain I try a lot. It just makes you try more but you [**shall/should**] always try your best in everything, even if you're playing someone rubbish. But you just think about it and think, 'Right I'm going to win this!' but I try my hardest in most matches really.

c) [This is part of an e-mail between two people who work in different parts of an organisation.]

   Yes well maybe we [**shall/should**] make an arrangement for the week after next now, so that we [**shall/should**] be sure to meet.

B Discovering patterns of use

1 Expressing probability

- Underline the uses of *shall* and *should* in the following extracts.
- Which form is used to talk about individuals' personal futures?
- Which form is used to talk about facts? ☞

a) [This is from an information leaflet from the fire brigade about smoke alarms.]

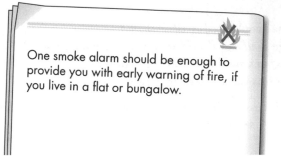

One smoke alarm should be enough to provide you with early warning of fire, if you live in a flat or bungalow.

b) [This is part of an e-mail from one friend to another.]

I have spent quite a bit of today trying to track down my luggage after a real nightmare of a trip back here. Anyway as I write (5.20 pm) it should be leaving Denmark and may even get back here by midnight so I can comb my hair at last!!

c) [This is part of a doctor–patient interview.]
Doctor: Em, what was I going to say? So, no, we needn't worry the neurologist today. That's no problem. Your bloods* are all okay. We shall probably leave you on this combination of tablets for some time.
Patient: Mm.
Doctor: Okay? Make you feel things are nice and stable. Then what we'll probably do is tail down the doses.

d) [This is part of a research interview with an unemployed young man, Tony.]
Interviewer: Are you optimistic?
Tony: No. No I'm, I'm afraid not, I don't think I shall ever get a job.

---

* Bloods, here, means blood tests.

Observations

- Both *shall* and *should* can be used to express your belief about a probable action or event.
- If you use *should*, these events can be happening now:

  'As I write (5.20 pm) it should be leaving Denmark.'

  or in the future:

  'By next Friday, it should be here.'

  Using *should* in this way is like saying 'According to what I know about the circumstances, [X] is happening (or [X] will happen)'. Because we cannot know exactly what is affecting the events, or will affect them, we have to use a modal which expresses probability. (If we want to sound more confident about the outcome, we use *will*.)
- *Shall* refers to future probability and is only used with first person pronouns (*I*/*we*) in speaking, and as a more general future form in formal writing. In speech, *shall* often alternates with *will* or *'ll* (as in example (**c**) above). *Shall* is slightly more emphatic than *will* (and much less frequently used).
- *Should* is interchangeable with *will* when expressing probability (but the meaning is less doubtful if the latter is used):

  'As I write, ~~it shall~~ be leaving Denmark.' (✗) (must have 1st person pronoun, not *it*)

  '~~As I write, we shall be leaving~~ Denmark.' (✗) (cannot use *shall* to refer to present action)

  'As I write, my luggage will be leaving Denmark.' (✓) (The writer is confident that the action is happening.)

  'On Friday, we shall be leaving Denmark.' (✓) (OK because first person, and future reference)
- Care needs to be taken because *should* has a further very common use (dealt with in **B2**, below) which is to express obligation or advisability.

  Compare:

  'I don't think I shall get a job.' (I probably won't get a job.)

  'I don't think I should get a job.' (I don't think that it is advisable for me to get a job.)

2 Expressing obligation and advisability

- **Look at the uses of *should* in the following extracts.**
- **Which ones could you replace with *shall* and which ones could you replace with *ought to*?** 🔑

a) [This is part of an e-mail from one friend to another.]

b) [This is from an information leaflet from the fire brigade about smoke alarms.]

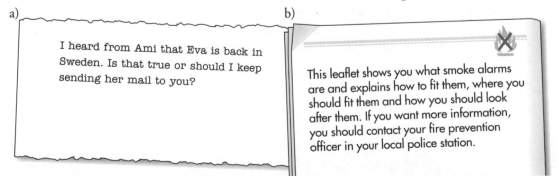

a)

> I heard from Ami that Eva is back in Sweden. Is that true or should I keep sending her mail to you?

b)

> This leaflet shows you what smoke alarms are and explains how to fit them, where you should fit them and how you should look after them. If you want more information, you should contact your fire prevention officer in your local police station.

c) [Mr Owen is being interviewed by a market researcher about his opinions on pensions.]

Mr Owen: What you have been paying for is, when you get … when you're taken ill, you should get the treatment, and when you retire you should have a reasonable income, retirement pension …

Interviewer: Mm.

Mr Owen: … and if you're taken seriously ill, then you should, you know, the government should provide for your healthcare.

> **Observations**
>
> - Depending on the context *should* can be used to express **obligation** or **advisability**.
> - When *should* is used to express advisability it can be replaced by *shall* (in the first person) with very similar meaning:
>   'Should I keep sending her mail to you?' (✔)
>   means:
>   'Shall I keep sending her mail to you?' (✔)
> - When *should* is used to express obligation (or strong advisability, rather than a suggestion) the two forms are not interchangeable. *Should* is then equivalent to *ought to*:
>   'The government should pay for healthcare for the elderly.' (*ought to*)
>   'The government ~~shall~~ pay for healthcare for the elderly.' (✗)
>   Compare:
>   'I should lose some weight.' (It would be a good idea if I lost some weight.)
>   'I shall lose some weight.' (I am determined to lose some weight.)
> In the second example, *shall* could be replaced by *will* (*'ll*), which would be the form most often used.

C Grammar in action

1 Making offers and suggestions

Look at the following extracts.

■ Do you think the speakers used *shall* or *should*? ⌾

a) [Jenny and Savithri are in the kitchen. They have had a snack, and Jenny wants to know whether she should put the cheese back in the fridge.]
Jenny: [**Shall/Should**] I just put this back as it is? Or …
Savithri: … Huh? You can leave it out if you want, 'cos I'll have a bit in a minute.
Jenny: All right.

b) [Dr Evans is with a patient when the phone rings.]
Dr Evans: Hi. Right … I've got somebody with me at the moment so [**shall/should**] I come down when we've finished and catch you? Oh right. Bye.

2 *Shall* and *should* in fixed expressions

- **Do you know the following expressions?**
- **Can you match them with the functions which are listed after them?** ☞

a) Shall we say five o'clock?
b) By the way, I should say, I might be late.
c) I should imagine he's not very pleased.
d) They certainly should.
e) He's about 35, I should say.

Functions:
guessing/speculating
suggesting/arranging
agreeing (strongly)
introducing an awkward point

D Follow-up

- Find a leaflet giving advice (e.g. at the dentist, doctor or advice centre). How many times is *should* used? Is *shall* used at all?
- Next time you are making arrangements in English, listen for people using *shall* and *should*. Do they use them in the ways you have learned in this unit?
- Look out for speakers or writers using *shall*. Can you find any examples which do **not** use the first person (I/we)?
- If you want more practice exercises, do the Further exercises at the end of the unit.
- If you want further details of points relating to this unit go to the Reference notes on pages 197–9.

Summary

- *Should* is used to express probability when a speaker or writer is not confident enough about the event to use *is* or *will*.
  Compare:
  'Tony is in the kitchen.' (definite, e.g. pointing through a window at Tony)
  'He will back in five minutes.' (definite)
  and:
  'Tony should be in the kitchen.' (Tony is probably in the kitchen, because I saw him there two minutes ago.)
  'He should be back in five minutes.' (Tony will probably be back in five minutes.)
- A second important use of *should* is to express advisability or obligation. The difference between these two functions often depends on the context:
  [Teacher to pupil] 'You should work harder.' (obligation)
  [Friend to friend] 'You should work harder.' (advisability)
- When weak obligation, or advisability is expressed (in the first person), *shall* and *should* are very similar in meaning:
  'Shall/should I get a haircut?' (✓)
  'Should he work harder?' (✓)
  'Shall he work harder?' (✗) (not first person)
- *Shall* is an alternative form of *will* which is only used with first person pronouns (*I/we*) and is slightly more emphatic and formal.
- *Shall* is used with first and second pronouns (*I/we/you*) to form offers and suggestions, and often in the context of making arrangements.

Further exercises ⚟

1 **Replace each of the words in bold in the following extracts with one of the following:**

    will probably   ought to

- **Next, try to replace each of the examples of *should* with *shall* and analyse why you can or cannot replace one verb with another in each case.**

a) [This is part of an e-mail.]

> We are in the process of starting the next set of interviews as part of the Survey of Modern Family Life. Could you please give me an idea of when we **should** be receiving the first lot of transcripts as the families will be interested to know. We are having a meeting with the interviewers tomorrow (22/5) and I would be grateful if you could let me know then.

b) [John, Julie and Peter are talking about family meetings and visits during holidays. Julie and Peter are married. Jenny is their young daughter.]

Peter: I as I said when the kids are small it's different …

John: Mm.

Peter: … but when they're older that's when the family **should** get together.

John: Right.

Peter: They **should** all come and bring their kids.

Julie: Or we **should** go to them.

Peter: Yeah. When Jenny's a grandma.

John: Yes.

Julie: Yeah. Or we **should** go to them, like, one Christmas they'd come to us and …

Peter: No, no. Christmas they **should** all come here.

Julie: Mm. Well you can do the cooking!

c) [Lucy, Anthea, June and Penny are four students. Anthea wants to lose some weight. She is going to visit different parts of Europe by train that summer. Lucy and June think that this will help her to lose weight.]

Lucy: Inter-railing* will help.

Anthea: Yeah.

June: Inter-railing **should** knock it off of you.

Penny: Inter-railing won't help 'cos you eat cheese and stuff all the time.

2 Decide whether these speakers used *shall* or *should.*

a) [Tony is talking about his plans with a friend.]

John: Mm. What about the New Year?

Tony: Em, you know, not not such a big thing. I think we'll have a very quiet New Year.

John: Mm.

Tony: May or may not see the New Year in, not even certain this year whether I [**shall/should**] bother.

b) [John is sending a present by mail. He wants to insure the parcel, and is filling out a form at the post office.]

Clerk: Just make that out.

John: Okay. Do I have to be specific?

Clerk: No.

John: What [**shall/should**] I put?

Clerk: Photograph frame.

John: Oh right. Okay. That is specific then.

Inter-railing is formed from 'Inter-rail' ticket – a form of ticket popular with students travelling in Europe.

c) [Mary and Dominic are taking part in a discussion about healthcare.]

Interviewer: Right. [**Shall/Should**] we stop treatment for people over a certain age?

Mary: No.

Dominic: No, I think.

Mary: If it's doing them good no.

Interviewer: Mm.

Dominic: Yeah they [**shall/should**] just carry on with the treatment.

3 Write sentences and exchanges using the following:

I should say ... (both uses)
I should imagine ...
He certainly should ...
Shall we say ...

Other modal forms

A Introduction

The other units on modality in this section have shown how modal verbs can be used for expressing how certain or necessary it is that something happens (e.g. *can, could, may, might, must*). In this unit we explore how some other verbs and expressions can also express similar meanings.

■ Underline the verbs in these extracts from real conversations which could be called modal, that is to say, that affect the degree of certainty or necessity expressed in the sentence. ⌐

a) I look forward to Christmas. It seems to be the only time the whole family gets together.
b) There have been burglaries in the neighbourhood, but I reckon we're safe here.
c) There are managers, and the junior staff are meant to report back to them.
d) I'm sorry, it's not my department. You need to contact the person who's responsible.

Observations

● From the exercise, we can observe other verbs that carry modal meaning. The speaker in each sentence is modifying or changing in some way the statements they are making. Try reading the same sentences again without the words you have underlined; they seem quite neutral, and do not so obviously give the speaker's perspective on how definite or necessary something is. Modality is concerned with speakers' and writers' perspectives and viewpoints.

B Discovering patterns of use

1 Contrasting meanings of other modal forms

Here are the sentences from **A** again. They have been changed.

■ How is the meaning different? Make notes. ⌐

a) I look forward to Christmas. It tends to be the only time the whole family gets together.
b) There have been burglaries in the neighbourhood, but we ought to be safe here.
c) There are managers, and the junior staff are to report back to them.
d) I'm sorry, it's not my department. You have to contact the person who's responsible.

2 Choosing between modal forms

In each of these pairs of sentences, the same verb is missing.

■ **Choose from the list of verbs to fill the gaps.** ○⇌

have to   ought to   tend to   seem to   be to   reckon   be meant to   need to

a) I .... have lost your letter. I'm sorry.
b) It .... be the case that nobody knew what was happening.

c) She .... be here answering the phone. I don't know why she isn't.
d) That plastic cover .... keep it dry, but it didn't work.

e) [People opening a pile of packages.]
   This .... be the last one. Let me just check.
f) You really .... pay more attention to what I tell you.

g) This .... be the coldest day of the year; it's absolutely freezing!
h) You .... take all your documents. If there's anything missing, they'll just send you away.

i) I .... the best way to get there is to take the bus.
j) This restaurant is .... to be the best in town.

k) You .... explain the situation to Barbara; she'll tell you what to do.
l) This system .... be changed; it just isn't working.

m) We .... like less crowded places when it comes to holidays.
n) I don't recommend this program. It .... be difficult to use if you aren't a computer expert.

o) The lists .... be ready by next Tuesday, without fail. Could everyone make a note of that please?
p) It .... be the happiest day of his life, but it ended in disaster.

- *Seem* is used when you want to say how things look to you, even though it is not certain that things are that way. It can be followed by a verb with *to* or a *that* clause.
- *Have to* is used to express an external obligation (see **B2(h)**), or to state that you are very sure about something (see **B2(g)**, and compare with *must* in Unit 8).
- *Tend* is used for what is normally, but not necessarily always, the case (see **B2(m)** and **(n)**).
- *Ought* is used to mean what the speaker thinks the **right** way to do something is (see **B2(f)**, and compare with *should* in Unit 9), and also to say that you are reasonably sure about something (see **B2(e)**).
- *Need* is used to express a polite instruction or a necessity (see **B2(k)** and **(l)**). When it is an instruction, it is followed by a verb with *to*. When it is used in a passive context, a verb with *-ing* can follow it (see **B2(l)**, which could also be expressed as 'needs changing').
- *Reckon* is used to lessen the certainty of something. It means that people think, guess or believe that something is so, without being absolutely certain (see **B2(i)** and **B2(j)**). It can be used in the passive (see **B2(j)**).
- *Be to* is a rather formal way of expressing either a decision or instruction from authority (see **B2(o)**), or what is or was destined to be (see **B2(p)**). See also Unit 5.
- *Be meant to* is used to express how things are intended to be, but they may not necessarily be so (see **B2(c)** and **B2(d)**).

C Grammar in action

1 Structures after other modal forms

■ **Put these eight sentences into two groups of four, on the basis of what they have in common in the grammatical form of their modal words in bold.** ⌘

a) He **seems not to** have noticed what was going on around him.
b) Falk **was reckoned** by many **to** be the best engineer of his generation.
c) They**'re not supposed to** face that way. Turn them round.
d) You **needn't** worry about the exams. You'll find them easy.
e) People **tend not to** care about the quality of fresh food nowadays.
f) They **were meant to** arrive before now. I don't know what's happened.
g) Students **ought not to** forget that someone has to pay their fees, even if they themselves don't.
h) You**'re bound to** feel tired after travelling half way around the world.

2 Choosing the correct completion

The modal expressions in this unit can be followed by a variety of different constructions.

Use a dictionary if necessary to check which of the possible continuations are appropriate for each of these verbs.

■ **Mark the boxes, as in the example, with a tick (✓) for yes, and a cross (✗) for no.** ⊙━

a) It seems	I've let you down.	✓
	as if everyone has a cold today.	✓
	starting to rain.	✗
	to have got burnt on the edges.	✓
b) It needs	that it's repaired.	☐
	to be looked at.	☐
	painting.	☐
c) It needn't	be so loud.	☐
	be looked at.	☐
	painting.	☐
d) It tends	that it lasts only a short time.	☐
	to break easily.	☐
	not to run regularly.	☐
e) It doesn't tend	that it lasts very long.	☐
	to last very long.	☐
	last very long.	☐
f) It ought	never to have happened.	☐
	be changed immediately.	☐
	not to surprise anyone.	☐
	n't matter too much how we do it.	☐
	to be forbidden.	☐
g) It didn't ought	to happen.	☐
	happen.	☐
	happening.	☐
h) Does it	seem right to you?	☐
	tend to happen often?	☐
	ought to be sent by airmail?	☐
	have to be covered?	☐
	meant to work only when the light is on?	☐

3 More modal forms

In this exercise, there are some new modal expressions not yet covered in this unit. They have meanings similar to those already presented, but the grammar that follows them may be different.

■ **Using a dictionary if necessary, mark the boxes in the table for the types of structure that are possible after the expressions. For example, if you think you can say 'it looks okay,' put ✓ or if you think it is wrong, put ✗. If you think that an item might be used, but only rarely, put a question mark.** ⚲

a)

	to be okay.	*okay.*	*that it's okay.*	*as if/as though it's okay.*
It seems				
It appears				
It looks				
It sounds				

b)

	to happen.	*that it will happen.*
It's bound		
It's likely		
It's liable		
It's probable		

c)

	it's the best way to do it.	*it to be the best way to do it.*
I think		
I guess		
I reckon		
I consider		
I suppose		

d)

	to be the best method.	*the best method.*
It's thought		
It's guessed		
It's reckoned		
It's considered		
It's supposed		

D Follow-up

- Collect more modal expressions, expecially ones which are not verbs, such as *maybe, perhaps, possibly, certain, likelihood*, and wherever possible, make a note of the contexts they are used in.
- Observe the degree of formality of such expressions too, e.g. *perhaps* is more formal than *maybe*; *is considered, is thought*, etc. are more formal than *I think, I consider.*
- If you want more practice exercises, do the Further exercises at the end of the unit.
- If you want further details of points relating to this unit, go to the Reference notes section on pages 199–204.

Summary

- A number of other verbs apart from the most common modals such as *can, will, may*, etc. also express modal meaning.
- A speaker or writer shows how certain, necessary, regular or predictable they think events are by using modals.
  Modal expressions therefore represent the speaker's or writer's viewpoint.
- Amongst the expressions that carry similar meanings to the most common modal verbs are verbs such as *seem, tend, have to, need, look, think* and *ought*.
  The structures which may or may not follow these expressions are quite complex, and must be learnt for each expression.
  Some are more formal and are associated with written contexts or very formal spoken ones, such as *be + to* (see Unit 5) and the passive voice of *think, consider* and so on.

Further exercises 🔑

1 Fill the gaps using these modal items. There may be more than one possible answer.

ought to   be to   have to   need   seem   tend to   be meant to

a) These blades .... break very easily and .... be replaced about once a month.

b) It .... unfair that she should have to do all the work.

c) We .... check to see if that flight is still operating before we fix the date for the trip.

d) You .... get a work permit if you want to work here. That's the law, I'm afraid.

e) It .... be signed by everyone. I can't understand why he hasn't signed it.

f) These papers .... be returned to the tax office by 31 July.

2 Make these sentences negative. If there is more than one way of making them negative, do it in each different way.

a) I tend to use salt when I cook.

b) Ought we to send those forms off to get our money back?

c) You have to write your telephone number in the box.

d) She seems to have noticed it.

e) I reckon it's worth waiting three weeks.

f) You need to fill out a form.

3 Which of the possible continuations are appropriate for each of these verbs? Mark the boxes, as in the example, with a tick (✓) for yes, and a cross (✗) for no.

Example: It seems
- she's not coming after all. ✓
- as if I'm the only one who cares. ✓
- getting wet. ✗
- to have got burnt on the edges. ✓

a) It needs
- that it's painted. ☐
- to be covered with something. ☐
- repairing. ☐
- be black. ☐

b) It needn't
- be eaten today. ☐
- cleaning. ☐

c) It tends
- that it gets dirty. ☐
- to stick to your hands. ☐
- not to grow very well in a cold climate. ☐

d) It doesn't tend   that it cooks very easily. ☐
to cook very easily. ☐
cook very easily. ☐

e) It ought

never to have been allowed. ☐
be closed for good. ☐
not to happen that way ☐
n't make any difference really. ☐
to be free. ☐

f) It didn't ought

to go like that. ☐
go like that. ☐
going like that. ☐

g) Does it

seem crazy? ☐
tend to work better at night? ☐
ought to be put in a plastic bag? ☐
have to be repainted very often? ☐
meant to include everyone? ☐

Part C

Choosing structures in context

A Introduction

1 Most students of English learn that there are three main types of conditional clause:

1   If it rains, I'll stay in. (*if* + present simple + *will* + verb)
2   If it rained, I would stay in. (*if* + simple past + *would* + verb)
3   If it had rained, I would have stayed in. (*if* + past perfect + *would* + perfect verb)

■   Describe the grammar of the following examples. (The first one is done for you.)

■   Do these fit the three types of conditional sentences given above? 🔑

a)   If he comes, I go. (*if* + simple present + simple present; this does not fit any of the three types.)[1]
b)   If she finds out, she's going to kill me.
c)   If you suffer from headaches, take Hedex.
d)   If you want it, why don't you go and get it?
e)   If you have toothache, you should go to the dentist.
f)   If David doesn't come, you must ring me.
g)   If they weren't so busy, they would help you.

2 What tenses do you think these speakers used?

■   Put the verbs in brackets into a suitable tense (sometimes more than one tense is possible, and the answer key will tell you which one the speaker actually chose). 🔑

[Sharon and her husband John are being interviewed as part of a survey. They are talking about a bid which their city is making for a 'millennium park'.]

John: If it ever [**get**] off the ground[2], it [**be**] a good thing for Derby, if it [**get**] off.
Sharon: What the park?
John: Yeah.
Interviewer: What do you think of that?
Sharon: Well I don't know. Do you know the latest? I [**wonder**] if that [**be**] what you meant. The millennium thing?
John: Yeah.

[1]This is sometimes referred to as the zero conditional.
[2]'To get off the ground' is an idiomatic expression meaning 'to happen' or 'to be launched'. It is often used with proposed complex projects, or business ventures.

3 What kind of text is the following? Where would you expect to see it? Why are conditionals used in the text? 🔑

> The consistency should be something like mayonnaise and, if you think it's too thick, add a little more of the cooking liquid. Taste and season with salt and pepper. If possible, leave to marinade for several hours. (If you can't get fresh chillies, you can use one level teaspoon of chilli powder instead.)

B Discovering patterns of use

1 Past tenses and conditionals

- Put (A) next to each of the following examples if it refers to a situation which did happen or (B) if it refers to a situation which might happen. (The first two have been done for you.) 🔑

a) It's not going to rain tomorrow. That's why we're going. If it rained, we'd just swim in the hotel pool. (B)

b) We chose the wrong place, I suppose, but we got used to it in the end. If it rained, we'd just swim in the hotel pool. (A)

c) I've got to paint the kitchen this week. If I had time, I would like to go to the cinema.

d) The course I attended kept me very busy. If I had time, I would go to the cinema, but it didn't happen very often.

e) Her car's broken down on the motorway. I would help if I could but my car is out of action today.

f) My daughter needed to speak French more. As long as she saved some of the money, we would try to send her to France every summer.

g) His school report is terrible. Unless things improve, we're stopping all his pocket money.

h) The government was in a dire situation but provided that the economy improved they would stand a good chance of being re-elected the following year.

Observations

- Conditional clauses are normally used when you talk about a possible situation, both in the past and in the future.
- Conditional clauses normally introduce conditions and, usually, another clause, linked to the conditional clause which explains the conditions or gives further information about consequences.
- Although there are many clauses which fit the 1, 2, 3 conditional patterns which you may have learned, there are many which do not.
- Most conditionals help us refer to situations which did not happen. But conditional clauses can refer to conditions which used to prevail in the past and which really happened.

2 Other conjunctions with conditional meanings

Other words or phrases apart from *if* can introduce conditions.

- Underline the words or phrases in the following examples which introduce conditions.
- Can *if* clauses substitute for all the conditional clauses? ⌐

a) Unless they change the team, they're going to lose the next match.

b) This article may be freely distributed provided that this copyright notice is not removed.

c) Supposing that we don't sell the house, we can still move next spring. There are always more buyers in the spring.

d) I'll let you borrow my Walkman on condition that you let me have it back next weekend.

e) She's just trying to find out whether or not her brother'll come to meet her at the airport.

f) She can't decide whether to go to university this year or to take up the job offer.

g) Given that three of Jane Austen's novels have been made into films in the last three years, do you think there are likely to be any more?

Observations

- *If* is not the only word we can use to introduce conditional clauses. Conditions can be introduced in different ways by a wide range of forms (e.g. *provided that, as long as, whether*). Most alternatives to *if* add greater formality or are more likely to occur in written contexts.
- The most common alternative to *if* is *whether* but *if* is still four times more frequent than *whether* in English.
- Some conjunctions can be used interchangeably with *if*:
  'This article may be freely distributed *on condition that / provided that / if* this copyright notice is not removed.'
  If is the less formal equivalent of these forms, but can be substituted for either of them.
- *Supposing (that) ... / given (that) ...* are used to speculate about future possibilities and can sometimes be replaced by *if*:
  '*Supposing that / given that / if* we don't sell the house, we can still move next spring. There are always more buyers in the spring.' (✔)
  but:
  'This article may be freely distributed ~~supposing that~~ / *if* this copyright notice is not removed.' (✗)

GLASBERGEN

"Thank you for calling the Weight Loss Hotline. If you'd like to lose ½ pound right now, press 1 eighteen thousand times."

3 *If*-constructions in speech

The following examples are all transcriptions of recorded speech.

- **Does the conjunction *if* introduce conditions?**
- **If not, what kinds of meanings are conveyed?** ⌐

a) [This conversation takes place in the entrance to a restaurant.]

Waiter: Good evening, sir.
Customer: Evening.
Waiter: Table for …
Customer: Four.
Waiter: If you'd like to come this way.
Customer: Can we put our coats here?
Waiter: Sure.

b) [Two friends, Tim and Jake, are opening a bottle of wine before dinner. Tim gives Jake a jug to pour the wine into.]

Tim: If you'd just like to hold this for me.
Jake: I'll open the bottle.
Tim: It's OK. How was the meeting with Jeff?

Note: It may help you to work out the meanings here if you compare the *if* clauses with alternatives introduced by imperatives. For example, *Come this way* 3(a) and *Hold this for me* (3b).

Observations

- *If* is used, especially in spoken English, to signal requests or invitations to do something. Using *if* in this way is less direct than using an imperative.
- An *if* clause can only be used in this way if the action is an **expected** part of the interchange:

    'If we could put our coats here.' (✗)

    'Excuse me, if you could direct me to the station…' (✗)

- The variety of functions which *if* clauses can perform is dealt with in more detail in the next section.

C Grammar in action

1 Functions of *if* clauses

Here are some more examples of recorded conversations together with an extract from a letter. The *if* clauses are in bold.

- What do you consider to be the main function of *if* in these examples? Here are some suggestions to help you: 🔑

    - to help to explain something or to introduce an explanatory example
    - to make a suggestion, usually in the form of an indirect request
    - to give a reason or reasons for something
    - to offer an interpretation

a) [A student, Sally, is talking in a university seminar.]
Sally: When he experienced that, he realised that all the other great prophets before him weren't Buddhas ... in those days it was just in the same religious tradition ... tradition of enquiry, **if you like**, into the spirit.

b) [Two students, Ben and Tony are talking in a kitchen about a forthcoming dance.]
Ben: Oh there's orange juice in the fridge as well **if you want a drink** ... erm, no, **if we have this** and go back to your house.
Tony: Yeah, help yourself ... there's scissors in the drawer **if you need to cut it open**.

c) [Some friends are looking at some photographs.]
Anne: It's the shorter of the two. **If you look at this photograph here**. Look back there.
Bella: Mm.
Anne: **If you look at this one** ... where is it?
Sue: No, it's the one before.
Anne: Yeah.
Bella: Yeah.
Anne: It's the shorter one of the two.

d) [From a formal letter]

> **If you would like to return your original insurance certificate to us**, we will issue a new certificate for your vehicle within three days.

Observations

- In spoken English, *if* clauses do not only introduce conditions, but carry out a variety of functions such as explaining, suggesting, or giving reasons.
- Whereas in writing we expect an *if* clause to be linked to a main clause, in spoken and informal contexts the *if* clause often stands alone as in **C1(a)** or **C1(c)**.

2 *If* in fixed expressions

■ **Using a dictionary to help you, if necessary, write four sentences making use of four of the following examples:** 🔑

if in doubt   if so   if not   if possible   if anything

if necessary   if only   if ever

Observations

- Many of the fixed and semi-fixed expressions in which *if* occurs can be expanded into clauses. Because they are shorter than clauses, they help speakers and writers use language more economically. They can be explained as forms of ellipsis. (See Units 23 and 24.)
- *If in doubt* is equivalent to 'If you are not certain/sure'.
- *If not* and *If so* are used to signal whether conditions have been fulfilled. They usually follow another *if* clause, or a question:
  'Look to see if it's raining. If so (if it is raining), I'm not coming for a walk!'
  'Is it warm today? If not (if it is not warm today), I'll stay in.'
- *If possible* and *if necessary* could also be expanded into clauses ('If it is possible', 'If it is necessary'), and refer to a situation or condition to which they are linked. However, unlike *if so* and *if not*, they function within the same sentence as the linked condition:
  'If possible, bring a copy of your birth certificate.'
- *If anything* is a fixed expression. It strengthens a statement:
  A: Educational standards are getting worse.
  B: No they're not. If anything, they're improving.
  Note that we cannot say 'if ~~something~~' (✗) or 'if ~~nothing~~' (✗).
- All the above can be placed either at the start or the end of the clause. *If only* and *if ever* generally start clauses, the first introducing wishes and the second strengthening a statement:
  'If ever you visit Malaysia, you must visit my family.' (if you visit)
- *If ever* and *if only* can both be separated by the grammatical subject of the clause:
  'If he ever/ever he had run his own business, he'd know how difficult it is!'
  'If I only/only I had a bit more money, I'd buy that hat!'

D Follow-up

■ Make up your own one-sentence advertisement for the following products. Use a conditional clause in the sentence. 🔑
a) soap
b) holidays on a tropical island
c) the second album by a pop group whose first album sold over half a million copies

■ If you want more practice exercises, do the Further exercises at the end of the unit.

■ If you want further details of points relating to this unit, go to the Reference notes section on pages 204–6.

Summary

- Although the three main types of conditional which are taught are useful, they are only a starting point for understanding and forming other patterns.
- Conditional clauses are used to refer to events or situations in the past which actually took place as well as to events or situations which might happen.
- Although a number of forms in English introduce conditional clauses, *if* is one of the most frequent; it is also one of the most frequent words in the English language and occurs regularly in fixed phrases.
- In spoken English, in particular, *if* clauses have a range of functions and do not only introduce conditions. One important function of *if*-constructions in speech is to act as a polite indirect imperative:

    'If you'll fill this form in, please ...' (Fill this form in.)

  This can only happen where the action that is requested is normally going to occur without question:

    ~~'If you'll lend me your~~ car, please. (✗)

- *If* clauses in speech can also:
  - introduce an explanatory example ('If you look at the figures for March, now ...')
  - make a suggestion ('If we move to another table, John will see us when he arrives.')
- *If* also occurs in a number of fixed and semi-fixed expressions such as 'If in doubt', 'if only', 'if ever', which are best learned as grouped vocabulary items.

"We've got the murder weapon and the motive ... now if we can just establish time-of-death."

The Far Side by Gary Larson © 1982 FarWorks, Inc. Used with permission. All rights reserved.

Further exercises ⚷

1 **Match these clauses to make conditional sentences.**

a) If you have lost money,	you'll stay slim.
b) If I went to Germany,	you must take the call.
c) If you don't eat too much,	the holiday would have been miserable.
d) If she liked spaghetti,	contact the police.
e) If David phones,	I would buy a bigger a car.
f) If the weather had not changed,	she must have been Italian.
g) If I were as tired as you,	I would visit Berlin.
h) If I had enough money,	I should take a holiday.
i) If you can't sleep,	I like drinking beer.
j) If they like wine,	take some sleeping tablets.

2 **These sentences are in two parts. In (a)–(f) fill in the gap with an appropriate verb and tense choice. In (g)–(l) complete the sentence with an appropriate conditional clause.**

a) If the sun shines, we .... go to the sea.

b) If David can't come, ... I ask Michael?

c) If the weather is warm, we .... eat outside.

d) If I pass the exam, my parents .... pay for my holiday.

e) If I went to England, I .... visit London first.

f) If you like beer, there .... a good pub in the next street.

g) If .... , take care.

h) If .... , they can try another shop.

i) You must let me know, if ....

j) If .... , we would cancel the party.

k) If .... , I would not have even spoken to her.

l) We would not have played the match, if ....

3 **Using a dictionary, if necessary, work out the contexts in which you would be likely to meet the following *if* phrases.**

■ Ask yourself if the phrase is more likely to be spoken or written, or whether it is an idiomatic use of *if* in a fixed phrase form (for example, 'We may not go to London more than once a year, if at all.'). One of the sentences is equally likely to be found in spoken or written context.

a) She earns £30,000 a year, if not more.

b) If you could just sign here for me. Thank you.

c) He was overweight, if not fat.

d) The weather looks a bit iffy.*

e) It's a rest, a holiday, if you like, that she needs.

f) If anything, he looked older than the other man.

Iffy means uncertain, i.e. the weather may change / become bad.

g) Few, if any, people wanted to buy the car.

h) If I could just come in here and make a point.

i) The trouble with her is that she's all ifs and buts.[*]

j) As if I would.

k) A: They may not get here by midday.
B: If at all.

4 The texts below are all complete one-line texts and appear as part of advertisements. Write brief notes on the following questions.

- What is the product, company or service which is advertised? (Where appropriate, the names of the products have been deleted.)
- Why is a single sentence used in each case?
- Why are conditionals used?

a) If you're still in the dark about Program Flash, the —— (*product name*) will throw some light on the subject.

b) If only everything in life were as reliable as a —— (*product name*).

c) If your colour TV goes up in smoke or robbers roll out your much-prized Persian carpet, you'll feel a lot happier talking to —— (*company name*).

d) Ask the deaf if silence is golden.

---

[*]*She's all ifs and buts* means that she is rather negative, she always thinks of reasons why something won't work.

Wh-*constructions*

A Introduction

1 Look at the sentences in column A and the alternative versions in column B.

■ Make some general notes on the sorts of situations where you think you would use the column B sentences.

	A	*B*
a)	We need more money.	What we need is more money.
b)	We did it by giving each person a number instead of a name.	How we did it was by giving each person a number instead of a name.
c)	We went wrong. We turned left instead of right.	Where we went wrong was that we turned left instead of right.
d)	I rang you because I needed to check something.	Why I rang you was because I needed to check something.

2 Here is part of an interview.

■ Why does the administrator use the *what*-clause in bold?
■ How does the *what*-clause link back to the first line of the extract?

[A hospital administrator is talking about the job.]
Administrator: I don't get involved in any day-to-day care. I'm not qualified to do that.
Interviewer: Right.
Administrator: I don't have the skills or the qualifications or the experience but **what I am qualified to know about** is that non-clinical aspects can give an important message about the type of care that's delivered.
Interviewer: Yeah.

Observations

- In general, using a *wh*-clause moves the emphasis to the first part of the sentence in some way, therefore the emphasis in **A1** column B above is on:

  '*What* we need ...'

  '*How* we do it ...'

  '*Where* we went wrong ...'

  '*Why* I rang you ...'

  We may need to make such emphasis for a number of reasons:

  – We may want simply to stress our opinion/viewpoint.

  – We may want to contradict what someone else has said or is thinking.

  – Perhaps we are answering a question, repeating part of it, e.g.

  A: So tell me, how did you do it?

  B: How we did it was by giving each person a number instead of a name.

  – We may want the sentence to stand out in its paragraph (or in a monologue in spoken language) as being the most important one in the paragraph.

- In the extract in **A2**, the administrator really wants to emphasise the contrast between her skills and qualifications and those of the clinical staff. The *wh*-clause links back to her sentence 'I'm not qualified to do that.'

B Discovering patterns of use

1 Choosing to use a *wh*-clause: in writing

Now we shall look more closely at sentences with *what*-clauses at the beginning, since these are by far the most common type of *wh*-fronted clauses in written and spoken English.

- **Find the *wh*-clauses.**
- **Choose which reason seems to be the most likely one for the use of the *what*-clause from the options given.** ⚷

a) [This is a newspaper article that mentions some popular British convenience and junk-foods.]

> Junk food may well be high in fat – but human beings also consist partly of fat, and no one says we're junk.
>
> What matters when you're young is that junk food tastes great – like burgers, crisps and hot dogs.
>
> When it comes to food, ignorance and pleasure go hand in hand.

Reason for *what*-clause:

  i) to contradict what the reader is thinking

  ii) to contradict the previous sentence

  iii) to focus on the writer's own viewpoint

b) [from a newspaper article on how to get a place at a university]

> If you want to continue into higher education, the prospects for getting a last-minute place at a university or college are good. What you need is a list of addresses, plenty of time, determination and a phone.

Reason for *what*-clause:

i) to focus on the main conclusion
ii) to contradict what the reader might be thinking
iii) to contradict the previous sentence

c) [from a newspaper article about world leadership in the future]

> World leadership in the new century will not be a question of new philosophy.
>
> Thinking globally will not necessarily mean thinking in a new and different way, because the most important things in life will always be the same, wherever you are in the world.
>
> What is most important, whether it's in a small factory or a huge international corporation is that human beings should always come before economic profit.

Reason for *what*-clause:

i) to focus on the writer's main argument
ii) to contradict the previous sentence
iii) to answer a question the writer thinks the reader is asking

2 Choosing to use a *wh*-clause in speech

In these examples, one of the clauses was a *wh*-clause.

- The clause has been changed to normal word order. Which one do you think was the *wh*-clause?
- Write out the *wh*-clause as you think it was in the original conversation. ☜

a) [A group of people at a dinner party are moving from the living room to the dining room.]
   Hostess: Will you bring the wine in from the other room?
   Host: I did bring the wine yeah, but I forgot to bring the candle. I'll just go back in and get the candle.
   Guest: Oh it looks lovely ... lovely.

b) [A hairdresser is telling a customer about her daily routine.]

Hairdresser: I mean I know if I've worked late then I won't be in till about half past seven.

Customer: Yeah.

Hairdresser: And then I have my tea and go straight to bed.

Customer: Yeah.

Hairdresser: I tend to read or watch television in bed at the moment.

Customer: Yeah.

c) [Two people, Mary and Joan, are talking about the problems faced by carers, i.e. people who stay at home to look after disabled or sick relatives on a full-time basis.]

Mary: If you asked a lot of carers if they want to be looking after their loved ones, they want to be there. They want the support in order to carry on and enable them to carry on doing that role.

Joan: Right.

Mary: It's the lack of support that brings them down, it's the lack of support that causes them ill health.

Joan: Mm.

Observations

- Sentences beginning with a *what*-clause are often used in writing to focus on the writer's main conclusion which they want to bring to the reader's attention.
  What-clauses are therefore important signals that the writer is **evaluating/taking a stance on something**:
  'What matters ...'
  'What you need ...'
  'What is most important ...'

- Almost any part of a clause can be focused on by using a *wh*-clause at the beginning of a sentence, and they can become quite complex:
  'What is important is taste.' (Taste is important; subject is focused on.)
  'What he bought with the money was a car.' (He bought a car with the money; object is focused on.)
  'How he behaved was terrible.' (He behaved terribly; adverb of manner focused on, note change to adjective.)
  'What he said was that he'd never been married before.' (He said that he had never been married before; reporting clause is focused on.)
  'Where he'd been hiding since the robbery was in the basement of his mother's house.' (He'd been hiding in the basement of his mother's house since the robbery; adverb of place is focused on.)

- Remember that however complex the construction, you must have at least two verbs in a *wh*-construction:
  'Where he lived in New York.' (✗)
  'Where he lived (*verb 1*) was (*verb 2*) in New York.' (✓)

C Grammar in action

1 Using other *wh*-clauses

Fronting of other *wh*-clauses is far less frequent than *what*-clauses, but it does occur.

Look at these spoken extracts.

- Underline where a *wh*-clause is fronted. (Look back at the examples in A for the types of clauses you might expect to find.)
- What is the effect of the *wh*-construction? ☞

a) [Richard is talking about how his attitude to his job has changed. He is a health-service manager.]

Richard: I mean, things have got better. Where I saw myself six months ago was very much a two-headed animal, a corporate beast with the need to have an overview of what was happening.

b) [Andrew, a researcher, is interviewing an old man, Douglas, about his early life.]

Douglas: They were very nice people, all of them, very good people.
Andrew: And where you lived, you always stayed in Layard Street, did you?
Douglas: Yeah, I never moved from there, never.

c) [Terry and Muhammed are having a conversation about Muhammed's job. Muhammed has just explained the structure in which he works.]

Terry: You seem to fulfil a very useful role.
Muhammed: Yeah it's interesting, it really is, and why I like this structure is that I'm able to develop a philosophy and I can propagate it by sitting on the quality group, quality committee.

d) [Jenny is telling Bronwen how she came to join a particular club.]

Bronwen: You've been in it a long time then?
Jenny: Yeah, quite a bit, and how I got involved in the first place was one of the women who ran it turned up at our office one day, and just, you know, we got talking and I said I was interested in it, you know.

2 Everyday expressions containing *wh*-clauses

Do you know the meaning of these common expressions?

- Write sample sentences and dialogues containing them.

No matter what   What's more   So what?
Come what may   What on earth

"I don't know how I ever got along without a computer. They make it so much easier to calculate the years, months, weeks, days and seconds until my retirement!"

Observations

- *No matter what*, and *come what may* are both expressions of determination, and show that a speaker means to overcome difficulties or objections:

  'I'm going to pass my driving test this time, no matter what / come what may.'

  The latter is more formal. They can come at either end of the clause.

- *What's more*, *So what?* and *What on earth* are all expressions of attitude. *What's more* is a more conversational equivalent of *Furthermore*, but is used to strengthen a statement, and can be seen as meaning 'And what is more important is …':

  'He's well-qualified. What's more he's got several years' experience.'

- *So what?* expresses a lack of support for what has just been said, often when a speaker has given an example to show a weakness in an argument:

  'There will be hundreds of new TV channels, but so what? The quality will be terrible.'

- *What on earth* is an exclamation expressing surprise. It can either stand alone, or be part of a clause:

  'What on earth! I thought you were in Venice!'

  'I don't know what on earth the hairdresser had done, but my hair looked purple!'

D Follow-up

- Look at an argumentative type of written text in English (for example, a newspaper editorial or a political column) and note uses of *what*-clauses. Change them back to 'normal' word order (as was done in the extracts in **B2** above). How does this affect the text? Does it improve or make it weaker in some way? (If you cannot find any texts of your own, do the exercise with the written texts in **B1**.)

- If you want more practice exercises, do the Further exercises at the end of the unit.

- If you want further details of points relating to this unit, try the Reference notes section on pages 206–7.

Summary

- In English, *wh*-type-clauses (those beginning with words like *what, where, how,* etc.) can be brought to the front of the clause and used as subject for emphasis. The reasons for fronting these clauses may be to signal evaluation (that it is the writer's or speaker's opinion, judgement or stance that is being flagged up), or to contradict an anticipated response from the reader/listener.
- Clauses with *what* are by far the most frequent, in both written and spoken English. Clauses with other words (*why, where, how*) do occur, but are less frequent.
- Speakers often use *wh*-clauses to shift the topic of the conversation on to something they wish to talk about, or else to anticipate a possible question the other person might ask, answering it before it is asked.

"What amazes me is that he can open the piano."

Further exercises ⌾

1 Rewrite the sentences using a fronted *wh*-clause with the word in brackets, as in the example.

Example: I usually take the dog for a walk on a Sunday. (what)
        What I usually do on a Sunday is take the dog for a walk.

a) His reason for not telling us was that he thought we wouldn't believe him. (**why**)
b) I misunderstood her in that I thought she was complaining. (**where**)
c) You really should have written it all down so there could be no dispute. (**what**)
d) The government must now pass a law forbidding such sales as soon as possible. (**what**)
e) It was a mystery to all of us why she should have gone without saying goodbye. (**why**)

2 Now turn these sentences back to 'normal' word order, without a fronted *wh-*clause, as in the example.

Example: Why the students were angry was that they hadn't been given their exam marks.
The students were angry because they hadn't been given their exam marks.

a) Where we got lost was that we turned left instead of right, just as you come into the village.
b) Why certain animals can sense when people are upset is a great mystery.
c) Who you ought to really be worried about is yourself, not your sister.
d) What I wanted to know was whether you were interested or not.
e) How she got herself in such a mess was that she got her foot caught in the hosepipe.

3 Fill the gap with *what, where, who, how* or *why*.

a) .... I'd really like to get to know is that good-looking cousin of yours.
b) .... the government has failed is in the relationship between exports and employment.
c) .... that cat found its way home from 100 miles away is incredible!
d) .... you really need more than anything is a good holiday.
e) .... all children should be given the chance of further education is that without it nowadays, you're unemployable.
f) .... George was trying to say was that we should go back to square one.

4 Match the *wh-*clauses on the left with a suitable clause on the right.

i)	Where I went wrong was	**A**	they hadn't addressed it properly.
ii)	Why she rang was	**B**	in not getting a receipt.
iii)	How they knew the answer was	**C**	that everyone had to promise to pay £50 to the next person after them.
iv)	Why the package never arrived was	**D**	to ask if there was any work available.
v)	How he arranged it was	**E**	someone had tipped them off.*

tipped them off means gave important, often secret, information to them.

13

It, this, that

A Introduction

1 **Look at this piece of spoken English, where the speakers are talking about traffic problems in Britain.**

- ■ **Make notes in the boxes below about the speakers' use of *this* and *that*.** 🗝

[Joan is asking her sister, Margaret, and Margaret's husband, Bill, about the long car journey they had coming to Joan's house. Joan comments on the traffic in general.]

Joan: The roads in this country are just too crowded, aren't they?

Margaret: It's not been too bad today. But there was, there was more traffic than I thought in Weymouth. I mean, we had difficulty …

Bill: Yes, yes, incredible, you can imagine in this weather.

Margaret: We, we stopped, we stopped and stood up on the, sort of, sea front, you know, and got all windswept in the storm and everything.

Bill: That was West Bay.

Margaret: That was West Bay, yes.

Bill: With the tea gardens.

	Example	*Reasons for use of* **this** *or* **that**
a)	in this country	
b)	in this weather	
c)	That was West Bay (×2)	

2 **Look at the next extract.**

- ■ **Think about the difference between using *it*, *this* or *that* to refer to some aspect of the situation. How do these uses fit with the notes you have made in 1, above?** 🗝

[Dorothy is telling Gerry a story about a minor road accident she was involved in.]

Dorothy: There was an incident that I don't think I'll ever forget, and **it** was when I'd just passed my driving test …

Gerry: Yeah, how long ago was **that**?

Dorothy: Er … fifteen, sixteen years ago.

Gerry: Aye.

Dorothy:	My youngest daughter was about five years old and I was taking her to the dentist, and I was coming down Southport Road near the police station and there was a line of traffic but I was at the front you know and there were …
Gerry:	Was **this** in the driving school car or in your own?
Dorothy:	No, no, **it** was in my own car.
Gerry:	Oh, **it** was in your own car, yeah, yeah.

B Discovering patterns of use

1 *It/this/that* in writing

Here we shall look at some ways in which *it*, *this* and *that* are used in writing to organise arguments or points in the text.

- Match the descriptions (i)–(iii) to the functions of *it/this/that* in the extracts (a)–(f). There are two extracts for each description.
- In extract (e) what does *that* refer back to? Is it style or is it the process of analysing style? ◎━

i) In this extract, the writer rejects an idea. *It/This/That* stresses that the idea is being rejected, pushed aside, distanced in some way.

ii) In this extract, a **new** aspect of the topic is introduced, using *it/this/that*. *It/this/that* focuses on the **new** thing that will now be discussed. *It/this/that* gives a signal that an important new point is being made.

iii) In this extract, *it/this/that* simply **continues** the topic of the text.

a)
The brain is our most precious organ – the one above all which allows us to be human. The brain contains 10 billion nerve cells, making thousands of billions of connections with each other. **It** is the most powerful data processor we know, but at the same time **it** is incredibly delicate.

b)
The Migration and Social Security Handbook was published this month. **It** is aimed at emigrants and immigrants, from business people to students and refugees.

c)
Coming out from the base of the brain like a stalk is *the brain stem*. **This** is the swollen top of the spinal cord, which runs down to our 'tail'.

d)
A quarter of Britain's strawberries have rotted following June's torrential rains. **This** has led to supermarket shortages and wreaked havoc with advertising campaigns.

e)
It is, of course, impossible to analyse style. **That** wouldn't be stylish, would it? And anyway, what is commendably stylish in one person is offensive in another.

f)
Lots of people don't like boxing; many would like to see it banned. But to have men decide for women that we really don't want to mess up our hair and get involved in such a nasty, aggressive business is a different issue. **That's** just plain sexist.

> **Observations**
>
> ● *It, this* and *that* can be used to refer to things in a text, but they function in different ways:
>   – *It* simply continues what we are already talking/writing about, without focusing in any special way.
>   – *This* is used to focus or highlight new, important topics in the text, making them immediate.
>   – *That* is used to distance ourselves from aspects of the topic.
> ● The ideas of making something immediate by focusing on it or making it distant by distancing ourselves from it are similar to the examples in **A** above.

2 *It/this/that* in spoken English

Look at some more spoken examples under (a) and (b) below.

■ Make notes in the boxes on the next page on why the speakers choose *it, this* and *that* (marked in bold). Here are some possible reasons to choose from. If you do not agree with these, add your own reasons. ☞

 – in question tags, e.g. *isn't it?/wouldn't it?* we do not normally use *this* or *that*
 – used to refer to the place where the speakers are at the moment
 – used to continue referring to something already being talked about
 – used for an important new topic
 – used for something just mentioned, but which is not going to be important in the story

a) [Iris, who is disabled and uses a wheelchair, is starting a story about how she was invited into the pilot's cabin during a flight from Cyprus to London. Because she is disabled, she had to be taken on to the plane in a special lift.]
Iris: Well, I don't know how I got **this** honour really. I had all the badges, you know, I used to be in the air force, and I'd spoken to two or three people, but when we got on the plane, they took me on first, because they had to lift me on, you know, with **that** lift, and the pilot was sat in one of the seats. There was nobody on the plane but me, and, I don't know, I must have said, either said something funny about flying, or he'd said something, noticed my badges, I don't know which it was …

b) [A customer asks for help in a bookshop.]
Customer: I wonder if you could help me.
Assistant: Yeah.
Customer: I'm looking for two books, one's a book on organisation. *Schools as organisations*, by Charles Handy. [Assistant: Oh, yes] Can you tell me where **it** might be?
Assistant: Yes, there would be one or two places we've got **it** on stock. [Customer: Yes] **It** might be in the business section, because all his books are generally at the business section. [Customer: Yes] But I doubt …
Customer: **That**'s on **this** floor, is **it**?
Assistant: Yeah, it's downstairs.

Example	Reasons for use of *it*, *this*, or *that*
1 how I got **this** honour	
2 with **that** lift	
3 tell me where **it** might be?	
4 we've got **it** on stock	
5 **It** might be in the business section	
6 **That**'s on **this** floor, is **it**?	

*I'm a mother, a wife, a business woman, a teacher, a nurse, a cook
and a housekeeper ... that's just 23 pounds per woman."*

Observations

- *It* is the most neutral word, simply continuing reference to what is already the topic.
- *This* and *that* change the focus on the topic in some way:
  - *This* increases the focus, for example, to introduce a new topic.
  - *That* decreases the focus, suggesting that the thing referred to is not going to be important, or that the speaker wants to distance him/herself from it in some way.
- Tags normally use *it*, even when they refer back to clauses where the subject is *this* or *that*:

  'That's on this floor, is it?'

C Grammar in action

Choosing between *it/this* and *that*

1 **Look at these examples of story-telling in spoken English.**

- **Why do think the speakers use *this* in the highlighted places?**
- **Could you replace *this* with *a*, *an* or *the*?**

a) [The speaker, Colin, is telling a story about an earthquake.]

Colin: **This** guy, this is true, there was a guy down in Mesa, and that town got, you know, it got really badly hit, there were all sorts of old buildings, you know, little old cottages, and everything fell, but he was in **this** hotel that had been badly built and he ….

b) [The speaker, Roger, is telling a story about a friend who travelled on a long-distance bus across Europe, and who ended up sitting next to a very large woman, which made his journey uncomfortable.]

Roger: My mate came down on his way to Australia, you know, from London and he was the last one to turn up on the bus at Victoria Coach Station. It was just packed, and the only seat left was next to **this** enormous woman and he said he went all the way across Europe in the bus with one buttock on the seat you know, and she just she was just knitting and eating …

2 **Here are two extracts from essays by learners of English, marked by their teacher.**

- **Why do you think the teacher crossed out *it* and asked the student to change the texts?**

a) [In this essay, the student is describing two questionnaires she did for a class project. Here she describes the first questionnaire.]

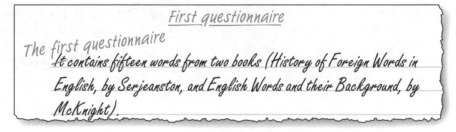

First questionnaire

The first questionnaire ~~It~~ contains fifteen words from two books (*History of Foreign Words in English*, by Serjeanston, and *English Words and their Background*, by McKnight).

b) [In this essay, the student is describing different ways of studying language, and has now come to talk about dialectology (the study of different dialects).]

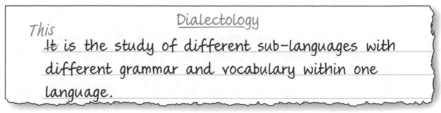

Dialectology

This ~~It~~ is the study of different sub-languages with different grammar and vocabulary within one language.

3 *That* in everyday expressions

Do you know the following common expressions?

- **When might people say them?**
- **Write some sample sentences or dialogues containing the expressions.**

That's that/it   That's all right/okay   That's right

D Follow-up

- Look at an editorial in an English newspaper, or any other text where someone is presenting arguments or opinions, and note how *it*, *this* and *that* are used to refer to the points the writer is making.
- If you want more practice exercises, do the Further exercises at the end of this unit.
- If you want further details of points relating to this unit, go to the Reference notes on pages 207–8.

Summary

- *It, this* and *that* can all be used to refer to things, situations and ideas, but do so in different ways.
- *It* continues the topic we are already speaking or writing about. *It* is not used to introduce a new topic (especially at the beginning of a text or a new section in the text).
- *This* highlights or focuses upon a new topic, or something new and important in the text. *This* is also used in spoken stories instead of *a/an* to introduce new, important people, places, ideas and things. *This* creates immediacy, and is used for things which are 'here and now' in the situation.
- *That* is used when we want to distance ourselves from an idea (or person or thing), or when we want to dismiss or reject an idea.
- *That* is also used to refer to earlier situations or anything which the speaker feels is distant in time or place.

Further exercises ☞

1 **Look at this extract of spoken English. Speaker A is telling B about crime incidents in his area. He starts a story about an elderly lady who burglars tried to trick by getting her to leave her house so that they could go in and steal things. In some places, you are given a choice of *it, this* or *that*.**

- Underline which one(s) could be used. It may be possible in some cases to use all of them.
- Give reasons for your choice(s). The key tells you which word the speaker originally used, and suggests why.
- What does 'that was that' mean towards the end of the story?

A: She's about eighty-odd. She had somebody knocking at her windows shouting "Fire! fire!" and **it/this/that** was just a trick to get her out of the house, you see.

B: Mm.

A: And er, she was very sensible, the old lady was, she phoned.

B: Good.

A: And how we heard about **it/this/that**, **it/this/that** was the following morning, the window cleaner came. I told him about **it/this/that**. He couldn't clean the windows because the detectives were there. The detectives came. **It's/This's/That's** how we heard about **it/this/that**.

B: Mm.

A: And **that was that**. **It/this/that's** about the only incident though ... Well, I had the flu. I finished up with ... **it/this/that's** got nothing to do with crime.

B: **That's** all right.

2 Here are some examples from written texts. Some of the examples of *it/ this/ that* have been changed from the original. Find them and correct them. (The key gives the original versions – remember very often one of the other forms is grammatically correct, but the writer uses another to focus the attention differently.)

a) Daniel felt his life did not begin the day he was born. That began when he first saw Mary in the schoolhouse sixteen years ago.

b) Daniel took the little package. He unwrapped this and then smiled. It's gold sovereigns, Mary. His eyes held wide. 'Sure', she smiled. 'That's for us to go to America. You've always wanted to go there. Let's go, Daniel, while we can get out.'

c) The forest was silent and so were the women. They walked steadily, cat-like. That moment had been long-rehearsed. Anna, from when she was a baby, knew that secret path into the forest and she approved of it.

3 Here are some idiomatic expressions using *it*, *this* and *that*. Using a dictionary if necessary, fill the gaps in the sentences using them.

this, that and the other   this is it   that's that   and that   that's it

a) A: Sally just doesn't understand the lectures, nor do lots of other students.
   B: Well, yes, ... , somebody ought to tell the lecturer, it's a desperate situation.

b) A: What were you talking to Joss about?
   B: Oh, ..., nothing in particular.

c) A: But I don't want to go!
   B: You'll do as you're told and .... ! No arguments!

d) A: So, ... for today then, we can go home now.
   B: Good.

e) A: What did she want to talk about?
   B: Oh, the exams, you know, grades, deadlines ....

A Introduction

1 Read the sentences below. Some of them are correct and others are incorrect or inappropriate.

- Draw two boxes and label them A and B. Put the correct sentences in box A and the other sentences in box B.
- Correct the sentences in box B.
- Try to think of three rules for when it is not appropriate to use the passive voice. ☞

a) The station was left by the train five minutes ago.
b) Languages are taught in every school in the country.
c) My jacket was made in England.
d) He was died by his brother.
e) Paper was invented by the Chinese.
f) The new road will be completed early next year.
g) Two litres are contained by the bottle.
h) The interview is being televised throughout the world.
i) A nice house is had by them.
j) You could see that he was going to be attacked by a large dog.

2 In the following extract from a real conversation no standard passives are used by the speaker.

- Underline all the places where a standard passive construction **could** have been used. (The first one has been done for you.)
- Do the forms you have underlined have anything in common? ☞

[The speaker is telling a friend about a car accident in which she was involved.]
I was just driving along talking to Jill and we'd, like, stopped at some traffic lights and then – bang! – there was this almighty crash and <u>we got pushed forward</u> all of a sudden. Jill nearly, you know, hit the windscreen. We'd got hit from behind. When I got out, I just looked and the whole bumper had, like, got sort of pushed in. When the police came, they called a local garage and had two recovery vehicles free my car. The lorry driver apologised and all I could say was, like, tell him to get his eyes tested.

- You have probably learned how to form passive sentences by changing the position of the object in a sentence and using the verb *be* + past participle. That is to say, standard passives are formed by 1) placing the object at the beginning of the sentence 2) using the verb *to be* + past participle or *have* + *be* + past participle which agrees with the first-placed item 3) placing the subject after the verb phrase in a phrase with *by* before the noun:

  'Seven candidates took the examination.' (active)

  'The examination was taken by seven candidates.' (passive)

- The key to **A1** contains further information about which verbs can and cannot be used in the passive, if you want to revise these. However, most of this unit looks at how speakers and writers use passive forms and when they are appropriate or not appropriate. It also introduces a greater variety of ways of constructing passive forms, for example the *get*-passive seen in **A2**.

B Discovering patterns of use

1 Omitting the agent

- Read the following extracts from written texts, and underline the passive constructions.
- Give the main reason or reasons *why* the agent, or person(s) responsible for the action or event, is omitted. ⌾━

a)

> The woods were visible from the back windows and it was clear why the house was called Commonwood House, because there were views of the common from all sides.

b)

> The hospital where Maggie in Little Dorrit was treated for fever is able to provide its impoverished patients with fruit and soft drinks ...

c)

> As a result of the 25-mile Challenge £200 was raised for the Cancer Appeal. Thank you to all sponsors and congratulations to Mrs Evans for her splendid contribution.

d)

> Most of the work was completed before the start of the nineteenth century. Thus the next chapter will focus on how land was farmed in Northamptonshire and Bedfordshire in the eighteenth century. Changes after 1700 will not be discussed.

2 The form and function of different passive constructions

- Sort the passive constructions in the following sentences according to their structure.

    Choose from the following structures:

    get + past participle

    have + object + past participle

    'standard' passive

- What contexts do you think they were used in? ☞

a) **This poor bloke who got charged** in nineteen eighty eight is still looking for justice.

b) If I went and worked and I earned two hundred and fifty a week, over the year it's a lot of money. But if **I was given that lump sum** right at the beginning of the year just think of the interest!

c) He **had his stitches taken out** yesterday.

d) **This woman was abducted** by a youth and er I think **her gold ring was taken off** or some jewellery and er that was a cause of concern for us because we are so close to the place.

e) So **do the results of that get fed back** into the management process then?

f) So I said 'Oh well we'll go down and **have it looked at** then. Down to the accident and emergency department.'

g) And they said 'What questions **do you get asked** most?' and they said 'Well one of the silliest ones **we often get asked** is "Do the crew sleep on board?"'

- Phrases such as 'I had my hair cut' or 'I got my leg stuck' are called **pseudo-passives**. They are not formed in the same way as passives but they are passive actions in that subjects have things done to them or for them.
- *Get*-passives are a little more informal than *have*-passives, and are more likely to occur in spoken than in written English. They are normally used without an agent.
- The *get*-passive should not be confused with the form of *get* which means 'become':
  'I get bored on long flights.' = I become bored on long flights.
- *Have*-passives should not be confused with standard passives in the present perfect:
  'The garage has been boarded up.' (standard passive, present perfect)
  'The garage has had its windows broken.' (*have*-passive, present perfect)
- Unlike standard passives, both *get*- and *have*-passives involve a subject ('**He** got robbed.'/'**My sister** had her house flooded.') and yet the meaning is that these subjects were completely uninvolved in the action described. This means that they can be used to give a strong sense of helplessness on the part of the subject, particularly in the case of *get*-passives. **C2** gives more details of how these different forms are used and the effect they have.

C Grammar in action

1 Contrasting uses of agented and agentless passives

- **Compare the following sets of sentences and make notes on the different meanings conveyed by each sentence.**

1. a) I was told you are leaving for another job.
   b) Somebody told me you are leaving for another job.
   c) Carol told me you are leaving for another job.

2. a) An increase in membership fees was suggested.
   b) I suggested an increase in membership fees.
   c) Somebody suggested an increase in membership fees.

3. a) The port was blockaded by French lorry drivers.
   b) The port was blockaded.
   c) They blockaded the port.

4. a) The government have put up taxes again.
   b) They've put up taxes again.
   c) Taxes have been put up again.

- The agent is omitted from passive sentences if:
  – we do not know who performed the action.
  – the agent or 'doer' is not particularly important. What is done is more important than who does it.
  – the agent or 'doer' is so obvious that it is not necessary to repeat it.
  – we do not wish to reveal the agent, either deliberately or out of politeness.
- In some cases the agent is omitted from passive sentences if it would be embarrassing to the agent to mention them or in order to deflect possible criticism. (e.g. 'I was told you were leaving us for another job'). Alternatively, a dummy subject (e.g. *they* or *somebody*) can also hide the real subject (e.g. 'They say you're leaving us for another job'). The agent is also normally omitted when the action is performed by a large group of nameless people (e.g. 'The whole city was rebuilt after the earthquake').

2 Typical uses of *get*-type passives

Get-passives are often used as alternatives to standard passive forms. The following passives, which are all formed with the verb *get* + past participle, have been collected from actual conversations.

- **Do the passives have anything in common?**
- **Are there any exceptions?**
- **What kinds of events were people talking about?** ⌐

got flung about the car   got killed   got locked out   got lumbered*

got criticised   got picked for the team   got sued   got promoted

got burgled   got beaten   got intimidated

3 Choosing between different passives

a) In the following extracts from recorded conversations both *get*-passives and passives formed with *have* + object + past participle are found.

- **What differences do you notice in the way the two passive constructions are used?** ⌐

i) [A married couple, Jill and Matt, are discussing with a friend, Carol, the hurricane-like storms which hit Britain in 1987.]

Jill: Remember those gales when our roof was blown off?
Matt: Yes, by that massive gust.
Jill: Then the pipes got frozen up and we had three plumbers come in to repair it all.
Carol: And they never even put out weather warnings.

Lumbered means to have to do things you do not want to do.

ii) [Two students are talking about a hairdressing salon.]

Ann: Your hair looks nice.

Toni: I had it cut by the new hairdresser in the Student Union building.

Ann: Not that place where I got my head stuck in the drier?

Toni: Must be, I suppose. Yes, that one.

Ann: Huh, and they still let them open.

iii) [Two friends are discussing whether to employ a lawyer.]

Don: Do you know how much lawyers get paid for an hour the best ones?

Simon: I don't care.

Don: Six hundred pounds an hour.

Simon: I don't care.

b) Some of the following sentences are more likely to be used than others, **even though they are all grammatically possible.**

- **Decide which ones seem most likely to be used, and mark with a star (*) any you think would not occur very often.** ⌇

i) I was rung up yesterday by someone trying to sell life insurance.

ii) A potted plant was given to me by my daughter on my birthday.

iii) I got my car fixed, but it cost the earth.

iv) Chips are not normally served at breakfast.

v) Every student was sent a letter demanding immediate payment of fees.

vi) I had my house burnt down last year. It was a nightmare.

vii) My hair was cut yesterday. Do you like it?

viii) I've always had my fees paid by the government.

ix) The roof was demolished in the storm last night.

x) Our house got broken into last night.

D Follow-up

- Find an English language newspaper. Read an article about a recent event which interests you. Underline any passive constructions. Is the agent named? If so, why? If not, why not? A common passive construction in such contexts is *It has been said that* or *It has been reported that*. Why is it common?
- If possible, video part of an English language soap-opera or drama. Listen for passives, and pseudo-passives. Do they fit the patterns and functions we have dealt with in this unit?
- If you want more practice do the Further exercises at the end of the unit.
- If you want further details of points relating to this unit, go to the Reference notes section on pages 208–10.

Summary

- The passive voice enables a writer or speaker to focus on who or what is affected by an action. The item which comes first in a passive sentence receives the most emphasis. The passive voice is formed when you use the verb *to be* with a past participle (e.g. 'The door is locked at 10.30 a.m.,' 'The wine will be delivered direct to your home,' 'The match is being shown on TV tonight').
- After modal verbs the base verb *be* or *have been* are used. (e.g. 'Who should be questioned about this?' 'She couldn't possibly have been criticised at work').
- The agent (the person or thing that performs an action) is omitted from passive sentences if you do not know or do not wish to reveal who it is. The agent can also be omitted if it is obvious who or what the agent is or if it is simply unnecessary to mention (e.g. 'Swimming in the lake is prohibited').
- If an agent or instrument (something used to perform the action) does need to be mentioned, then the words *by* and *with* respectively are used (e.g. 'She was told off by the teacher,' 'He was attacked with a knife').
- Passives are not normally formed from stative or intransitive verbs (e.g. 'Carol seems right for the job.' 'The job is seemed right by Carol. (✗)).
- Pseudo-passives (often with *have* or *get*) are common in informal English. They also have subjects which have things done for them, to them or which happen to them (e.g. 'My car got broken into last night', 'I had my hair cut').
- Pseudo-passives with *have* are normally used when somebody does something for you or when you arrange a service, usually by an expert or professional. *Get-* passives are very common in spoken English, are likely to be used without an agent and are most often used when the speaker considers a situation adverse or problematic.

Further exercises ⚷

1 Using these words, form five sentences in the passive voice.

Leonardo da Vinci	sing	the telephone
Christopher Columbus	paint	the *Mona Lisa*
Alexander Graham Bell	invent	*Born in the USA*
Tolstoy	write	America
Bruce Springsteen	discover	*War and Peace*

2 Match the two parts of the following sentences. The first one, (i) + (a), has been done for you.
Example:

i)	Food prices	a)	... have been increased. (✓)
ii)	The metal	b)	... was opened by a pop star.
iii)	The centre of the old town	c)	... are all manufactured in Singapore.
iv)	The video recorders	d)	... should be heated up to a high temperature.
v)	The other candidate	e)	... must have been interviewed earlier in the morning.
vi)	The new supermarket	f)	... is being rebuilt.

3 The following sentences are not very formal. Turn them into impersonal, formal public notices by using the passive voice. In some cases the infinitive has to be changed into a noun. The first one has been done for you.

i) You are not permitted to smoke here.   (Smoking is not permitted here.)
ii) You should keep your dogs on a lead.
iii) You must not park your cars on the grass.
iv) You are not allowed to dive in the swimming area.
v) We speak English here.
vi) You can pay your fees at the entrance.

4 The following extract is from a children's school Science book. Use the verb in brackets to form the passive voice throughout the extract. Make notes on why there is no mention of agents in the extract.

Double glazing ....

When houses are .... (**double glaze**), only a relatively small amount of heat is .... (**lose**) through the windows. Double glazed windows have two panes of glass and air is .... (**trap**) between them, preventing escape of the heat. Double glazing also ensures that condensation is .... (**reduce**) and noise is .... (**decrease**). Heating bills can be .... (**reduce**) when double glazing is .... (**install**). People living near busy roads or airports also find that double glazing has to be .... (**fit**).

5 Write two sentences using these lists of words. One sentence should be a passive, the other sentence a pseudo-passive. Make notes on the differences between the sentences.

Example:
i) hair   cut   last Wednesday   Snips
   a) I had my hair cut last Wednesday at Snips.
   b) My hair was cut last Wednesday at Snips.
ii) house   break into   last night
iii) must   driving licence   renew   by January
iv) car   fix
v) always   club fees   pay   my parents

6 Here are three headlines from national newspapers in Britain. They each report the same event but the messages are different. Say what you think about the different meanings.

A IBM dismisses 500 factory workers.
B 500 factory workers dismissed by IBM.
C 500 factory workers dismissed.

Headline A uses the active voice because ...
Headline B uses the passive voice because ...
Headline C uses the agentless passive because ...

Position of adverbs

A Introduction

Usually, English adverbs are found in one or more typical places in clauses.
Read (a)–(i) below, which are extracts from real conversations.

- In your own words, can you describe the places where the adverbs are in the clause? (The adverbs to focus on are in bold type, and the first one is done for you.)
- Why is (i) wrong? ⌐

a) I've never had a holiday like it **in my life**. (Place of adverb: the end of the clause, after the object.)
b) **In the meantime**, I'd met your mum.
c) They **sometimes** get here early.
d) I don't **normally** eat seafood.
e) I've **never** had a holiday like it in my life.
f) We **usually** have tea for breakfast, and coffee later.
g) She's **always** ready to help.
h) I'm **always** being accused of things I haven't done.
i) She moved **closer** her chair and spoke to him in a low voice.

Some terms you might find useful when talking about adverb positions are in the following table:

clause			
subject	*auxiliary verb(s)*	*main verb*	*object/complement*
Everyone		loves	a holiday.
Dennis	has	lost	his keys.
The man	is being	questioned.	
I		am	unhappy.
She	did	forget	it.

Despite the surge protector, Marty still shorted out on too much coffee.

B Discovering patterns of use

1 Extending the rules about adverbs

Here we extend the rather simple rules we made in **A** by looking at some examples from real conversations.

In each pair of sentences which follow, one of the versions is the **real conversation**, and the other is not.

■ **Which one do you think is the real conversation?** ☞

a) [The speakers are talking about how few women get important jobs. B is of the opinion that this is typical, but A disagrees.]
i) A: I know of instances.
   B: Yeah, there are always going to be exceptions.
ii) A: I know of instances.
   B: Yeah, there are going always to be exceptions.

b) [The speakers are talking about going to the doctor's.]
i) A: And when you first got the problem, did you immediately go to the doctor's
   B: Yeah.
   A: Or did you wait a while?
ii) A: And when you first got the problem, did immediately you go to the doctor's?
   B: Yeah.
   A: Or did you wait a while?

c) [The speakers are talking about the young person's railcard system for travel in Britain.]

i) A: So they don't ask you to show the card?
   B: No I've never been asked to show it. There were three guards on the train today and I got never asked to show my railcard.

ii) A: So they don't ask you to show the card?
    B: No I've never been asked to show it. There were three guards on the train today and I never got asked to show my railcard.

■ **Based on a), b) and c) above, what rules could you make for:**

adverbs with the *going to* future?   Rule: ....

adverbs with the *do/does/did* in questions?   Rule: ....

adverbs with the *get*-passive form?   Rule: ....

2 Adverbs between the subject and the verb

In **A** we saw how adverbs can come **between** the subject and the main verb.

■ **Based on examples (a)–(f), what types of adverbs usually occur in this position?**

■ **Why is *honestly* in different positions in (e) and (f)?** ☞

a) I **just** hope you don't have to make that decision yourself.
b) It **really** hurts when you say that.
c) I've **never** noticed it until now.
d) He **frequently** misunderstands even simple things.
e) I don't **honestly** think my kids will pay for my healthcare.
f) He believed that he had dealt **honestly** with his customers.

3 More than one adverb

Look at the texts below, and study the adverbs. Texts (a)–(c) are all about small countries.

■ **Try and make a general rule for the word order when there is more than one adverb in a clause. Remember, adverbs often describe the time, the place and the manner of, or reason for, doing something, or the frequency of something (how often or how many times it happens).**

(To help you, each sentence has two boxes after it in which you can make notes of the order, as in the example.) ☞

Example
[newspaper report]

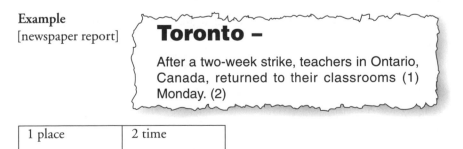

Toronto –

After a two-week strike, teachers in Ontario, Canada, returned to their classrooms (1) Monday. (2)

1 place	2 time

a) Reunion/[Economy and the land]

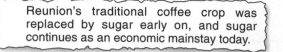
> Reunion's traditional coffee crop was replaced by sugar early on, and sugar continues as an economic mainstay today.

┌─────────────┬─────────────┐
│   │   │
└─────────────┴─────────────┘

b) St Pierre and Miquelon/[History and politics]

> Basque fishermen found their way to the islands in the sixteenth century, and French settlement began in the seventeenth century.

┌─────────────┬─────────────┐
│   │   │
└─────────────┴─────────────┘

c) Solomon Islands/[History and politics]

> Hunter-gatherers lived on the islands as early as 1000BC.

┌─────────────┬─────────────┐
│   │   │
└─────────────┴─────────────┘

■ **Now check which statements seem to be true, based on (a)–(c), above.**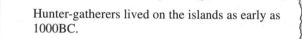

	True	False
i) Manner adverbs usually come before time adverbs.	☐	☐
ii) Place adverbs usually come after time adverbs.	☐	☐
iii) Time adverbs usually come before manner adverbs.	☐	☐
iv) Place adverbs usually come before time adverbs.	☐	☐

■ **Now do these sentences in the same way as (a)–(c) above.**

d) The hospital was on red alert three times during December.

┌─────────────┬─────────────┐
│   │   │
└─────────────┴─────────────┘

e) I arrived an hour late because of the traffic.

┌─────────────┬─────────────┐
│   │   │
└─────────────┴─────────────┘

f) I have been back and forth – ninety mile round trip – several times each week.

┌─────────────┬─────────────┐
│   │   │
└─────────────┴─────────────┘

g) The computer is designed to help people who cannot write normally because of a physical disability.

┌─────────────┬─────────────┐
│   │   │
└─────────────┴─────────────┘

C Grammar in action

1 Adverbs and style

Look at examples (a)–(c).

- **What is special or unusual about the position of the adverbs in bold in these examples?**
- **What would the word order be in an informal, spoken version of the report in (c)?** ⊙━

a) [radio news announcement]
   The government has decided to postpone **indefinitely** an agreement on the easing of the trade barriers with South America.

b) [The speaker is contributing to a discussion about feminism. *Just 17* is a popular magazine aimed at teenage girls.]
   Many of the Editors of *Just 17* … have always stated **in public** their commitment to female equality and to producing magazines which don't patronise girls.

c) [extract from an American newspaper]
   Washington: The US Senate **on Sunday** approved a bill that would compensate Indian tribes in North Michigan for short-changing their ancestors in a 19th century land deal.

2 Adverbs at the beginning of clauses

- **Compare these two texts (a) and (b), also about small countries.**
- **Underline any adverbs which are placed at the start of sentences.**
- **In what way are they different?**

a) [History and politics]

> **Niue**
> More than one thousand years ago Niue's first inhabitants arrived either from Samoa or another eastern Pacific island. In 1774 Captain James Cook of Britain came to Niue, calling it Savage Island because of the hostility of the inhabitants. The island did not come under British rule until 1900. In 1901 Niue was annexed to New Zealand, and the island became a self-governing territory of New Zealand in 1974.

b) [History and politics]

> **Qatar**
> No strong central government existed in Qatar before Saudi Muslims gained control in the late eighteenth century. Ottoman Turks occupied the region from 1872 to 1916, when Qatar became a British protectorate. Although oil was discovered in 1940 on the Western side of Qatar's peninsula, the outbreak of World War II postponed exploitation for another nine years.

D Follow-up

- As you read English texts, collect any examples of unusual positions of adverbs, and try to understand why the adverbs are used in those positions.
- Does your own language, or any other language you know normally have adverbs between the verb and the object? If so, what kinds of adverbs may be used in that position: time, place, manner, frequency, reason?
- Go back to the two texts in **C2**, about Niue and Qatar, and try changing the positions of the time adverbs. Are the texts you produce by doing this different from the originals? In what way? Are they better/not so good? Why?
- If you want more practice exercises, do the Further exercises at the end of the unit.
- If you want further details of points relating to this unit, go to the Reference notes section on pages 210–13.

Summary

- Adverbs can occur in most places in English clauses, but it is only in rather formal styles (especially journalism) that they are used between the verb and the object.
- When auxiliary verbs are used, the neutral position for adverbs is after the first auxiliary verb.
  The position after the first auxiliary verb is commonly used for short adverbs, negative, intensifying and indefinite frequency adverbs, and for adverbs expressly signalling speaker/writer viewpoint.
- When more than one adverb is used after the verb in the same clause, there is a normal, neutral order for their use (manner–place–time).
- The normal order can be changed for special emphasis and foregrounding. This is often done in order to organise the text in some way, for example around a time-frame, or around a series of places or locations.

Further exercises ☞

1 Put the adverbs in their most typical, neutral position in these sentences, as in the example.

Example:
I didn't realise what was happening. (**quite**)
I didn't quite realise what was happening. (**short adverb after first auxiliary verb**)

a) They're going to sell up and move out. (**probably**)
b) I got thrown out of my seat. (**suddenly**)
c) The tickets are on sale. (**twice a week**)
d) I did my duty. (**simply**)
e) I couldn't think of any reason to say no. (**honestly**)
f) He's the first to complain. (**usually**)
g) She wouldn't allow it. (**under any circumstances**)
h) Would you sign the bottom, please? (**just**)
i) We have dinner at 6.30, you know that. (**always**)
j) She always dealt with her clients. (**honestly**)

2 Here is a text about the Spanish island of Ibiza. An Ibicenco is a native of the island. In the right-hand column, there are some adverbs which were in the original text. Can you guess where in the clause each adverb occurred? The clauses of the text are divided up, with the adverbs that were in each clause alongside.

Text	Adverbs
(sentence 1) There were two taxis: this number had rocketed to three.	in 1943 on the island by the early sixties according to popular memory
(sentence 2) Almost more remarkable is another pair of statistics relating to private cars.	(no adverbs)
(sentence 3) Remembers one eminent Ibicenco, there were 'twenty or thirty' cars. Ibiza has the highest number of cars per head.	in the mid-fifties on the whole island in Europe now
(sentence 4) A handful of ancient buses ploughed their way some of which had only one service a day; necessitating long queues.	into town from the villages in the early hours of the morning in village squares

3 Here are some sentences with adverbs in unusual positions.

- Why is the position unusual, what is the effect of these unusual positions and if they suggest a special style, what style is it?
a) The government cancelled immediately all contact with the terrorists.
b) I never ever would have thought that she would do such a thing.
c) She's been really longing to meet you for ages.
d) Three times a week I've driven up that motorway, for the last ten years.
e) I shall, in any case, be writing to you soon to let you know our decision.

Around the noun in context

A Introduction

1 **Look at the following. Extracts (a) and (b) are short film reviews taken from an Australian magazine while (c) is part of a conversation between a doctor and a pregnant patient.**

■ **Put *the* in the brackets where you think it is needed, or leave a blank if you think no article is needed.** 🔑

a)
> ( ) Tensions between ( ) three middle-aged couples after a blonde stranger arrives are explored in a 1984 Greek film.

b
> A hideous comic-book monster comes to ( ) life and terrifies a creepy house where a student lives. ( ) monster is scary but ( ) film is not.

c) Stella: I've only seen (…) midwife once.
   Doctor: Right. Right. Okay. Did she explain to you what (…) 'case-load midwifery' involves?
   Stella: That I would actually see her right from (…) beginning. [Doctor: Mm] when she books me in, to (…) end, basically (…) delivery. She would hopefully deliver (…) baby if I wanted her to deliver it.
   Doctor: Mm.

Observations

- You probably found *tensions* and *three middle-aged couples* in **A1(a)** easiest to decide on. These do not need *the* because they are 'new' plural things in the text; they have not been mentioned before.
- In **A1(b)**, *the monster* and *the film* are both already part of the text, they are already mentioned, so they take *the*.
- In **A1(b)** we have the expression *come to life*. This expression never has *the* before 'life', and can be learnt as a fixed form. The reason it never has *the* is that *life* is being used in a very general sense to refer to something abstract. Compare *music, love, death*, which are also often used in this way (e.g. 'I'm not afraid of death', 'Life without music would be nothing').
- In **A1(c)** *the* is used to refer to single, specific things in relation to the situation: *the midwife, the delivery, the baby* and so on. When the reference is more general, countable nouns are put into the plural: 'Young babies need a lot of sleep.' You may be familiar with these types of rules for the use of *the*. In this unit we are going to explore more uses of *the* and try to make some new, more generally useful rules.

B Discovering patterns of use

1 Modified noun phrases

These sentences, taken from a women's magazine, contain noun phrases with *the*. The noun phrases are in bold and the main nouns are underlined.

■ **What do the noun phrases have in common?**

a) <u>The state</u> **of women's health** in the 1990s reflects <u>the price</u> **of progress**.
b) <u>The role</u> **of women** in today's society has been achieved through centuries of major cultural changes.
c) In this special health report we look into <u>the causes</u> **and** <u>cures</u> **of your six most common health complaints**.

■ **Why do the next examples of noun phrases with prepositions not have *the*?**

d) What makes us different from <u>women</u> **of past decades** is our range of choices.
e) Only in America ... psychologists for pets! In California, <u>owners</u> **of mentally disturbed dogs** are now paying for pet psychologists to help them.

Observations

- All the nouns in **B1(a)**, **(b)** and **(c)** are followed by a phrase starting with a preposition (*of* in these examples). You may have learnt this rule: when a noun has a phrase with a preposition after it (e.g. 'of women in today's society'), use *the* before the noun. But this is not always so.
- In **B1(d)** and **(e)** there **is** a prepositional phrase, but the meaning of 'women' and 'owners' is still general and open-ended. Compare this with:
  'The women of the other team all came from Cairo.'
  'The owners of the three dangerous dogs had to pay a fine.'
  Here *the team* and *the three dangerous dogs* limit the meaning of *women* and *owners* to a definite, specific group of people which you, the reader, are already familiar with, so we need *the*.
- The same is true with sentences with relative clauses:
  'People who drink and drive should go to prison.' (**any** people, it does not matter who)
  'The people who made this mess should be ashamed of themselves.' (that **specific** group who made the mess)
- It is not the presence of a prepositional phrase or relative clause which decides whether *the* is needed or not. What is important is whether we are referring to 1) someone or something unlimited, open-ended, unpredictable, or 2) someone or something limited to a specific person, thing or group that the listener or reader can be assumed to be familiar with or to understand the reference to. In type 1) we do not use *the*, in type 2) we do.

2 *The* in specific contexts

Some uses of *the* are best observed in real contexts, because the use of articles is strongly affected by context. Here is the beginning of a story which Peter is telling about a funny incident involving ice-cream.

- Underline each time he uses *the* and make notes as to why he does so in each case.
- Peter could have said 'a little sweetshop'. What difference would that have made to the meaning?
- Why does Peter use *the* with 'door' and 'deep-freeze' even though he has not mentioned them before?

Peter: We went into the little sweetshop just up the road here, and we walked straight in the door, and the shopkeeper was on the phone, and we walked straight in, and just turned to the right, and there was the ice-cream deep-freeze, and we noted that it was a 'Walls'* deep-freeze and we knew exactly what we were looking for, the ice-cream called Magnum ...

Observations

- Once Peter mentions a sweetshop, he can **assume** that everyone will know that it has a door and a deep-freeze for ice-cream. We could also talk about other things always associated with shops, and would naturally use *the*:
  'the shop window,' 'the shelves'
- Peter also knows, when he says '**the** *phone*', that no-one will ask 'which phone?' because we all know that he means the telephone in the shop. Other examples are:
  'When I came in she was listening to *the* radio.'
  '*The* post was late this morning. I wonder if *the* postwoman's ill?'
  'It was in *the* newspaper, so it must be true.' (understood as 'the newspaper I, or you and I, read', or 'one of the well-known ones that people read')

C Grammar in action

1 Choosing to use *the*

The word *the* has been taken out of the following examples of conversation.

- Where would you insert *the* in the following examples? ☞

a) He said his name was Paul McCartney. I knew he wasn't Paul McCartney, but he was a good singer anyway.

b) [at an airport check-in desk]
   Airline official: How many bags are you checking in?
   Passenger: Just one.

c) Receptionist: So it's just one person then?
   Bill: No, no, it's for two of us.
   Receptionist: Oh, I'm sorry. Right, two persons.

Walls is a popular brand of ice-cream.

d) The last time I saw her was three weeks ago. She was in England for one week. She phoned me on Wednesday and we met on Friday.

> **Observations**
> - Particularly in speaking, *the* can be used to highlight the specific nature of something for emphasis. One common use is *the* + proper noun when referring to a famous person or place:
>   'I live in Rome, not the (/ði:/) Rome, but a little village in Wales.'
>   'I knew he wasn't the (/ði:/) Paul McCartney.'
> - In **C1(b)** and **(c)** *the* is used in front of *one*, (*Just the one*) and *two*, (*It's for the two of us*) simply for emphasis.
> - When *the* is used in front of days of the week (or months of the year), it shows that there was a clearly specified week (or year) being referred to:
>   'She rang on the Wednesday and we met on the Friday.'

2 *The* in proverbs

■ **English proverbs often contain *the*. What do these common proverbs mean?** ⌐

a) The early bird catches the worm.
b) When the cat's away, the mice will play.
c) The grass is always greener on the other side of the fence.

■ **Which of the proverbs above could you use about someone who ... ?**

i) always says their friends have more interesting jobs than them.
ii) plays around with the boss's computer when the boss is on holiday.
iii) always queues for hours outside shops where there is going to be a sale.

D Follow-up

■ Always make notes of any use of *the* which strikes you as unusual or interesting. This might apply to certain names such as streets with *the*. In London there is 'The Strand,' and a lot British towns have a street called 'The High Street.' Equally, note names which do **not** have *the* where you might want to say *the* (e.g. 'Central Park' in New York, 'Sydney Harbour' in Australia).

■ Look out for the use of *the* at the beginning of novels and short stories to create a feeling of familiarity and as a way of bringing the reader into the world of the story. Writers often use *the* in this way to make you, the reader, feel as if you share the world of the character(s). Here is an example from the opening lines of a story by Ernest Hemingway:

The train went on up the track out of sight, around one of the hills of burnt timber. Nick sat down on the bundle of canvas and bedding the baggage man had pitched out of the door of the baggage car.

- Train yourself to observe details of usage such as these in your reading and listening. Always note them down.
- If you want further details of points relating to this unit, go to the Reference notes section on pages 214–17.

Summary

- Most uses of *the* show that 'I (the writer/speaker) can assume that you (the listener/reader) know who/what I am referring to'.
- When a noun is 'new' in a text or conversation, or when the reference is very general, *the* is not normally used.
- Once a topic has been introduced, a speaker/writer can use *the* to refer to people/things that are normally present in that situation. For example, if someone is telling a story about a flight they were on, they can refer to 'the pilot', 'the plane', 'the airport', 'the food', etc., without having to be more explicit.
- Some uses of *the* are more idiomatic.

Note: the Further exercises for Unit 16 are combined with those for Unit 17. You can find them at the end of Unit 17, on page 122.

Articles 2: a /the /no article

A Introduction

Look at these examples of the use of the word *book(s)*, taken from real spoken situations. In (a) there is *a* (the indefinite article), in (b) there is *the* (the definite article) and in (c) there is no article.

■ **Read these three rules for the use of articles. They are unfinished. Match them to (a), (b) and (c), and complete the rules.** ⊙━

Rules for the use of articles:
1 If the speaker limits something or specifies a particular set, then ...
2 If the speaker is referring to one example of a general class of things, then ...
3 If the speaker is referring to all and any examples of a general class of things, then ...

a) [customer in a bookshop]
    Customer: I'm looking for **a book** by Charles Handy, *Schools as Organisations*.
    Assistant: *Schools as Organisations*, it might be in Educational.

b) [Another bookshop; this time the customer is unhappy. The shop does not have the book he is looking for.]
    Customer: You don't have it? You never have **the books** I need.

c) [A small child is trying to tear a book. Her mother gets angry.]
    Mother: No, no, that's horrible! You don't do that to **books**!

Observations

● In general, the three rules above are very useful for a wide range of uses of *a, the* and no article.
● *A* refers to one member of a class of things (e.g. 'She has a dog and a cat.'). *The* refers to a thing or things that are assumed to be familiar to speaker and listener because they are limited or restricted in some way. In (**b**) above, the things referred to are only those specific books that a particular customer is likely to want.
● No article is used for open-ended reference to any or all members of a class (in the case of (**c**), all books the child might ever touch).

In this unit we look further at the use and non-use of articles, and some typical problems you may meet.

B Discovering patterns of use

1 No article and *a* with uncountable nouns

a) Uncountable nouns are usually not used with *a*. However, *a* is used with uncountables for particular types of meanings.
Look at these examples of uncountables:

i) **A washing powder** I've found to be extremely good is 'Snow'.
ii) This seems to be **an excellent oil**; the engine's running very smoothly.

■ **Complete this rule.**

A/an can be used with uncountables if the speaker or writer ...

b) **Some uncountable words have different meanings when used with *a/an*.
What is the difference between:**

i) *chocolate* and *a chocolate*?
ii) *iron* and *an iron*?
iii) *glass* and *a glass*?

■ **Fill the gaps with *a* if you think it is necessary, or leave the space blank.** ☞

a) I've spilt some wine; get .... cloth.
b) When you're in town, can you get .... paper? The printer has run out.
c) Is there .... chicken in this hamburger? It tastes as if there is.
d) When you're in town can you get .... paper? I want to get the football results.
e) After walking for about an hour we came to .... wood.
f) .... cloth has to be imported. That's why clothes are expensive.
g) If you want to make a fire you'll need .... wood.
h) I ran over .... chicken near a farm today. It had obviously escaped.

2 *a/the*/no article with particular classes of noun

■ **What rules can you make for the use of *a*, *the*, and no article in relation to the following contexts?
(If you find this difficult, read the text on the next page, which contains the kinds of context you are being asked about.)** ☞

a) When mentioning someone's profession or job, use ...
b) When mentioning very famous families, use ...
c) When mentioning someone by name, who everyone in the world knows use ...
d) When using the *-ing* forms of verbs as nouns, use ...
e) When mentioning the names of countries, use ...
f) When using words referring to someone's house or home, use ...

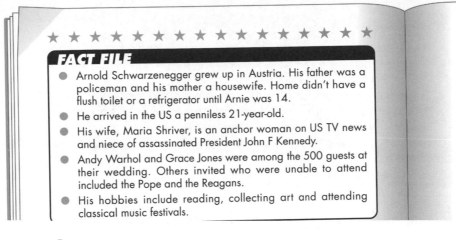

c Grammar in action

1 *a* versus *one*

a) **In these extracts from real texts and conversations some words are missing. What do you think the people actually said?**

■ **Fill the gaps with *a(n)* or *one*.** ☞

i) [Trevor is talking about the town where he lives.]
Trevor: It's not a very big town anyway, it's only .... hundred thousand people.

ii) [Doris is talking about an exotic food experience she and her husband, David had.]
Doris: It was full of garlic. David took .... mouthful and shot out of the room!

iii) [A customer in a film-processing shop asks how long his enlargements will take.]
Customer: When will they be ready?
Assistant: They take .... week.
Customer: .... week, right, thanks very much.

iv) [Francis is telling Nell how to make a cake.]
Francis: A hundred grams of flour to .... egg, yeah, mixed up in the bowl.
Nell: Right.

b) **Look at these two further examples of *one*. Why do you think *one* is used instead of *a*?**

i) [Sian is talking about restaurants she goes to in London with her best friend.]
Sian: There's **one** place we go to which is a Mexican restaurant, and they have a happy hour between 5.30 and 7.30.

ii) [Martyn is remembering horrible tricks he and his schoolmates used to play on other boys when they were kids.]
Martyn: There was **one** lad they used to terrify, they used to tie dead birds on the inside of his desk!

2 *This* instead of *a* in spoken stories and jokes

- **Read these extracts from real spoken stories.**
- **Why do the speakers use *this* instead of *a*?**

a) [A woman is telling a story about standing in the wrong queue for something.]
So I go in **this** queue, and I'm waiting, so I saw them taking names and writing things down, so I had **this** feeling I was in the wrong place, so I thought to myself, 'Oh I'm going from here,' but as I was stood at the table **this** person said, 'Now then, you're next!'

b) [Two men are gossiping about a woman they used to work with.]
First man: Apart from George she hasn't really met any nice people, eligible nice people I know of, perhaps I don't know enough.
Second man: There was **this** guy that she was really madly in love with, that went on and ended up working on an oil rig somewhere.
First man: Really?
Second man: Oh yes, she really was, really loyal. Very struck on* him.

c) [A student is telling a joke.]
Student: **This** girl goes up into this farmhouse and she's looking for a job, and the farmer says, 'Okay, you can ...' (etc.)

---

* *Struck on* means to be very fond of.

D Follow-up

■ Look out for uses of *a* and no article with days of the week. Sometimes, the differences are very slight and subtle. For example – 'On Sunday,' 'on Sundays,' 'on a Sunday,' can be used to generalise: 'The shops are closed on Sunday / on Sundays / on a Sunday'. You will hear all three in British English. (See also cartoon below.)

■ Think of your language or some other language you know. Is the equivalent of *this* used instead of *a* in jokes and spoken stories to focus on characters and places and things in the story?

■ Study Unit 23 on ellipsis to see examples of when the articles are omitted in informal spoken language.

For other uses of *a* and no article which often cause difficulties, see the Reference notes, pages 214–17.

"It feels more like a Wednesday to me."

Summary

● *A*, the indefinite article, is the normal, neutral and most typical way of referring to a single example of something.

● We only use *one*:
   – when we want to be particularly emphatic or dramatic, meaning 'no more than one'.
   – when we are explicitly contrasting numbers, e.g. two kilos of flour and one litre of water, or in technical mathematical contexts.
   – when we want to highlight something/someone in a report or story, and make them our topic.

● No article is used for general, open-ended reference to classes of things.

● No article is normal with uncountable nouns, but *a* is used when the meaning is 'a type/kind of.'

● Some uncountable nouns have quite a distinct meaning when used with *a*.

● *This* is used for special focus instead of *a* in reports, stories and jokes in informal spoken language.

Further exercises (Units 16 and 17) 🔑

1 Which nouns would you put *the* before in these sentences?

a) I'll meet you at university at three o'clock, outside room 26.
b) Dog needs to go to vet. Can you take him?
c) When I got up, I noticed car windscreen was covered in ice.

2 Fill in the nouns which fit the **topics** that these people are talking about, as in the example.

> **Example:**
> He owned a huge ..estate... . The land and the buildings were worth millions.

a) What did you think of that .... ? I thought the atmosphere was good, but the service was slow.
b) I think for me, when it comes to choosing a .... , the conditions and the prospects are more important than the salary.
c) I don't think I'll ever use that .... ; the ingredients are impossible to get hold of and the instructions are too complicated anyway.
d) What did you think of his latest .... ? I thought the plot was tedious and the characters were unrealistic.
e) It was a most dreadful .... ; the survivors had to spend the night on a cold mountainside.

3 Put *the* or leave a blank in the brackets in these sentences.

a) I think ordinary people in Vietnam must have suffered terribly during
(   ) years of their war with America.
b) I feel very sorry for (   ) people who have to live in (   ) cities which they absolutely hate because they have no choice.
c) (   ) role of (   ) computers in (   ) society will only be truly understood when (   ) historians look back on (   ) end of the twentieth century.
d) (   ) humans can never really understand what (   ) animals think and feel, or whether they experience (   ) pain and (   ) suffering in the same way that (   ) people do.
e) (   ) children of (   ) single-parent families often suffer (   ) discrimination in (   ) countries where (   ) marriage is still considered essential.

4 Here are some quotations from famous people. Decide whether *the* is necessary in the gaps.

'All .... good books are alike in that they are truer than if they had really happened.' (Ernest Hemingway, 20th century American novelist)
'.................... worker is .... slave of the capitalist society; ....
female worker is .... slave of .... slave.' (James Connolly, Irish 19th century political thinker)
'.................... happiest women, like .... happiest nations, have no history.' (George Eliot, real name: Mary Ann Evans, English 19th century novelist)
'.................... non-violence is .... first article of my faith.' (Mahatma Gandhi, 1869–1948, Indian statesman)
'.................... success is counted sweetest by those who ne'er* succeed.' (Emily Dickinson, 19th century American poet)

5 Here are some lists of things connected with the same topic. Which ones of them would normally have *the* in front of them when you refer to them? Do as in the example. Tick those that would have *the* and put a cross by those that do not.

Example:

(things to do with space) sun ✓ moon ✓ Mars ✗ universe ✓
(things to do with media and communications) Internet e-mail phone press
(things to do with sport) tennis Olympic Games crowd world record
(things to do with food and drink) chef menu kitchen breakfast
(things to do with politics) Prime Minister democracy economy state

6 In this passage of real speech, decide whether it is necessary to put *the* / *a* / no article in the gaps.

[Laura is talking about her friend, Melanie, who was looking for a part-time job.]
Laura: Well no Melanie's actually still a student and she has ten hours of lectures a week, so she works in McDonalds in her spare time, 'cos she needs .... money, and she works in McDonalds in Hatfield in .... big shopping centre. In fact she wrote, she got .... application form and sent it in, and she didn't hear from them, and we went to .... cinema .... one day, and I said to her, 'Look, why don't you just go in and ask them?' 'Cos she wasn't on .... telephone, you see. I said, 'They may well have been trying to ring you.' So she went in again and they couldn't find her application form, they gave her another one and fixed an interview with her at that time, so I think it was .... fact that she went back again ...

7 Where could you put *the* in the following?

a) Nora: It was a terrible week, wasn't it, d'you remember?
   Marco: Yes, we had snow on Monday and floods on Thursday!

b) More you study English, harder it seems to get.

Ne'er means never. It is rarely used in contemporary English.

Unit 18   Complex noun phrases

A Introduction

The following texts are all taken from 'small ads[1]' or 'personal ads' in newspapers in which people offer some item or service for sale or in which they are looking for a romantic friendship. In order to be effective, a lot of information has to be 'packed' into noun phrases.

■   **Complete each sentence beginning in the left-hand column (a)–(f) with a suitable ending from the right-hand column (g)–(l).** ☞

a) Delightful country house hotel	g) with private lake frontage and jetty.
b) Unique four-bedroom lodge[2] set in own grounds	h) independent-minded, mid-twenties partner.
c) Lightweight cross-training shoe	i) sport-loving, energetic companion.
d) Attractive, fun-loving male seeks	j) with dual-density midsole.
e) Air-conditioned rooms	k) with private bath and WC[3].
f) Slightly balding but fit and active divorcee seeks	l) with log fires and oak beams.

[1] *Ad* is a very common shortening of *advertisement*. We use the shortening here because these kinds of advertisement are very rarely referred to as anything else.
[2] A *lodge* is a particular kind of house, generally found on the land of another, bigger property where it may have functioned as the home of a kind of security guard or *lodge keeper*.
[3] *WC* stands for *Water Closet* and means lavatory or toilet. The full form of WC is never used these days, but the abbreviation is very common in these kinds of advertisement.

- Noun phrase structure in English can be very complex. You have probably learnt that the order of adjectives before the noun is quite fixed (*Unique four-bedroom lodge* not *four-bedroom unique lodge*), that meanings can vary depending on word order, and that a variety of structures can come after the noun:
  – prepositional phrases (*rooms with **private bath***)
  – relative (or reduced) relative clauses (*lodge **set in own grounds***)
- Additionally, words before the main noun (which pre-modify it) and after it (which post-modify) often contain further sub-modifications inside them. For example: 'a **slightly balding** divorcee', 'a house with **carefully restored** oak beams'.
  This unit looks at patterns of pre- and post-modification in speech and writing, and how they can vary. (See also Unit 22, where we give examples of how speakers present information to listeners in far less complex ways than some of the examples in this unit.)

B Discovering patterns of use

1 Noun phrases in speech and writing

The following extracts describe people and places as part of a narrative recount.

- **In each case underline the noun phrases.**
- **Analyse how modification is structured.**
- **Do you notice any differences in how the noun phrases are structured in the spoken and written recounts?** ☞

a) [This is part of a newspaper report.]

Balamurali Ambati graduated last week from the Mount Sinai School of Medicine in New York at the age of seventeen. Dr Ambati, a native of Vellore, India, moved to Buffalo, New York, with his family when he was three. He was doing calculus at four. At eleven, he graduated from high school and co-authored a research book on AIDS with his older brother Jaya. He plays chess, basketball and ping-pong and is just learning to drive.

b) [This is part of a holiday guide book.]

Dar-es-Salaam, as capitals go, is a new and fresh face on the holiday map ... The shanties, bazaars and marshalling yards have given way to clean streets and plate-glass facades ... Banks and insurance blocks dominate the skyline, for Dar-es-Salaam's monuments are not to the past but to present prosperity.

c) [A nineteen-year-old girl, Sally, is talking about the town in the north of England where she and her family live.]

Sally: I quite like living in Sheffield, I mean, there's lots of good clubs and the sports facilities are great, like swimming baths, most of them brand new, and there's the Don Valley sports and athletics centre … and you're only twenty minutes away from the Peak District, one of the loveliest parts of England, with all kinds of walking, country pubs and that …

2 Variation after the noun

Adverbs, adjectives and noun phrases are more restricted as post-modifiers of nouns and tend to refer mainly to time or place (e.g. the appointment **the following day**; a month **ahead**; the trip **overseas**; the park **nearby**). More typical is post-modification by means of prepositional phrases and, especially, relative clauses.

- ■ **Underline the post-modification in the following examples. (The first one has been done for you.)**
- ■ **In which example(s) do you think the context is more likely to be spoken than written? (In each case the headword (main) noun is in bold.)** ☞

a) That's the **bit** that we don't tend to know quite so much about.

b) There's just so many **things** that we've got to tell them about and that they've got to just sit down and listen to.

c) A similar situation occurs in the **region** of the Nile Basin where farmers are forced to use irrigation techniques in order to subsist.

d) While we were on one of those Breton holidays, she swam so far out that she met the only other **person** who could swim, who turned out to be an Austrian and that was the **beginning** of our link with Austria, and the next day Emily went to **Graz** where the woman lived, and your grandfather and I followed the next summer, I think.

Observations

- ● Noun phrases can be quite simple or quite complex in structure. Complex noun phrase structures can allow a lot of information to be conveyed in relatively few words.
- ● Information before the noun (in pre-modifying structures) often creates a more descriptive style and occurs in advertisements and in descriptions of people and places; information after the noun (in post-modifying structures) creates a style in which information about the noun is either expanded or defined more precisely. Nouns which are both heavily pre- and post-modified are more likely to occur in written English.
- ● Complex pre-modifying structures are particularly common in written academic English, while complex post-modifying structures are also common in spoken English. In spoken English, information can also be built up around different headword nouns more gradually and in smaller chunks.

C Grammar in action

1 Varying the structure of noun phrases in context

- **What do you notice about the underlined noun phrases in the following examples from scientific textbooks?**
- **What are the changes in structure as this noun phrase is repeated and can you explain them?**

a) There are <u>forces of friction</u> whenever solid surfaces slide over each other. The friction forces always act in the opposite direction in which an object or surface is moving.

b) The explosion produced <u>a chain of molecules</u> which were diffused throughout the atom. Such molecule chains are now recognised by physicists to be instrumental to atomic diffusion.

c) <u>The population of the batch culture</u> multiplied within a short space of time. However, some batch culture populations did not survive and investigations were conducted to explain their disappearance.

> **Observations**
>
> - When a noun phrase is first introduced it normally consists of a noun with an *of*-construction as post-modifier.
> - When the information contained by this phrase is repeated, it is taken as knowledge which can be assumed and it is normally repeated in the form of a noun plus noun structure. Thus, in *a chain of molecules … molecule chains* the change is to a pre-modified noun phrase which condenses the information, and also signals that it is given or already referred to.

2 Apposition

Noun phrases can sometimes be placed alongside one another. This feature is called apposition.

A standard example of apposition is:
'My neighbour, a school teacher, has been helping our daughter with maths.'

- **What differences do you notice in the use of nouns which are placed together in the following written examples (a–c) and spoken examples (d–f).** ☞

a) The Queen, the head of state, will attend the conference in Singapore.
b) Her brother, David James, also plays for the club.
c) Single neural cells or neurones form a lower layer within the brain.
d) When you got inside the garage the first thing you saw was the jack* – his jack.
e) We were on holiday in Southern France near a large campsite, the Bois de Perigord.
f) I'm going to see my tutor, Dr Johnson, about a change of course.

---

*A *jack* is a piece of equipment which allows heavy weights, such as a car, to be raised.

D Follow-up

■ Next time you are reading an English language newspaper, choose the opening sentences of a couple of articles and analyse the complexity of the noun phrases. How many examples of complex structures can you find? Why do you think newspaper language has complex noun phrases?

■ If you want more practice exercises, do the Further exercises at the end of the unit.

■ If you want further details of points relating to this unit, go to the Reference notes section on pages 217–218.

Summary

● What goes in front of a noun and what follows a noun can create different styles of English. Different structures are used to create spoken and written styles.

● Pre-modifying structures help to produce a more descriptive style. Post-modifying structures help to produce a more defining style. Complex pre-modifying structures are common in advertising, poetry and in journalistic prose. Both scientific and academic writing as well as informal conversational styles can be characterised by more complex post-modifying structures.

● In spoken English, information, particularly about people and places, is built up gradually around a headword noun phrase. In spoken English noun phrase apposition tends to be used at the end of clauses rather than at the beginning of clauses. Noun phrase apposition at the beginning of clauses is more usually associated with written styles of English.

Further exercises ⌫

1 **The following two sentences occurred in a recent TV news broadcast. Keeping the content of the sentences the same, rewrite the second sentence so that you form four separate sentences. The first sentence has been done for you.**

a) Publication of the framework document has set the scene for an intensification in the next four months of an already bustling Anglo-Irish political scene in Belfast, London and Dublin.

i) The framework document has been published.
ii) It has set the scene for an intensification of the Anglo-Irish political scene.
iii) The political scene is already bustling.
iv) The political scene will intensify in the next four months in Belfast, London and Dublin.

b) The programme for restoration of the inner cities seems to penalise those least able to look after themselves and those occupants of council houses who have not already received grants for repairs.

2 In order to convey a lot of information in a short space, newspaper headlines often employ noun plus noun structures. Sometimes three or four nouns occur together in one headline.

Make up headlines from the information given in the short preceding sentence. The first one has been done for you.

a) Businessman David Howells is expected to fly home to Britain today after he was freed from jail in Nigeria.

Suggested headline: JAILED BRITON'S FREEDOM FLIGHT

b) Hollie Roffey, the world's youngest heart transplant patient, died yesterday when her new heart failed after she developed breathing difficulties.

c) Both sides in the rail dispute meet today to decide on the pay claim submitted by over 25,000 signalmen.

d) Families of Lencom Engineering employees, who had been promised weekend breaks in five-star luxury hotels in Southern Spain learned yesterday that the company had gone bankrupt.

e) Two England footballers were detained late last night at Hammersmith Police Station, West London on charges of causing a disturbance of the peace, after police were called to a night club in the early hours of the morning.

3 Underline examples of apposition in the following sentences and texts.

a) The phrase interim share dividend is simply another way of paying less than they should.

b) The film *One Fine Day* is just about as sentimental as they can get.

c) His Royal Highness Prince Charles.

d) Some satellite TV channels such as Sky Two show news programmes all day.

e) In the film *David*, an apprentice welder, is made redundant and has to find a new employer. In a series of hilarious episodes he meets Rosie who advises him that the best way to make money, real money, is to work as a male stripper.

4 Formal names for services and for official organisations usually involve noun phrases in which the main noun is modified by other nouns. Create names for the following services, jobs and organisations.

a) a service which provides information about careers

suggested name: careers information service

b) a kit which is used for repairing a motor car body

c) an officer who is responsible for preventing crime

d) a program which protects computers from viruses

e) a certificate which shows that your car is insured

5 Rewrite the following sentences which each contain some complex noun phrases to form at least three separate sentences. Keep the content the same as far as possible.

■ What context do you think the sentences come from?

a) Imaginatively restored Georgian terraced family house with fitted kitchen leading to spacious patio and 40 sq. ft[1] vegetable garden.

b) A full, fourteen-day money-back guarantee on all our home protection policies and expert claims advice via our special Claims Action Line.

c) The sloeblack[2], slow, black, crow-black fishing-boat-bobbing sea.

d) A bullish AGM[3] statement by Psion chairman David Potter sent shares of the hand-held computer group to a five year peak of 374p.

[1] *Sq. ft* is short for 'square feet', a measurement.
[2] *Sloeblack* is a word made up by the writer, but a 'sloe' is a small fruit which is a very dark purple colour.
[3] *AGM* stands for Annual General Meeting.

A Introduction

- Read the following extracts. As you read, try to imagine what kinds of text they are, letters? business correspondence? e-mails?
- Which is the most formal, and which is the least formal in style?
- Fill in the gaps in the texts with a preposition (for example *to* or *of*). ☞

a)

> Dear Sonia
>
> I hope that you had a good time [1] (...) the family, and that it wasn't too crowded [2] (...) London. I'm still trying to finish that essay [3] (...) the position of middle managers [4] (...) company restructuring.

b)

> Dear Michael Evans,
>
> Thank you [6] (...) your message. Joan is absent [7] (...) the office [8] (...) present and will return [9] (...) 13 March, the day you are [10] (...) the office. Her extension is 5732 if you would like to contact her then.

c)

> Dear Stella
>
> I'm sorry that I did not answer your message. I had just got back [11] (...) a lecture tour [12] (...) America. I do know Jenny Klaus. We were [13] (...) university together as a matter [14] (...) fact. She lives [15] (...) the Isle of Man now, but we meet [16] (...) time [17] (...) time. I hope you'll spend a couple [18] (...) days [19] (...) us when you are here [20] (...) the summer, and perhaps the three [21] (...) us can meet?

Observations

- Prepositions can be a difficult aspect of English because of their variety, and the difficulty of deciding whether to use one. In this unit we try to make them easier to learn by asking you to think whether they:
  - are being used to show the physical location of something ('in the library'), or relations between objects/items ('He moved towards his car'). **or**:
  - because another word in the clause or phrase forces us to use it ('the importance of the proposal'. 'He was accused of the theft'). This use is dealt with further in **B2**.

The unit also deals with prepositions in short question forms, and in idiomatic expressions.

B Discovering patterns of use

1 Basic use (e.g. location) versus other uses

Read the following extracts.

- Fill in the table which follows the extracts.
- Which of the extracts contains only basic uses of prepositions (type A)? Can you think why this is? (Part of the exercise has been done for you.) ⚷

a) [sowing instructions]

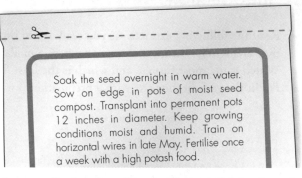

Soak the seed overnight in warm water. Sow on edge in pots of moist seed compost. Transplant into permanent pots 12 inches in diameter. Keep growing conditions moist and humid. Train on horizontal wires in late May. Fertilise once a week with a high potash food.

b) [Sally is drying a silk jumper after hand-washing it. She is explaining how she dries it.]

Sally: Yeah it's a hand wash in cold water 'cos it's silk. And then wrap it in a towel and put it in a spin drier to spin dry it, and then dry it flat on a towel on a table.

c) [Two people are discussing a friend who is ill.]

Jenny: She could have given up and then perhaps she wouldn't be in so much pain but because she will insist on not being a complete invalid she is in constant pain.

Extract	Type A (physical location, time, relations between objects)	Type B (grammatically connected to another word in the clause)
a)	in warm water	
b)	in cold water	
c)		in (so much) pain

"We dazzled them with our presentation, we amazed them with our concepts! They were all set to sign, but nobody in our office uses pens anymore."

2 Understanding the rationale for prepositions

Although it is difficult to guess which preposition you should use, you can begin to learn more about them by thinking about which words they depend on in their clause.

Look at the following extracts from e-mails.

■ **Decide which word(s) form a grammatical unit with the preposition.** ☞

a) I hope that you had a good time (with your family).
b) Thank you for your message.
c) We were at university together.
d) We meet from time to time.
e) Joan is absent from the office at present and will return on 13 March, the day you are in the office.

> **Observations**
> - Although a preposition is structurally linked to the following word (as in *with your family, for your message*), the choice of preposition can also be dependent on a word which precedes it:
>   – verb + preposition: *insist on not being a complete invalid* (**B1**(**c**));
>   *thank [x] for [y]*.
>   – adjective + preposition: *be absent from [z]*.
> - Some words must be **preceded** by a particular preposition:
>   preposition + noun: *in pain* (**B1**(**c**)); *on 13 March* (**B2**(**e**)).
> - A good dictionary, or a large reference grammar will describe these structural combinations in more detail.

c Grammar in action

1 Prepositions in short question forms

a) **Which prepositions are missing from these conversations?** 🔑

i) [Mary is telling her husband that her sister will visit.]
Mary: Barbara is coming tonight.
John: Barbara? What …?
Mary: She wants to.
John: Oh just visiting, you mean.

ii) [David is remembering a very icy winter when it was difficult to drive.]
David: It took me about five hours to get home.
Raj: Where …?
David: Wimbledon [laughs]. A drive of fifteen miles!
Raj: [laughs] No!

iii) [Three friends are talking about the engagement of someone they know.]
Paula: Oh Jenny Adams has just got engaged.
John: Has she?
Henry: Mark found that out.
Joan: Oh right. Who …?

b) **Complete the following table. Choose prepositions which you think could be used after each of the following *wh*-question words to form short questions (e.g. *What for?*). (Note that not all the *wh*-question words can be used with a preposition.) One of the answers has been completed for you. Brackets around a word indicate that this is a rare usage.** 🔑

for   in   on   about   of   from

with   at   until   by   during

wh-*question words*	*prepositions*
who	
what	
where	from/to/(until)
when	
why	
which	
how	

2 Prepositions in idioms and fixed expressions

Many prepositions form fixed expressions which function as a unit, and are like idioms in that they cannot be altered (e.g. changed in tense, or made singular if they are plural).

- **Do you know these expressions? Use them to complete the sentences which follow.** ⚏

  From [x] to [y]:

  from bad to worse

  from time to time

  from start to finish

a) My investments are not doing very well, in fact, they're going ...

b) I've just had a terrible holiday. The whole thing was a disaster ...

c) A: Do you still play football?   B: A bit, yeah ...

in [*x*] *of*
in favour of
in charge of
in danger of

d) Are you .... the new road tax?
e) Ask the manager. She's .... customer relations.
f) I think we're .... taking opinion polls too seriously.

D Follow-up

- Use short question forms + preposition (*What for?*, *Where from?* etc.) to create a mini-dialogue.
- Next time you are reading, spend some time analysing the prepositions in the text. Underline each one in a paragraph, and decide why it is used.
- When you are learning new vocabulary, always try to learn the relevant prepositions that go with the word. Try to learn it in a memorable phrase, rather than in isolation.
- If you want more practice exercises, do the Further exercises at the end of the unit.
- If you want further details of points relating to this unit, go to the Reference notes section on pages 218–21.

Summary

- The choice of preposition is not simply dependent on meaning. It is very often dependent on a preceding verb or adjective.
- When learning prepositions, it is useful to consider which other words in a clause cause it to be used (e.g. is it the preceding adjective or is it the following time expression?).
- Prepositions are retained in short questions (and answers) in conversations (e.g. *What for?*).
- When you are checking information you have already been given, the preposition precedes the *wh*-question word:
    - A: Send that to New Haven.
    - B: Sorry ... to where?
- When you are asking for new information the *wh*-question word precedes the preposition:
    - A: We'll send it for checking.
    - B: OK. Where to?
- Prepositions occur in a number of fixed expressions which can have an adverbial function (e.g. *from time to time*) or act like adjectives after be (e.g. *in favour of*). These need to be learned as complete units.

Further exercises 🔑

1 **Can you guess the correct prepositions in these extracts from conversations, interviews and e-mails?**

of (×3)   from (×3)   in (×2)   to   after   at

a) [This is part of a conversation between two sisters.]
Oh I've had a letter this morning (....) America, (....) my friend (....) America. But (....) the letter she puts er 'I'm an old lady now I'm sixty four.' I thought 'Heavens! that's as old as I am.'

b) [This is part of an e-mail.]

> Hi Tony – it was really great to hear (....) you so soon and you exactly summed up my feelings. I have spent quite a bit (....) today trying to track down my luggage (....) a real nightmare (....) a trip back here.

c) [This is part of an interview about family life.]
Interviewer: What about your schooldays? What do you remember and what did you enjoy?
Tony: I hated English and loved maths.
Interviewer: Uh huh. Why's that?
Tony: I was absolutely rubbish (....) English.

d) [This is part of an interview about healthcare.]
Researcher: Will there be much consultation?
Interviewee: Yeah, er part (....) the process will be talking (....) er the GPs.

2 **In the following conversations, the speakers' utterances have been listed separately. Work out the correct order for the original conversation.**

a) [John and Ellen are in the car. A 'growbag' is a plastic bag of soil which gardeners use to grow plants such as tomatoes easily at home.]
John: Have you got to call for a growbag tonight?
John: Cutler's have got 'em.
John: We could go up and get one. I want three er 'Moneymaker' or 'Alicante' tomato plants.
John: Eh?
John: Yeah.

Ellen: Where from?
Ellen: I'll go and get them tomorrow.
Ellen: Have they? Oh all right then. Well, do you want me to call on the way?
Ellen: Well I was going to get them tomorrow. Haven't got any money tonight.

b) [Andrew has met someone in the pub called Brian.]

Andrew: Do you live round here?

Andrew: Somerset. That's where they make the er cider.

Andrew: Where from?

Brian: Well er originally I was from the south of England, from Somerset originally.

Brian: Yeah I, no I'm I'm here visiting you know for a while.

Brian: Cider apples. Yeah.

3 Match the expression containing prepositions in the left-hand column with the correct meaning in the right-hand column.

a)

expression	*meaning*
from day to day	in different locations
from place to place	on different days
from strength to strength	deteriorating
from bad to worse	improving
from time to time	throughout
from start to finish	occasionally

b)

expression	*meaning*
in excess of	as
in place of	more than
by way of	instead of
by means of	with/using
on behalf of	in someone's place

Exploring spoken grammar in context

Unit 20 Direct and indirect speech

A Introduction

1 Look at this piece of spoken English, where a woman, Mary, is talking about something that happened when she was on holiday with a friend called Dulcie. She tells her friend Danny what they said to each other.

■ In what way are her reports of what was said different from the way we normally report speech in written text (such as novels, newspapers)?

Mary: So, we'd been wandering round in the morning, doing the usual thing, came back and had lunch and I said, 'What would you like to do this afternoon, Dulcie?' She said, 'Oh, Mary, let's go to bingo.' Now, bingo is never ever my cup of tea[1] [Danny: No] but seeing that I was supposed to be with her I'd to fall in with[2] her. [Danny laughs] 'All right then, Dulcie, where do we go now to bingo?' 'I don't know,' she said, 'but we'll find out.' So we walked along and we saw this hall and she said, 'I think that's it.' So I saw a lot of people and I said, 'I don't know Dulcie, doesn't look like a bingo hall.' So she said, 'Well, go in the queue,' she said, 'and find out what's happening.'

"The doctor told my husband to double his physical activity, so now he changes channels with both hands."

[1] *Not my cup of tea* means 'not what I normally do or like to do.'
[2] *Fall in with* means do the same as.

2 In each pair of sentences below, changes have been made when direct speech is reported indirectly. In the third column, note what changes have been made. The first one has been done as an example. 🗝

	Direct	*Indirect*	*Changes*
a)	'I'll be arriving at six,' Laura said.	Laura said she'd be arriving at six.	*will → would* *I → she* subject and reporting verb moved to start of sequence
b)	She asked, 'Do you want me to bring my guitar?'	She asked if we wanted her to bring her guitar.	
c)	'What are you building?' he asked.	He asked (us) what we were building.	
d)	'I think,' she said to me, 'you've come to the wrong room, you know.'	She said she thought I'd come to the wrong room.	
e)	'You will be ready at three, I hope, won't you?' she said to me.	She said she hoped I'd be ready at three.	

Observations

- In written texts, it is normal to report questions with a verb such as *ask* or *enquire*, so a written report of Mary's first question might typically be:

  '... and I asked, "What would you like to do this afternoon Dulcie?" '

- In novels, we often get verbs such as *reply* or *answer* when someone answers a question, whereas here, Dulcie's answer to Mary's question is also reported with *say*.

- In some novels (but not usually in newspaper reports), we do get reported speech without a statement of who said the words, as in: *All right then, Dulcie, where do we go now to bingo?* This is very common in informal spoken language. In this kind of spoken language we also find 'double' reporting verbs, as in: So she said, *'Well, go in the queue,' she said, 'and find out what's happening.'* This helps to make the speech report more dramatic and 'real'.

- You are probably familiar with the structural changes we asked you to revise in **2**, above. This unit helps you learn more about the differences between speech reporting in natural conversations and narratives, and written speech reporting.

B Discovering patterns of use

Direct speech in writing versus informal speech reporting

Some types of direct speech reporting are very common in written texts such as novels, short stories, etc., but we hardly ever use them in informal spoken language.

Look at the following sentences (a)–(f) from a famous early nineteenth century novel, *Ivanhoe*, by Sir Walter Scott and (g)–(h) part of Mary's spoken narrative.

- Make notes about the main differences between the speech reporting in the two extracts (a)–(f), and (g)–(h).
- Why do you think the writer chose direct speech instead of indirect speech in (a)–(f)?
- Change the utterances (a)–(h) below into indirect speech. ☞

a) She then uttered a loud shriek, and exclaimed, 'He is down! He is down!'
b) 'Who is down?' cried Ivanhoe.
c) 'The Black Knight,' answered Rebecca.
d) 'Front-de-Boeuf!'[1] exclaimed Ivanhoe.
e) 'Who yield[2]? – who push their way?' said Ivanhoe.
f) 'The ladders are thrown down,' replied Rebecca.

g) Mary: I said, 'What would you like to do this afternoon, Dulcie?' She said, 'Oh, Mary, let's go to bingo.'

h) [Mary and Dulcie go to what they think is the bingo hall: Mary tells how she asked Dulcie why so many people were queuing up. This is Dulcie's reply.]
Mary: So I go back to Dulcie and she says, 'All right Mary, will the bingo be starting soon? I can't see any chairs and tables.' 'No,' I said, 'We're in the wrong place.'

Observations

- Direct speech is a good way of creating a very vivid and dramatic picture of the events reported. Indirect speech makes events less dramatic, as you will probably notice in the indirect versions of **B(g)** and **(h)**.
- In everyday conversation, we can use *say* for direct reporting of questions. We do not have to use *ask* (see **A1**). *Say* is also used for the answer. Therefore, in (g) and (h) the verb *answer* would have sounded too formal/written.
- In conversation, we can use *say* at the beginning, in the middle and at the end of a direct speech report. We don't usually invert the verb and subject (**not** ~~said she~~ (**✗**)).
- *Say* can cover most types of direct speech report in conversation. Other verbs such as *exclaim*, *reply*, *answer*, etc., are very seldom used, but are much more common in written dialogues (see **B(a)–(f)**).
- Note also that in informal stories, speakers can often switch from past tense to present when reporting speech. The present tense, as used in **B(h)** highlights/emphasises the speaker's words more than the past tense.

---

[1] *Front-de-Boeuf* is the name of a character in the story.
[2] This is an outdated type of structure only found in old literature.

C Grammar in action

1 Choosing to use speech verbs in continuous forms

Look at these examples.

■ **Why do you think the speech verbs are used in their continuous forms?** ⌐

a) [Tom is telling a bit of village news to a neighbour.]
   Tom: Brian was saying the village hall nearly caught fire last night!

b) [Dick has just heard a piece of news from his daughter.]
   Dick: Caroline was saying that five mortar bombs have been discovered at Heathrow Airport.

c) [John is commenting on how quickly companies respond to job applications.]
   John: My son is with the Electricity Board and he was telling me that they have this sort of procedure as well. They have to reply initially within, well I can't remember the number of days.
   Bill: So two or three working days.
   John: That's right, that sort of thing.

> **Observations**
>
> ● We can use the *-ing* form when we want to concentrate on the **content of the topic** of what someone said, rather than their actual words. This is particularly so when we are introducing a piece of news or a new topic into the conversation.
> ● Note that the tense does **not** have to change in the way it did in the examples in the table in **A2**: in **C1(b)** above, Caroline probably said,
>   *Five mortar bombs have been discovered* ... Dick reports her words using the same tense.

2 *Ask* + passive voice

Although *ask* is not used much in direct speech, it is frequent in indirect speech, and is often used with the passive (including the passive with *get*) and the *to*-form of the verb.

Here are some examples taken from authentic recorded English:

■ **What do you think the people actually said in (a)–(c)? Change the examples into direct speech.** ⌐

a) [The speaker is talking about a difficult job he has in the health service.]
   I was asked to do this job and I didn't have any choice.

b) [A teacher is talking about teaching.]
   Oh you know I've been asked to do some GCSE* English next term.

c) [someone talking about a difficult task at work.]
   And I got asked to do it 'cos they wanted, you know, a good presentation.

*GCSE means 'General Certificate of Secondary Education' and is an exam taken by 16-year-olds in the UK.

3 Ask + wh-clauses

Ask is also frequent in indirect speech in conversation with *who/what/when/where/why/how* clauses to report questions.

Look at the following examples.

- **Write out the questions in direct speech.**

a) I phoned up the hospital and asked who I should address the letter to.
b) Well, you don't interfere do you, so I asked him what the arrangements were.
c) I asked him how to get there, but it sounds a bit complicated.

You might have told me who Simon was when I said to bring him along!"

D Follow-up

- Look at a few pages in a novel or short story in English and see how many different speech reporting verbs you can find in the direct speech of the characters. Think of how you might make those same reports in ordinary conversation.
- Do the same with a newspaper, looking for examples of quotations of the words of politicians, famous people, etc. Are the reports the same as in the novel/short story? Are they the same as / different from everyday conversation?
- If you want more practice exercises, do the Further exercises at the end of the unit.
- If you want further details of points relating to this unit, go to the Reference notes section on pages 222–4.

Summary

- In general, informal spoken language is much more flexible than written language.
- Word order in informal speech reports does not always follow the rules of formal writing (e.g. questions may still retain question-word order in indirect reports).
- Some reporting verbs are hardly ever used at all for direct reports in informal spoken language, e.g. *exclaim, whisper, cry. Say* is used for most direct reports, regardless of how the words were originally said. Verbs like *exclaim, whisper* and *reply* are typical of novels and short stories. Verbs like *ask* and *answer* are normally only used in indirect reports in informal spoken language.
- The past tense with *-ing* is very common in indirect reports in informal spoken language. It emphasises the content rather than the words actually used, and is common when new topics are introduced into the conversation or when a special bit of news is reported.

Further exercises ☞

1 Here are some informal, spoken-style direct speech reports. Keep them as direct reports, but make them a more formal, written, style, using verbs such as *shout, shriek, ask, exclaim, wonder* or any other suitable ones.

a) She said, 'What time are you all leaving?'
b) 'Help! Help!' he said, 'I'm stuck! Pull me out!'
c) 'Is it possible they've disconnected the phone?' she said.
d) 'I don't believe it!' he said.
e) 'Arggh! It's a rat! Take it away!' he said.

2 Which of these reports would sound most natural if the continuous form of *say* or *tell* were used instead of the past simple form. Why?

a) Mary: Are you sure?
   Philip: Yes she definitely said 7.30, not 7.45.

b) Jim: Fred told me they're going to close that pizza place.
   Carmen: Yeah? That's a pity. We go there quite a lot.

c) Terry: I said to Nora the other day, you know, the kids are out of control.
   Marie: That's right. My sister's a teacher and she told me it's getting worse in her
           school.

d) Lisa: Hmm, that was a big mistake, I can see that now.
   Joe: I said you shouldn't do it, didn't I, but you wouldn't listen.

e) Ali: Jill asked if you'd had any further thoughts about the car.
   Brian: Well, no, I don't want to sell it. I told her that the other day.

3 What do you think the people reported actually *said*?

a) She wondered if I might be interested in working for her.
b) I got asked to sit on the committee the other day.

c) Bill was telling me he was rung up by someone trying to sell him car insurance at eight o'clock in the morning.

d) He was shouting at me to come and give him a hand and calling me useless.

e) He was complaining about the noise the kids were making.

4 Suggest ways of making direct speech reports for these remarks for a newspaper (i.e. keep the quotation marks, and add a reporting verb).

a) (the Prime Minister) 'We shall never increase taxes unless it is absolutely necessary.'

b) (famous film star Gloria Fox) 'I have not been asked to play Juliet in the new film.'

c) (footballer Joss Konran) 'Someone asked me recently why I don't go abroad and earn more money. The answer is I want to play for my own country.'

Tails (post-posed elements of clauses)

A Introduction

1 Look at these extracts from conversations.

- Contractions such as *he'd*, *it's*, *I'll* make the extracts informal. Mark any other words or phrases which make the conversations informal.
- Which of the extracts (a)–(d) is the most formal? Rewrite it to make it sound more informal. 🔑

a) A: Did Max help you?
   B: Yes, he moved all my books.
   A: He said he'd try and help out.
   B: He was very helpful, Max was.

b) A: It's not a good wine, that.
   B: I'll still try some.
   A: Where's your glass?

c) A: What are you going to have?
   B: I can't decide.
   A: I'm going to have a burger with chilli sauce, I am.
   B: It's a speciality here, chilli sauce is.

d) A: That's a very nice road.
   B: It runs right across the moors.
   A: Then it goes through all those lovely little villages.
   B: Yes, the villages are beautiful.

2 Which of these sentences is more likely to be used in formal situations and which is more likely to be used in informal situations? (Remember that in informal situations it is often difficult to plan and prepare what to say and therefore to make things clear for your listener.) Mark each sentence in the pair (F) formal or (I) informal. 🔑

i)   a) Gandhi was a great leader.
     b) He was a great leader, Gandhi was.
ii) a) He smokes too much, David does.
     b) David smokes too much.
iii) a) It's very nice, that road.
     b) That road is very nice.
iv) a) You're always getting it wrong, you are.
     b) You're always getting it wrong.

v)   a)   I'm a bit lacking in confidence, I am.

        b)   I am a bit lacking in confidence.

vi)   a)   Hong Kong is an exciting place.

        b)   It's an exciting place, Hong Kong is.

vii)   a)   They're not cheap, those clothes aren't.

        b)   Those clothes aren't cheap.

viii)   a)   That's a very nice beer, Fortuna is.

        b)   Fortuna is a very nice beer.

Observations

- The words added at the end of a sentence in spontaneous speech often involve repeating nouns and pronouns from an earlier part of the clause. They are called **tails**. They make the sentence more informal, and you can use them yourself when you want to sound more casual, or learn about them to improve your understanding of spontaneous conversation with English speakers.

- Due to their informality you should avoid using tails in, for example, the formal parts of a business presentation or a formal interview.

- In conversation we often want to give emphasis to statements. Tails can help us to do this. Tails are single words or phrases which occur at the end of a clause and extend what has already been said. A tail often consists of a phrase which extends a pronoun or demonstrative; it normally occurs as a complete phrase even though the subject phrase which is put at the front of the clause may be contracted, e.g. *It's an exciting place, Hong Kong is.*

- Notice that tails often occur in statements in which the speaker is evaluating things and saying positive or negative things. You get tails in sentences in which there are words like *exciting*, *very nice*, *great*, *too much*, or *a bit lacking*.

B   Discovering patterns of use

1   Nouns and pronouns in tails

Look at the following conversations.

- **What do you observe about the order of words in the tails?**
- **How do they compare with tag questions, e.g. *She does, doesn't she?* in (d)?**

a)   A: Did David make it on time?

     B: No, he was late. He was very cross, David.

b)   A: She's a very good tennis player, is Hiroko.

     B: I know. She always beats me easily.

c)   A: Did Max help you?

     B: Yes, he was very helpful, was Max.

d)   A: Have you heard her sing?

     B: Yes, she sings beautifully, Laura does.

     A: She does, doesn't she?

e) A: Have you been to Singapore?
   B: Yes, but it's far too hot for me, Singapore.
   A: It's not just hot, it's humid as well.

Observations

- The word order of tails is more flexible than that of the standard tag-questions you may have learned. In a tag-question, the auxiliary verb comes before the noun and the verb is made negative or positive in opposition to the rest of the clause:
  'She doesn't, does she?'
- Tails are often used when a speaker wants to emphasise information or ideas using word order.

2 Position and order of tails

Now look at the following sentences. The sentences are all typical spoken sentences. The tails here are repetitions or occur with question tags.

■ **What do you observe about the position and order of the tails?** ☞

a) I went there early. It would be about seven o'clock, it would. It wasn't dark yet.
b) It's difficult to eat, isn't it, spaghetti? You have to suck it into your mouth.
c) It'll melt, won't it, the ice-cream?
d) She's a good tennis player, Hiroko is, isn't she?
e) You hardly ever show emotion, you don't. Don't you have any feelings for her?
f) She still hasn't finished, hasn't Maria.

Observations

- Many tails consist of a noun or pronoun and a verb. A tail often extends a pronoun or noun or demonstrative which has occurred earlier in the clause. In a tail the noun can either follow or precede the verb (e.g. *He was very helpful, Max was*; or *He was very helpful, was Max*; *She still hasn't finished, hasn't Maria*; or *She still hasn't finished, Maria hasn't*).
- When a pronoun comes first in a clause and the tail is formed with a noun then the noun normally makes the comment stronger e.g. *He was a great leader, Gandhi was.*
- The noun can also be used as a tail on its own (e.g. *He was very helpful, Max*; *It's an exciting place, Hong Kong*).
- When pronouns occur in tails the word order of the preceding phrase is repeated; otherwise the sentence may be heard as a question e.g. 'You're stupid, you are', You're stupid are you?; 'It would take about half-an-hour, it would', It would take about half-an-hour would it?.
- Tails can occur with tag questions and can be placed either before or after the tag (e.g. *She's a good player, Hiroko is, isn't she?*, *It's not easy to eat, is it, spaghetti?*).
- When the tail repeats a verb which is not the verb *to be* or an auxiliary/modal verb then a *do* verb is used (e.g. 'She sings very well, she does'; 'They complain all the time, they do').
- Tails always agree with the phrase to which they refer (e.g. 'It's not a good wine, that isn't'; 'She'll never pass the exam, won't Toni'). Negative adverbs such as *hardly, scarcely*, etc. normally keep a negative tail (e.g. 'He scarcely speaks, he doesn't').

C Patterns in action

1 Using tails to express attitudes

- Underline the tails in the following utterances which are taken from authentic recorded spoken English.
- Are any utterances used to help the speaker express an opinion? ⌇⟲

a) It'll surely melt, won't it, the ice-cream?
b) It's a nice garden for growing vegetables that of yours.
c) She's a lovely singer Kay.
d) They do take up a lot of time, I suppose, kids, don't they?
e) It can leave you feeling very weak, it can, though, apparently, shingles*.
f) I'm going to have Mississippi mud pie I am.
g) It's really cold this wind isn't it?
h) Look how far that comes out that bit of wood.
i) You wonder if it's ever going to stop this rain.
j) It's normally only made of plastic that sort of stuff.

2 Now fill in the gaps in the following sentences with an appropriate tail. In each case more than one word is normally required to fill the gap. ⌇⟲

a) She's the best **she is**.
b) You're too slow ....
c) I'm ready to play now ....
d) It would be about two centimetres long ....
e) It's a sweet wine ....
f) Cats just lie in the sun all day ....
g) They're getting even more powerful .... computers.
h) It would take about an hour ....
i) Carol's passed all her exams ....
j) You've watched too many horror films ....
k) Carl and his sister watch TV all day ....

Observations

- Tails help us when we have positive or negative things to say. Tails are often used in connection with names of people, places, etc. and allow us to express our attitude to them.
- Tails can also emphasise the subject or the main topic of a sentence, and so help the listener better understand your point.

Shingles is a form of illness in which the skin becomes very painful. Older people sometimes get shingles when they have been in contact with children who have chickenpox.

3 Interactions and tails

Look at the following extracts from conversations.

■ **How do the elements underlined in each conversation relate to one another?**

a) [Tony is explaining how the family all became ill with colds. Jimmy is his son, Jenny is his wife.]

Tony: 'Cos he he's a very busy person <u>isn't he</u> <u>Jimmy</u>. [He laughs.]
Jenny: [nods]
Tony: <u>Young Jimmy is</u>, mm. But er we started getting colds then, <u>didn't we</u>?

b) [Marion, Anna and Gill are discussing a friend who has become a famous singer.]

Marion: <u>Yeah</u>. He's er becoming, <u>you know</u>, er a name.
Gill: Oh <u>yeah</u>.
Anna: Definitely is.

Observations

- Speakers use both tag questions and tails to develop a point in exchanges with other people. As Tony is speaking in **C3(a)**, he is observing what his wife is doing and using the alternative clause structures to ask and answer his own questions with his wife's support.
- Equally, in **C3(b)** the three girls support one another, and Anna's comment *Definitely is* almost functions as tail comment on Marion's point.

D Follow-up

■ **Rewrite the following dialogues to make them sound a little more informal.** ☞

a) A: Here's the menu. What do you fancy?
   B: It's certainly a nice menu.
   A: I'm going to have steak and chips.
   B: I fancy the spaghetti but I always manage to drop it down the front of my shirt.

b) A: I like them. David and Jean make a nice couple.
   B: Do you reckon they'll get married eventually?
   A: David is still lacking in confidence, I suppose, and Jean is a bit too young at the moment isn't she?

c) A: Sophie will never lose weight.
   B: She hardly ever eats cakes or chips.
   A: I should eat less. I'm far too flabby.

■ If you want more practice exercises, do the Further exercises at the end of the unit.
■ If you want further details of points relating to this unit, go to the Reference notes on pages 224–5.
■ The main rules for tails are given on the next page in the Summary.

Summary

- Tails normally involve a word or words which repeat or extend or rephrase a word or words which have appeared previously in the sentence. Sometimes the tail involves a whole noun phrase (e.g. 'It never occurred to me, the danger I was in').
- The same sentence can be given a more formal, less spoken tone by putting such a tail as the subject of the sentence in place of *it* (e.g. 'The danger I was in never occurred to me').
- Tails are also used for emphasis and for highlighting or evaluating key moments in narratives. But if tails are used throughout a narrative or throughout every conversation utterance, it would be unusual because we do not want to stress everything we say.
- Tails are only used in very informal writing, such as personal letters, postcards and popular journalism. They are much more common in informal, spoken language.

Further exercises ⌐

1 Fill in the gaps in the following sentences with an appropriate tail, using the names from the brackets. You can add further words, if you wish.

   a) It's a very good film, *Shadows is*. (Shadows)
   b) He's always late .... (David)
   c) She watches TV all day .... (Alison)
   d) They're playing live next week .... (REM)
   e) He talks a lot doesn't he .... ? (Carl)
   f) It affects a lot of people .... (migraine)
   g) She's the best swimmer in the class .... isn't she? (Claire)
   h) It's a strong beer .... (Fortuna)
   i) It's getting very expensive these days .... (London)

2 Re-tell this narrative, adding tails where appropriate.

> It was late at night and typically, the last bus had gone. So I decided to walk home. I was really cross with Jeff. He'd left the party early because he had to be up early for work the next day. Anyway, as I walked along our road, I heard a car behind me. It was really dark. I became very frightened and started to run. A man got out of the car and started to follow me. I ran more quickly and then he began to run more quickly too. By the time I reached our house he had caught up with me. I turned round. It was Jeff. He'd come after me to apologise ...

3 Rewrite these sentences so that the tail is the clear subject of the sentence. The first one is done for you.

   a) It never occurred to me, the danger I was in. (The danger I was in never occurred to me.)
   b) That was the book I wanted, the one with the picture on the front.
   c) It was a strange feeling, walking into that place.
   d) They're far too hot, those countries where it's all humid.

Unit 22 Heads (pre-posed elements of clauses)

A Introduction

1 **Look at these extracts from conversations. In each case the third line of each exchange sounds particularly informal.**

■ **Rewrite each of the third lines in these extracts so that it is more formal and grammatical.** ⌾

a) A: Did you get back early?
B: Yes, I did. Someone was attacked last night on the underground.
C: A city like London, it's not very safe at night.

b) A: Where are you going all together?
B: Probably just Southern Ireland.
C: Most places in Ireland, they're really quite cheap.

c) A: How was the first day?
B: Fine, thanks. The teachers seem nice.
C: The teacher with glasses, he seems very nice.

d) A: The film was a bit sentimental.
B: Was it?
C: Yes, the people in the audience, they all started crying when the dog died.

2 **The following exchanges all involve questions and answers. They are all informal conversational exchanges. Rewrite the questions so that they sound more formal.** ⌾

a) A: That house on the corner, do they live there?
B: Yes.
A: It looks very nice.

b) A: The girl who drives the Ford, is she his sister?
B: No. She's a cousin.
A: Really?

c) A: That black jacket, is it yours?
B: No, it's not.
A: It must belong to somebody.

d) A: The shop by the traffic lights that's open until nine, did you say it's gone out of business?
B: Yes, they've sold to a garage.
A: Pity. I wanted to get some wine.

- Unit 21 showed how items in a clause can be repeated at the end of the clause and that these help speakers show their attitude to something. We term these items tails.
- This unit looks at how speakers manipulate clause structure at the opening of clauses. These items are called 'pre-posed' items, or heads. They are an example of a special kind of **fronting** device (see glossary). For example:

  'A city like London, it's not safe at night.'

  In **B** we look at the structure of these elements, and in **C** we deal with why speakers use them.

B Discovering patterns of use

1 Which grammatical structures can function as 'heads'?

Look at the following extracts from conversations. The fronted items are in bold.

- **What kind of grammatical items are fronted?**
- **How do they relate to the next part of the sentences?**
- **What is the effect of fronting?**

a) [conversation in a changing room before taking a swim]

Andy: **Ancient Chinese proverb**, if you're warm enough when you start, you'll be too hot when you've finished.

Bill: Good one that.

b) [Joan is teaching her daughter, Janice, how to make a cake.]

Joan: Okay, one more time, **eggs, flour, water and sugar**, break the eggs and whip the mixture then …

Janice: Put it in the pan and heat it up.

Joan: Gentle heat, don't forget.

c) [Two brothers are talking in a pub with a group of friends.]

Mark: **Well, the time I nearly crashed the car**, I was driving late one night …

Tom: You'd forgotten to turn your lights on.

Mark: Yes, and I just didn't see the car in front.

d) [Two students, Gary and Jeff, are in a college common room.]

Gary: Right, **Englishman, Irishman and a Scotsman**, the Englishman he says …

Jeff: I've heard this before.

Gary: Let me finish …

2 Heads with different subjects

- Fill in the gaps in the following conversational extracts.
- Analyse whether the fronted or pre-posed* item is the same as the grammatical subject which follows it. ⌐—

a) The man from Leeds we met on holiday, his .... wrote to us last week.

b) My secretary, Ann, her .... has won a car in a newspaper competition.

c) Carol's friend in Tokyo, her sister, her .... is coming to stay with us next week.

d) One of my flatmates, Sue, her .... have sold everything and moved to Australia.

e) This friend of ours, ... has just got married.

f) Mr Campbell's brother in Scotland, his wife, ... has invited us to stay in the family cottage.

Pre-posed is a more technical grammatical term. The more economical term, *head*, is used more often in this unit. Both terms refer to a process of fronting grammatical units.

- Speakers use a wide variety of elements in pre-posed positions. These can range from a single proper noun:

  'John, he's nice'

  To an extended relative clause:

  'The man from Leeds we met on holiday, his sister ...'

- The head item does not have to be the same as the following subject.

  Note also that the pre-posed item can be a more general class of things, or a broader event, than the item it refers to later in the utterance:

  'Okay, **eggs, milk, flour**, break the **eggs** ...'

  'The **team that won the league**, their **goalkeeper** ...'

- Like tails, pre-posed elements are different from *wh*-constructions (see Unit 12) because they **repeat** an element which occurs in the clause, rather than moving it to the beginning of the clause within a different structure:

  'The results are interesting.'

  'What're interesting are the results.' (*wh*-clause)

  'The results, they are interesting.' (pre-posed element)

- Most pre-posed elements refer to subjects in the following clause. However, it is possible for them to refer to other items, for example objects:

  'Those shoes with low heels, I really like them.'

- Section C deals with **why** speakers use heads.

C Grammar in action

1 Why do speakers use heads?

Look at the following extracts from real conversations.

- Underline the parts of the sentences which are fronted.
- How are they different from the fronting which occurs in the examples in A1?
- Why do you think speakers introduce people into conversations in this way in A1? ☞

a) This friend of ours, his son's just gone to university.

b) Madge, one of the secretaries at work, her daughter got married last weekend.

c) Pat was really upset; apparently, Brian, they suspect he's got heart disease.

d) The chap in Cardiff I bought the car from, his brother was saying they're going to close down the school.

e) His cousin in London, her boyfriend, his parents bought him a Mercedes for his birthday.

2 Fronting in narratives

- Underline the main pre-posed unit at the beginning of these narratives. (a) and (c) are people telling stories, (b) is from a TV cookery programme and (d) is the opening to a joke.
- Why does the speaker focus on the topic in this way? ⌐

a) I didn't tell you, did I, that time on the way back from Hong Kong, well, we were just about to land in Bahrain when ...

b) So, just the milk, the flour and two eggs and you mix the milk and flour together and then ...

c) Now, listen, an old country proverb, if the plants don't grow on the same ground, find new ground.

d) Right, a man in a pub with a parrot on his shoulder, he asks for a pint of beer and the parrot, he asks for a gin and tonic ...

Observations

- Heads help a speaker (or writer) to show what or who is significant.
- The amount of information fronted depends on how much the speaker thinks the listener(s) already knows.
- The fronting process links new information to what is already known. For example, in the following:

  'Carol's friend in Tokyo, her sister, her son is coming to stay with us next week.'

  the speaker and listener both know Carol, and know or have already spoken about the fact that she has a friend in Tokyo. Although the **final** element in the sequence, the son, is the relevant information (i.e. he will be arriving soon), putting *her son* at the start of the sentence would not be 'listener friendly':

  'The son of the sister of the friend of Carol who lives in Tokyo is coming to stay next week.'

  This is grammatically correct, but difficult to comprehend because the word *son* is so distant from the main verb.
- In narrative, pre-posed units can highlight the main characters, or setting, or even give a summary of a key point.

D Follow-up

- Revise the ideas in this unit by writing out at least three observations about heads based on your study of this unit. One observation has been made for you. Cover the Observations and Summary until you have completed your own observations then read all the observations and the summary to see if you have remembered the main ideas.

  1 Heads can help listeners to comprehend better by highlighting key information for them at the beginning of a sentence or utterance.

  2 ....

  3 ....

  4 ....

- Record part of a radio or television programme. Can you find any examples of heads?
- If you want more practice exercises, do the Further exercises at the end of the unit.
- If you want further details of points relating to this unit, go to the Reference notes section on page 225. (Fronting in relation to *wh*-clauses is dealt with in Unit 12.)

Summary

- Pre-posing or fronting identifies for a listener that a place, person or event is important. It is common in spoken English in the form of heads, but some forms of fronting are also used in written English.
- Heads are regularly made up of structures without a main verb in a main clause. This element is then followed by a pronoun which normally becomes the subject of a following sentence (e.g. 'That leather coat, it looks really nice on you').
- Sometimes the pre-posed unit is not the same subject as the main subject in the main clause, but it is likely to be logically connected to the fronting unit (e.g. 'My friend, Janet, her sister has just emigrated to Brazil').
- Also note that it is possible for clause elements other than the subject to be pre-posed (e.g. 'The house we were looking at when you visited, we bought it!').
- Heads are different from *wh*-clauses (Unit 12) or adverb fronting (Unit 15) because they repeat a clause element.
- Heads can sometimes work like titles for chapters to a book, framing what is to follow and orientating the listener or reader (e.g. 'The time we were living in Hong Kong, we ...').

Further exercises ☞

1 Fill the gaps in the following sentences with an appropriate fronting unit. Compose each unit from the sentence in brackets. The first two are done for you.

a) New York, it's got to be the most exciting city.
   (New York has got to be the most exciting city.)

b) The weather in Spain, I think it will definitely be better.
   (I think the weather in Spain will definitely be better.)

c) .... , you know him.
   (You know the man with the T-shirt.)

d) .... , I really like her.
   (I really like that girl with the brown eyes and dark hair.)

e) .... , is that where they live?
   (Do they live in that big house in front of the park?)

f) .... , is that his brother?
   (Is the boy who drives the VW his brother?)

g) .... , are they yours?
   (Are the trainers with the red stripe yours?)

h) .... , they're the most popular dish with children.
   (Pizzas are the most popular dish with children.)

2 Make the following more informal by putting head elements at the start.

a) Most castles in Spain are really impressive.

b) The English football team are always losing.

c) That laptop computer is very reliable.

d) Is that boy with dark curly hair a friend of yours?

e) Do they live in that house with the large garden?

f) He owns the very fast red cabriolet sports car.

g) Montpellier is a city with lots of old buildings in the centre.

h) Supermarkets which sell fresh bread are very popular.

i) Is the girl with brown hair and glasses his sister?

j) Most Australian wines are not expensive.

3 Choose your own fronting unit for the gaps at the beginning of the following utterances.

a) .... , he seems very nice.

b) .... , it's too crowded for me.

c) .... , I like that kind of thing on Sundays.

4 Rewrite the following sentences first with a head and then with a *wh*-construction.

Example:

I saw that man with a sports car again yesterday.

That man with a sports car, I saw him again yesterday.

Who I saw was that man with the sports car again yesterday.

a) The files about the yearly results are ready.

b) I've brought that software you wanted to see.

c) The figures for March are terrible.

d) Mr Brown's secretary's sister from Australia is coming to work here.

Ellipsis 1: at the start of clauses

A Introduction

1 **Look at these extracts from conversations.**

- **Mark places where you feel words may be missing, write a fuller version of the sentences you have marked, and compare the two versions.** 🔑

a) [Jim is telling Ken what route he took in his car to get to Ken's house. Mistham is the name of a small town.]
   Jim: And I came over by Mistham, by the reservoirs.
   Ken: Oh, by Mistham, over the top, nice route.
   Jim: Colours are pleasant, aren't they?
   Ken: Yes.
   Jim: Nice run[1], that.

b) [Two brothers are talking.]
   Matt: Are you late?
   Roman: Yes, really late.
   Matt: What time's[2] the film start?
   Roman: Seven-thirty.
   Matt: You've got half-an-hour.
   Roman: Any chance of a lift in your car?

c) [Paul is cooking rice in a microwave oven. Ingrid is watching him.]
   Ingrid: Didn't know you used boiling water.
   Paul: They reckon it's quicker.

2 **Would each of the following be acceptable in formal situations? If not, why not?**

a) Are you ready yet? / You ready yet?
b) Too late. / It is too late.
c) Fine, thanks. / I'm fine, thanks.
d) I'm not sure really. / Not sure really.
e) Is she French? Yes, she's French. / Is she French? Yes, French.

---

[1] *Run* can be used to mean journey or route.
[2] *What time's* here means 'what time **does**.'

B Discovering patterns of use

1 Simple patterns of ellipsis in conversation

Look at the following extracts from conversations.

- Mark places where you think ellipsis is used at the start of clauses.
- List the words which you think could be added in a more formal context, and try to categorise them according to grammatical structure. ⊙━

a) A: Want another coffee?
    B: Yes, thanks.
    A: Like some more cake as well?
    B: Yes, please. But it'll make me fat.

b) A: Did you knock on the door?
    B: I did. Nobody at home.

c) A: Seen Mike lately?
    B: Yes, I saw him last night actually.

d) A: Heard the joke about the monkey and the glass of beer?
    B: Don't you remember you told me it last week at the party.

2 The development of ellipsis in conversational exchanges

Look at these examples of real conversations between customers and people serving them.

- In each case a speaker repeats something, but uses ellipsis in one of the repetitions. Can you find the examples?
- Why is ellipsis used in some places and not in others? ⊙━

a) [A customer has bought the wrong part for his car.]
    Garage repair man: What was it? Renault?
    Customer: … I brought it up after you'd closed. I had to buy this one. So …
    Garage repair man: … What was it? A Renault?
    Customer: No. Em this one. The em Fiat Panda.

b) [Later in the same conversation, the customer asks about another car. The garage man is explaining that once a car is registered, you cannot change the number plates.]

Garage repair man: No. You can't change the plate after it's been registered.
Customer: I didn't know that.
Garage repair man: No.
Customer: Didn't know that. Amazing.

3 Ellipsis in written text

Here is a written text which contains several examples of ellipsis at the beginning of clauses.

- Which words could be added if the text was written out more fully? ⌇

JUST TESTING

Easter Eggs
Available in four sizes. A hollow milk chocolate egg with milk chocolate buttons. Minimum 14 per cent milk solids and 25 per cent cocoa solids. Really nice chunky chocolate. A big favourite with our testers.

Observations

- In informal conversations we can often leave out the subject *I* at the beginning of what we say:
  'Didn't phone yesterday.'
- In informal conversations subjects and auxiliary verbs can also be left out. Sometimes they are left out together:
  'Ready yet?,' 'Finished?'
- Sometimes a determiner and the dummy subject *there* (*is/are*) can also be left out:
  'Any tea left?' (not 'Is there any tea left?')
- Ellipsis occurs commonly with verbs such as *see, hear* and *think* in questions and in replies. In questions, *have you* and *do you* can be dropped with these verbs:
  'Seen Matt lately?'
  'Heard you were ill.'
  'Think he'll ring?'
- Before questions such as *Do you want ...?* and *Would you like ...?, Do you* and *Would you* can be dropped.
- Speakers use ellipsis when they feel certain a listener can understand the message without a full form. Therefore there is often more ellipsis at later stages in conversations.

C Grammar in action

1 Contrasting effects of ellipted and non-ellipted constructions

In this section we will observe more about ellipsis and how it is used. Once again it helps to compare full forms with reduced forms.

Read the following instances of ellipsis from real conversations.

- **How would the remarks sound if the full grammatical forms were used?**

  Example: Jill: Hi! Haven't seen you for a couple of weeks.
  Jill: Hi! I haven't seen you for a couple of weeks. 🔑

a) Tom: What's it like where you live?
   Ann: I like it, very happy there, must say.
   Tom: Bit of a change from London, I suppose.

b) Mona: Did you see that on telly a while back?
   Phil: Yeah, think so. Rings a bell.*

c) [Mary is talking about a busy town centre.]
   Mary: I sat on a bench there and honestly, never seen so many people.

d) [David is telling Jim about a car accident.]
   David: Happened right in front of the police station.
   Jim: Really?

e) Audrey: I came by bike, along the river.
   Cath: Bit dangerous there isn't it?

f) Helen: When can you bring the car round?
   Mike: On Friday.
   Helen: Sounds good. Thanks.

g) Jean: He's been ill because of the weather.
   Rob: Because of the weather?
   Jean: Yes, far too cold for him.

Observations

- Words that can be left out at the beginning of a sentence include: articles and determiners, possessives, auxiliary verbs, personal pronouns and the dummy subject *there*.
- Note that such words are not normally omitted in fixed phrases, and can generally only be omitted when the item is the subject of the sentence:

  'Wind's strong, isn't it?' (✔)
  'I can't stand up in the wind!' (✔)
  ~~'I can't stand up in wind'~~ (✗)

  'Pub's closed.' (✔)
  'Coming to the pub?' (✔)
  ~~'Coming to pub?'~~ (✗)

---

* *Rings a bell* is a colloquial expression. It means that the speaker can nearly remember something, or has a slight recollection of it.

2 Ellipsis in narratives

Look at this story which Amy tells her friend Barbara.

- **Is there much ellipsis in it?**
- **Would you normally expect to use a lot of ellipsis when telling an informal story like this one?**

[Two cousins are remembering a journey. Yarmouth, Norwich and Fareham are towns in the Eastern part of England.]

Amy: I remember that journey. We went from Yarmouth, when we had the car, and we went into Norwich, and there's a ring road round Norwich, and this road to Fareham was off this ring road. Well, we turned right, if you remember.

Barbara: Oh I can't remember.

Amy: And we went right round this ring road, I bet we did twenty miles, and when we came back it was the next one on the left to where we'd started.

Observations

- Ellipsis is a natural part of conversation, but is mainly used when the speakers do not expect or want a strong focus on what they are saying.
- In narratives such as the one above it would be unusual to see much ellipsis because the speaker wants the listeners to concentrate on the story. Ellipsis also functions when the speaker can assume knowledge on the part of a listener. Telling a story usually involves giving listeners **new** information.

D Follow-up

- Write a dialogue about three friends who are planning an evening out. Where would ellipsis be natural? Try to include one of the following somewhere in your dialogue.

  don't know   haven't been there   too far/expensive   seen it

  If possible, act out your dialogue with two close friends. Do you feel natural using these expressions? If so, why? If not, why not?

- If you want more practice exercises, do the Further exercises at the end of Unit 24.
- If you want further details of points relating to this unit, go to the Reference notes on pages 226–31.

Summary

- Ellipsis is used in informal situations, especially in conversations in which the speakers know each other well and in conversations which are relaxed and friendly. Very often the meaning is clear from the context, and speakers do not need to be very explicit.
- *I* as a grammatical subject is frequently left out at the beginning of what we say. This is especially common with mental verbs like *hope, think, expect, believe*. In replies these verbs are followed by *so* (e.g. *hope so, think so*. See the next unit for more information about this).
- Ellipsis often occurs at the beginning of common evaluative expressions or comments such as *(I) don't know, (It) sounds nice, (I'll) be seeing you, (It's a) pity we've missed it.*
- Subjects and main verbs can be left out, especially in questions and answers (e.g. *(Are you) ready yet? Yes, (I'm) ready, (Would you) like another coffee?*). Ellipsis occurs frequently in replies and responses.
- As a conversation develops, ellipsis is more likely to occur. When people know what the topic is, and who is speaking, it is not always necessary to repeat things unless a word needs to be stressed for some reason.

Note: the Further exercises for Unit 23 are combined with those for Unit 24. You can find them at the end of Unit 24, on page 171.

"There! There! See it, Larry? ... It moved a little closer!"

A Introduction

1 First cover the text below with a piece of paper. Then slide the paper down till you see a line across the page and stop.

'I'm off,' she said.   a) Who are these people?
'Don't go,' I said.
'I must,' she said.   b) What is the situation?
'Where to?' I said.
'Not far,' she said.
'Let's talk,' I said.
'No time,' she said.

....

'Someone else?' I said.   a) Is it any easier to work out what is going on now?
' 'Fraid so,' she said.
'Thought so,' I said.
'Guess who?' she said.   b) Who is the person referred to in 'Guess who?'
'Don't say,' I said.
'I must,' she said.
'OK,' I said.

....

'Your friend,' she said.
'My Vauxhall *Astra* [1]!' I said.
'You knew,' she said.

■ Now read the dialogue from the advertisement again and mark places where you feel more words would be needed if this was formal, written language (for example, *I thought so* instead of just *Thought so*).

2 Look at this Nissan advertisement for a car.

■ What three questions could you ask to give these answers?

It has.   It does.   It can.

> **Observations**
>
> ● In Unit 23 we looked at how words can be omitted from the start of clauses. This was one kind of ellipsis. In this unit we discuss ellipsis after the verb in spoken English, and describe how speakers use it naturally in conversation.

[1]A *Vauxhall Astra* is a car, and the text is an advertisement for it.
[2]This advertisement in no way reflects the current marketing strategy of Vauxhall Motors.

B Discovering patterns of use

1 Replying correctly using ellipsis

a) **What rules could explain the following examples?**

Question/remark	Wrong reply	Right reply
Is she French?	She may.	She may be.
Maybe he's lost it.	He might.	He might have.
Will you be ready?	I might.	I might be.

b) **Which response would you choose in the following?** ⌐━

A: Is Paola ill?
   a) She must.
   b) She must be.
   c) She must be ill.

B: Have you rung Laleh about the party?
   a) No, but Julia might.
   b) No, but Julia might have.
   c) No, but Julia might have rung Laleh.

Observations

- You have probably already learned that when you reply to a question, you do not repeat the main verb:
  - A: Can you swim?
  - B: 'Yes, I can ~~swim~~.'
  - A: 'Does he like fruit?'
  - B: 'Yes, he does ~~like it/fruit~~.'
- If the modal verbs (*must, can, will, may*, etc.) are used in the perfect tense with *have*, or with the main verb *be*, then these verbs **are** repeated.
  One reason for this is that there can be confusion between present perfect and future uses of modals:
  - A: Have you rung Laleh?
  - B: No, but Julia might. (might phone in the future)

  or:
  - B: No, but Julia might have. (might have rung her already)

---

2 Ellipsis of verb + *to*

Here are some more examples of ellipsis involving verbs and replies to questions.

■ **What is important to notice about B's replies in the following conversation?**

A: Do you want to come with me tonight?
B: Yes, I'd love to.
A: Okay, I'll pick you up at eight, then.
B: Okay, but only if you really want to. You don't have to. I could get a taxi.

C Grammar in action

1 Formal and informal structures

■ Examine the following dialogues and then tick the columns to indicate whether you consider the exchanges to be formal or informal or incorrect. ⊙━

	formal	informal	incorrect
a) A: Spent all your money? B: Afraid so.			
b) A: Coming out for a meal? B: No money. Sorry.			
c) A: Would you like a lift in my car? B: I have my own car, thank you.			
d) A: Would you like to marry in Cyprus? B: Like to.			
e) A: Can I have chips, beans and a sausage? B: So, you want chips, beans and and a sausage? A: Yes, I want chips, beans and a sausage please.			
f) A: So it happened in front of the police station? B: Yes, in front of.			

2 Ellipsis in well-established contexts

- Where do you think the following exchange took place?
- Who are A and B?
- Can you find any ellipsis?

(Cover the Observations box below while you do this exercise.)

A: Can I have a second class stamp please, love?

B: You can.

A: Thank you, love.

B: There we are [gives stamp] and one penny. [gives change]

A: Mm. Last of the big spenders*, eh?

B: Thank you.

A: I bought a new book of ten first class when I was in town today and I've left them at home in my shopping bag.

B: Have you? Oh dear.

Observations

- The exchange in **C2** takes place at a post-office counter. A is the customer and B is the post office clerk. The clerk uses ellipsis of the kind we have been looking at when she says *You can*, and *Have you?*

- In addition, because this is a well-established context, the speakers do not have to be fully explicit about everything they say. For example, the clerk does not say *Here is your stamp*, but *There we are*, a very common expression when someone is handing something to someone else. Equally, when the customer explains about leaving the stamps behind, she can just say *I bought a book of ten first class*, and does not have to add the word *stamps* because this is already assumed knowledge.

D Follow-up

- Choose one of the dialogues in this unit. Record yourself saying it, or rehearse it with a friend. How natural do the ellipted clauses sound to you?

- Are there similar processes for reducing clauses in your own language? If so, can you use them in any context, or are they only for informal conversation between friends?

- If you want more practice exercises, do the Further exercises at the end of the unit.

- If you want further details of points relating to this unit go to the Reference notes section on pages 226–31.

---

*As it sounds, a *big spender* applies to someone who spends a lot of money. 'The last of the big spenders' is an idiomatic, jokey, expression, generally applied to someone who is very careful with their money (i.e. the opposite of a *big spender*).

Summary

- In informal conversations verbs are often left out, especially if the meaning can be easily understood from the context or if the verb does not need to be stressed.
- When auxiliary and main verbs occur in replies, especially in short answers to questions, the main verb is normally left out. In such cases the subject is not normally omitted. (e.g. A: Have you finished? B: Yes, I have. not B: Yes, ~~have~~. (✗))
- When there is more than one auxiliary verb, ellipsis most often occurs after the first verb. A second auxiliary is normally included if there is a change in the modal auxiliary (e.g. A: Carol ought to be invited. B: Yes, she must be / she has been already).
- *To* and *so* are used instead of the whole infinitive of the verb if the meaning is clear, particularly in fixed phrases such as *hope so, love to.*
- Auxiliary verbs can be left out before personal pronouns. They cannot normally be omitted before the personal pronoun *I* or the pronoun *it.*
  e.g. 'You ready?' ('Are you ready?'); 'Jill say anything?' ('Did Jill say anything?'); 'Why ~~I done that~~?' (✗) ('Why have I done that?') (✓)

Further exercises 🔑

1 Cross out (as in the example) words that you feel might be left out in informal conversation in these mini-dialogues.

Example: A: ~~Would you like~~ some more coffee?

B: A little drop please ... that's fine.

a) A: Have you seen Roger at all this morning?
    B: No, I haven't seen him since yesterday.
    A: I wonder where he is.
    B: Yes, it's strange he hasn't come.

b) A: Did Veronica leave a letter for me?
    B: I think so. I saw it here somewhere.
    A: It doesn't matter. I'll come back later.

c) A: Did you go out with Beryl after all?
    B: Yeah, I didn't really want to go. I just felt I had to really. I'm sorry I did go now.

2 Now do the opposite. Expand these extracts so that they have a more formal, complete grammatical structure, as in the example:

Example: A: Like to go out tonight? (Would you like to go out tonight?)

B: Yes, love to. Anywhere in mind? (Yes, I'd love to. Do you have anywhere in mind?)

a) A: Know anyone who does translations?
    B: Funny you should say that, yeah, met a man just the other day, said he was setting up an agency.

A: Don't do Chinese to English by any chance, do they?

B: Wouldn't have a clue. Could give you his number, if you like, got it here somewhere.

b) A: You going to do that exam after all?

B: S'pose so. Trouble is, just can't be bothered studying for it.

A: Why should you? No-one else seems to be working. Why don't you just do it?

B: Could do I suppose.

3 In this conversation, some words have been left out which really should be present, and which are not normal examples of ellipsis. Put in the necessary words.

A: Have you heard from Raj lately?

B: Yeah. I got a letter other day.

A: Really? What he say?

B: He wants me to come to India for a holiday.

A: Great! You going?

B: Am thinking about it. I'd like, but it costs a fortune.

A: Well, better start saving. Go for it. I would.

4 Here are some phrases from the Vauxhall advertisement you studied earlier:

thought so   *I must*   *no time*   *'fraid so*

■ **Where do they fit into this conversation?**

'D'you fancy a cup of coffee?' he said.
'Sorry, ... ' she said.
'More problems?' he said.
' .... ' she said.
'Him again?' he said.
'Yes,' she said.
' .... ' he said.
'How did you guess?' she said.
'Your face,' he said. 'Please, don't go.'
' .... ' she said.

5 In the following mini-dialogues, which have been made up, the speakers are being a little too formal with each other.

■ **Rewrite the dialogues so that they use ellipsis and sound a little more friendly and informal.**

a) A: Are you ready yet?

B: Yes, OK.

A: How far is it to the station?

B: It's about ten minutes to the station.

A: The station's next to that supermarket, isn't it?

B: I think it's next to the supermarket.
A: We're going to be late.
B: It doesn't matter.

b) A: Would you like a coffee?
B: Yes, I would like a coffee please.
A: Do you take sugar?
B: Yes, I do take sugar. I take two teaspoonfuls, please.

c) A: Would you like to go out tonight?
B: Yes, I'd love to go out tonight. Did you have anywhere in mind?

d) A: I think the school's over there on the left.
B: Yes, the school's over there on the left.
A: I wonder if we'll enjoy the concert.
B: I hope we'll enjoy it.

6 **Complete the replies to the following questions using the verbs given.**

i) A: Will Jo be at the party?
B: Yes ....   (**hope**)

ii) A: Are you buying those shoes?
B: Yes ....
before they all go in the sales.   (**want**)

iii) A: Is Winston bringing some music?
B: Well, ... him ....   (**asked**)

iv) A: Are you coming with us?
B: Yes, I'd ....   (**love**)

7 **How could the speakers in this rather formal conversation use the kinds of ellipsis we have been looking at to make their talk sound less formal?**

Maria: Why don't you come with us tonight?
Bob: Where are you going?
Maria: Oh, just for a meal. Come with us.
Bob: Mm, well ...
Maria: Wouldn't you like to come?
Bob: I want to come, I mean, I'd like to come ... but ...
Maria: Why don't you come then?
Bob: I've no money.
Maria: Have you spent it all?
Bob: I'm afraid so.
Maria: What did you buy?
Bob: Oh, it was nothing special.
Maria: I could lend you some.
Bob: Would you lend me some? Thanks.
Maria: It's no problem. You should have said.
Bob: Yes, maybe I should have said.

Discourse markers

A Introduction

1 The following three texts (a)–(c) contain discourse markers (in bold).

■ Choose one of the functions listed below, and decide which applies to
them. ☞

i) helps readers to take steps in the right direction, usually in a sequence
ii) marks a boundary between topics
iii) indicates an alternative point of view
iv) expresses an attitude to what is being said

a) [This is from a magazine for teenagers.]

> **First**, reassure him that you still like him a lot and that
> you're not interested in seeing other guys. **Then**, tell him
> that his jealousy is making you feel trapped. **Hopefully**,
> this will make him back off. **But**, be prepared to remind
> him that you need some space, as possessiveness
> **actually**, can't be cured quickly.

b) [This is from an information leaflet.]

What is a Conservation Area?

These areas which are **then** designated as Conservation Areas derive their special qualities from the buildings, their traditional details, materials, scale and form. Equally important, **however**, is the way in which buildings and spaces relate to each other, the patterns of streets, open spaces and trees are important.

Conservation Area status does not rule out the need for new development which is sometimes necessary to maintain an area's economic and social vitality. **Rather**, it aims to direct any changes so that the existing historic and architectural character is respected and the new can sit sympathetically alongside the old. **It follows that** there will be views in favour of retaining existing buildings wherever possible.

c) [The following extract is from a university seminar. Alison is just completing a prepared talk to the seminar group. Dr James Blandford is the tutor.]

Alison: An example of this, at the moment French troops have helped to prop up the routed Rwandan army after its defeat … and that's it.

Dr Blandford: **Good**. Thank you very much indeed. **OK, so**, there's about three or four major points you want to talk about … **right** … which you were going to try and identify. The first of them is …

2 The next extract is from a conversation recorded between two retired teachers, Graham and John, who are talking about other teachers they both used to work with.

- Underline any words or phrases which you consider to be a discourse marker.
- What do each of the markers help the speaker to do? ☞

Graham: Well, she's like Aubrey was, I mean, Douglas was the sort of person who would never have made a great career.

John: No, no, that's true.

Graham: And there are people like that, who are very good at what they do.

John: Yeah.

Graham: I mean, Douglas is very talented both in and out of the classroom, you know, good teacher, good diplomat, nice bloke …

Observations

- Discourse markers are words or phrases which help us to structure and monitor a stretch of written or spoken language. You have probably learned how to use them in writing to help readers understand your ideas.
- In this unit the main focus is on the most frequent markers in spoken discourse.

B Discovering patterns of use

1 Discourse markers for listeners versus speakers

Read both of the extracts, which are examples of recorded conversations in which discourse markers are used.

- Underline the words or phrases which you think function as discourse markers.
- Say whether you think each chosen marker mainly: ☞

i) focuses on the listener, checking that the listener follows what is being said and/or makes sure that a speaker does not sound to a listener too certain or dogmatic.

ii) focuses on the speaker, helping the speaker to structure what she/he is saying.

a) [This conversation was recorded in a post office. Reg is a post-office clerk; Jennifer is a customer. The book they refer to is a book of stamps which can be bought monthly to pay for a television licence fee.]

Jennifer: Right.

Reg: They're doing it, they used to do it in book form years ago and I think they're starting again.

Jennifer: Right.

Reg: So you, you know …

Jennifer: 'Cos she's probably not going to be in her own home for a year, so we just want to do it for a month at a time, to see how she goes, right …

Reg: She can always change the address at a post office where she goes to.
Jennifer: Yeah.
Reg: If she does take a yearly one out, you know.
Jennifer: Right, okay, and the other thing I need is this …

b) [This conversation involves members of a Christian group discussing their beliefs.]

Helen: Yeah, well, I mean, in some ways, you know, I think you should make the difference but it's pernickety* as well, because when I have, you know, when I do go out with the guys and just talk to them … I try to just, sort of, hope my life isn't affected, you know, by my faith in that sense …

Raj: But is that because of your faith, or because you've got a bit of a conscience?

Liam: Mm.

Helen: Well, I see, I don't know, I think it is my faith because it comes from that feeling of doing wrong.

Moira: Isn't our faith, isn't our conscience affected by our faith?

Raj: Yeah, but …

Helen: No, no, I'm not trying not to generalise in that sense … I mean, you can be a good person and not a Christian, we all know that …

Observations

- Some of the most frequent discourse markers in spoken English are: *okay*, *well*, *you know*, *I mean*, *actually*, *right*, *I think*, *'cos*, *so*.
- Markers such as *right*, *okay*, and *well* normally occur at the beginning of utterances and indicate a boundary between one part of a conversation or one topic and another. *Well* and *I mean* and *I think* indicate that further comment and more details will follow.
- Markers such as *you know* check that your listener understands you and that you both share the same viewpoint.
- Markers such as *I don't know* and *I think* are sensitive to listeners and tend to soften opinions.

---

2 The variety and function of spoken discourse markers

The following dialogue, which has been slightly adapted, was recorded at a meeting of publishers who are preparing a book (similar to this book) which is for learners of the English language.

- Rewrite this dialogue removing the discourse markers which are in bold. How does the conversation now sound? What has changed in the relationship between the speakers?
- What kind of discourse marker is the phrase *There's something I wanted to ask you?*
- Write down **three** other discourse markers which function in a similar way.

Pernickety is a colloquial word which here means complicated.

[A publisher's meeting. *Changes* is the title of a book.]

Gill: **Right**, **okay**, but it's all under control.

Seamus: It's actioned.*

Gill: **Jolly good. There's something I wanted to ask you**, um … when are you going to start handling reprints? 'Cos I need some advice about reprints for *Changes*.

Mac: … It would take me about three months, **I would think**, to get an angle on it, but I'm not getting it until June.

Seamus: Linda's coming in in June, yeah.

Mac: **So**, until June.

C Grammar in action

1 Contrasting formal and informal discourse markers

Read the following text.

■ **What would be the effect if the discourse markers shown in bold in this advertisement were changed to the ones shown?**

Mind you → On the other hand
what's more → moreover

[The text is an extract from an advert for Subaru cars. The advert tries to persuade couples to buy two cars in order to make sure that neither loses out and that their life together stays happy. The Justy is the name of one of the cars.]

Gripping stuff, Subaru four-wheel drive.

The world and his wife's favourite, in fact. With one and a half million four-wheel drives to prove it.

Mind you, it only takes two to make a perfect marriage.

The Justy for one. The world's first 1.2 4WD supermini.

A poetic little mover. 3 valves per cylinder. 5-speed box. 3 or 5 doors.

From only £6,198 **what's more.**

---

*Actioned is a word from business contexts. It means that a task has begun, i.e. action has been taken in relation to a problem or task.

2 Discourse markers in casual conversation

- **Write an explanation for learners of English of the discourse markers which are in bold in this text:**

[In the following recorded conversation a married couple are planning a summer holiday with the help of a friend.]

Jan: **You know, like**, if you got the earliest train in the morning and then just got the last train back at night …

Sue: The only thing is, when I opened that up at Brugge, first thing it said in it was 'Don't stay in Brugge,' – no, it says, 'Don't stay in Brugge '**cos** it's dear'.

Jan: Is it?

Dave: Yeah.

Sue: Yeah, it does say that …

Dave: **Well**, maybe then we could do that; go to the Hook of Holland, go to Amsterdam, '**cos** Delft isn't far from Amsterdam is it?

Jan: I thought Delft was miles from Amsterdam.

Sue: Don't think so.

Dave: **Well, I mean**, it's only, Holland's only small, it's not a big place …

Sue: [reading from a guide book] 'Its museums are named as one attraction … hold some of the country's finest collections of Flemish …'

Dave: **You see**, I'd never get her into a museum to look at art.

D Follow-up

- If possible, record part of an English language drama from radio or TV. Listen out for the most common discourse markers (*well, OK, right* and so on). Are they used in the ways we have talked about in this unit? We would predict that *well* is frequently followed by a negative comment, or a refusal – is this the case in your examples?

- Look at your favourite English language textbook. Are there any dialogues in it? Do they use any discourse markers? If they don't, do you think this is a problem?

- If you want more practice exercises, do the Further exercises at the end of the unit.

- If you want further details of points relating to this unit, go to the Reference notes section on pages 231–2.

Summary

- The most frequent discourse markers in spoken English are: *okay, well, you know, I mean, right, actually, I (would) think, so, 'cos, you see,* and *I don't know*.

- Discourse markers usually occur at the beginning of utterances and signpost how a listener is to interpret what follows: for example, mainly as part of a logical or temporal sequence, as part of shared knowledge, or as part of statements which should not be taken too dogmatically. Discourse markers can also sometimes do several of these things at the same time.

- Whole phrases and clauses such as *I was saying* and *I just wanted to ask you* can also function as discourse markers.

- Spoken discourse markers can also cluster together, e.g. *well, I mean; I don't know, I think; you know, I think; right, OK*.

- Some discourse markers soften the content of a statement so that a speaker does not sound too definite or dogmatic.

Further exercises ⚷

1 Fill in the gaps with an appropriate discourse marker from the list:

a) A: How are the team playing at the moment?
    B: ...., they're playing well but the tactics are poor.
    (Well/So/Right)

b) A: What subject do we study next?
    B: ...., we move on to the tricky question of the Norman invasion.
    (Right/I mean/You know)

c) A: What is your view of the risks of cigarette smoking?
    B: Well, ..., it depends on your age and on other aspects of your life style.
    (I mean/so/'cos)

d) Go to London for the day .... it'll give you a break.
   ('cos/you see/okay)

2 The following discourse markers (in bold) are markers which are more usually used in a more formal written style. Change the markers to more informal spoken discourse markers which have a similar meaning. Choose from the following: *but, so* (×2), *what's more, you know what I mean.*

a) The whole room was in a mess after the party. **Consequently**, I had to clear it up.
b) He fell out of a first floor window, though he didn't hurt himself. **Moreover**, he was drunk.
c) **In conclusion**, I'm meeting Jack at six o'clock tonight.
d) **Alternatively**, it's important to book early for the New Year celebrations.
e) **You appreciate what I am saying** I am sure.

3 Here is an extract from a real recorded conversation. The conversation consists entirely of discourse markers:

- **Is the extract from the beginning or end of the conversation?**

Carol: So, anyway.
Frances: Well, you know.
Carol: Right.
Frances: Okay then.
Carol: Okay.
Frances: Good.

Glossary

You are probably already familiar with most of the grammar terminology used in this book, but there are a few terms you may not be familiar with which are centrally related to the kind of grammar we present in the book. These are explained here.

Note: a word in bold type with → afterwards indicates that you should see the separate heading for that item.

Clause

A **clause** is a unit of language based around a verb. All clauses, except imperatives and clauses with **ellipsis** (→), have a subject, and many have objects and adverbials too. Clauses may be *finite* (i.e. with a verb that changes for tense, person, number), or *non-finite* (i.e. with a verb that ends in an -*ing* form, or with a past participle, or with the infinitive form).

Examples of clauses:

'She loves nursery school.' (finite: subject–verb–direct object)

'He never laughs.' (finite: subject–verb)

'I knew the answer, but didn't tell her.' (two clauses: 1 finite: subject–verb–object–linking adverbial; 2 finite: subject–verb–indirect object)

'Listening to that music, I forgot all my troubles.' (Two clauses: 1 non-finite: -*ing* form of verb–adverbial; 2 finite: subject–verb–direct object)

'To get there by six, you'll need to leave here at about 5.30.' (Two clauses: 1 non-finite: infinitive verb–adverbial; 2 finite: subject–verb–verb–adverbial–adverbial)

Clauses are the building blocks of sentences in written language. In all language, they are the most basic unit of communication.

Discourse markers

Discourse markers are words or phrases which are normally used to mark boundaries in conversation between one topic or bit of business and the next. For example, words and phrases such as *right, okay, I see, I mean,* help speakers to negotiate their way through talk indicating whether they want to open or close a topic or to continue it, whether they share a common view of the state of affairs, what their reaction is to something, etc. For example, people speaking face to face or on the phone often use *anyway* to show the wish to finish that particular topic, finish the whole conversation or perhaps return to a previous topic. Similarly, *right* often serves to indicate that participants are ready to move on to the next phase of business.

Ellipsis

Ellipsis is common in spoken discourse. It occurs in writing where it usually functions *textually* to avoid repetition where structures would otherwise be redundant. For example, in the sentence 'We ran for the bus but missed it', it is clear that *we* remains the subject of both clauses; or in the sentence 'The chair was broken and the table too', where it is clearly unnecessary to repeat the verb *was broken*. Ellipsis in spoken English is mainly **situational** (i.e. affecting people and things in the immediate situation), and frequently involves the omission of personal subjects, where it is obvious that the speaker will remain unambiguous. This feature is especially common with verbs of mental process: for example, '(I) think so', or '(I) wonder if they'll be coming to the party'. Such ellipsis also occurs with main or auxiliary verbs where meaning can be relatively easily reconstructed from the context.

Fixed expression

The term **fixed expression** describes language which is in some way pre-formulated or prefabricated, that is, language forms which are routine and patterned. A significant proportion of all language comes into this category and, indeed, speakers would find it difficult to communicate if everything that was said had to be inventive and original. Fixed expressions play an important part in spoken language in particular in reinforcing shared knowledge and social conventions, and referring to common cultural understandings. Examples of fixed expressions include: *as a matter of fact, once and for all, at the end of the day, a good time was had by all, honesty is the best policy, carry the can, an open-door policy* and *as far as I am concerned*.

Fronting (or pre-posing)

Fronting refers to the movement of an element from its 'canonical' position and its relocation as the first element in a construction. Taking the sentence 'I dedicated my life to that man and his music', we can front the indirect object as follows: 'To that man and his music I dedicated my life'. The process allows a focus or emphasis to fall on the fronted or pre-posed element.

Heads

The term **heads** (sometimes called pre-posed elements in clauses) is used to describe structures which identify for a listener that something we are referring to is important. Heads are common in spoken English. Heads frequently consist of structures without a main verb which are **fronted** ($\rightarrow$) for emphasis and then followed by a pronoun to ensure that the listeners can follow:

'**That leather coat**, **it** really suits you.'

Sometimes whole clauses can be heads:

'**The house we were looking at when you visited**, we bought it.'

Several linked subjects can be stacked together:

'**My friend, Janet, her sister** has just emigrated to Brazil.'

Heads are very rare in written English but other forms of **fronting** do occur in written English.

Intransitive verbs

An intransitive verb is a verb which does not take a direct object. For example, 'an hour **elapsed**' or 'The actress **blushed** several times during the interview'.

Modality

This is a term used in grammatical and semantic analysis to refer to meanings connected with degrees of certainty and degrees of necessity, obligation, or desirability, expressed mainly by verbs but also by associated forms. A modal verb may express more than one kind of modality: for example, the sentence 'He must be in bed' can either be a conjecture (he must be in bed because he can't be found anywhere else) or an order/obligation ('he must be in bed by nine o'clock'). Modality can also be signalled by modal adverbs such as *possibly, probably, presumably, definitely,* as well as by related adjectives and nouns (see the Reference notes, Units 6–10). Modal forms are an interpersonal aspect of grammar and are central to all spoken and written language use; in conversational discourse they serve to mark out personal relationships and to convey important features such as politeness, indirectness, assertiveness, etc.

Stative verbs

A stative verb is a verb which expresses states of being or processes in which there is no obvious action. For example, 'I **know**'; 'I **believe** you are right'.

Tags

Tags are strings of words consisting of an auxiliary verb and a pronoun with or without *not* which are normally added to a declarative statement. The polarity of the tag is most typically, but not always, the reverse of that found in the main clause, that is, a positive clause takes a negative tag and vice versa. The following examples of tags (in bold) all meet this broad definition:

'Frascati's nice, it's nice to drink, **isn't it?**'
'She's a lovely girl, **she is.**'

A: Have you noticed it always disappears?
B: Yeah, it does, **doesn't it?**
A: I've got two now, yes, it does always disappear, **doesn't it?**
B: Yeah right.

'He isn't coming, **is he?**'
'Sound really bossy, **don't I?**'

In these examples there are also other features of tags to note. In the second example, two positive clauses are found together. Such forms do not necessarily demand a reply; instead they often serve just to establish a shared, mutual view of things. All the above data are taken from informal conversational interchanges. Tags are an essential feature of grammar in use in informal and intimate contexts of interaction and are particularly appropriate to contexts in which meanings are not simply stated but are negotiated and re-negotiated.

Tails

The term **tails** (sometimes called post-posed elements in clauses) describes the slot available at the end of a **clause** (→) in which a speaker can insert grammatical patterns which amplify, extend or reinforce what they are saying or have said. Examples of tails (in bold) include:

She's a really good actress, **Clare**.

Singapore's far too hot for me, **it is**.

He's quite a comic **the fellow**, you know.

It's not actually very good, is it, **that wine**?

Tails often serve to express some kind of affective response, personal attitude or evaluative stance towards the topic of the **clause** (→).

Reference notes

Choosing between perfective tenses

Present perfect and adverbs

- **Present perfect** is used with words such as *when, once, after, until, as soon as,* to refer to points in the future when something will be completed:

    A: *So shall I give you a ring **when I've sorted** the bill out?*
    B: *Yeah.*

    *Tell me **after I've eaten** my dinner because I want to enjoy it.*
    ***As soon as you've gone** away I'll think 'I wonder if Alan did so-and-so?'*
    *We aren't going to know the answer to that question **until we've cloned**[1] a human.*

- When these words are used to refer to points and periods of time in the past separated from the present moment or context, they are used with the past simple tense:

    [Somebody talking about a fainting attack] ***When I woke up** I didn't know where I was.*
    ***Once** the initial shock **was** over, Mr Coldman had to settle into his new role.*
    ***As soon as I knew** that was the case, I was appalled.*

- Some adverbial expressions can be used with the **present perfect or** the **past simple** tense, depending upon the speaker's or writer's point of view. *Today, this week/month/year, recently, before, once,* and *already* may all be used in both ways.

- If the events are considered as happening at a definite point in the past, then the **past simple** tense can be used:

    The house was sold recently. (The speaker is thinking of a definite point when the house sale took place.)
    ***Did you see** everybody you wanted to see **today**?* (The speaker considers that the relevant part of *today* is finished, i.e. when it was possible to see everybody.)

- If the events are seen as relevant to the moment of speaking or writing, then **present perfect** can be used:

    [loudspeaker announcement on a train]
    *To all passengers who **have recently joined** this service. My name is Chris and I'm your chief steward.* (The announcer focuses on the fact that the passengers are on the train now.)

[1]To *clone* something means to make an exact genetic copy.

I haven't asked her yet, I haven't seen her today. (Speaker considers that today has not finished yet, and it is still possible to see her today.)

- Be careful with the expression *It/This is the first time ...* Normally it is used with present perfect, not past simple or present:

  *It's going to be quite interesting driving home tonight 'cos **it's the first time I've used** the car in the dark since I put my headlights back in*. (preferred to: *It's the first time I'm using* (✗))
  This is the first time we've celebrated Devali [2]. (**not**: *This is the first time we celebrated* (✗))

- *Already* is another word that usually occurs with present perfect, not past simple, when it refers to something that has happened before now (often unexpectedly):

  *Look how much **Holly's done already**!*
  *Our common purpose, as **Matthew Brewer has already said**, is to exchange views.*

  Similarly, *yet* is normally used with present perfect, since it refers to time up to now:

  Has Jim arrived yet? (preferred to: *Did Jim arrive yet?* (✗))

- *Since* and *ever since* can occur with **present perfect** or **past simple**, depending on the speaker's/writer's viewpoint. They are especially flexible in informal spoken language:

  *She's been a bit nervous **ever since we got burgled**.* (informal spoken: speaker thinks back to the **point** when the burglary happened.)
  *It's ages **since I've seen him**.* (informal spoken: speaker thinks of *ages*, the 'time up to now', as more important than the point at which he last saw the person mentioned.)

- If there is a definite reference to past time or to time up to now, then the choice of tense is more determined:

  *I saw him last April and I **haven't seen** him **since then**.* (time up to now, **not**: *I didn't see him since then.* (✗))
  *How's your health been **since I last came?*** (definite point in the past: the last visit)

  Note in this last example, that the verb in the **main** clause is in present perfect (*How's your health been ...*), not past tense, because it refers to the period of time from the point where the speaker last came, up to the moment of speaking.

- In spoken and written journalistic styles, **present perfect** is occasionally used to stress the current importance of events, even if definite past time adverbials are used. This usage is restricted and relatively uncommon:

  [Speaker is speaking in 1998, i.e. **not** during *the early 1990s*.]
  ***We've lost** so much of our manufacturing industry in the 1980s and early 1990s.*

---

[2]'Devali' is an important Hindu or Sikh festival held in October or November.

Present perfect continuous versus present perfect

- It is sometimes said that **present perfect continuous** (*have + been +-ing*) is used only for things that are still continuing. This is not true. The continuous form (as with all continuous tense forms) emphasises the action or event itself, whereas the simple form puts more emphasis on the results of the event:

> [looking out of the window at daybreak]
> *It's been raining*. (The rain has stopped now, but it still looks wet.)
> *It must have snowed during the night. The lawn's white.* (The emphasis is on the result, that the lawn is white, rather than on the snow itself.)

Sometimes the difference is not so important, and either form can be used:

> *She lives in France. **She's been living** there for five years. (**or**: **She's lived** there for five years.)*
> ***She's lived** in this area a long time. (**or**: **She's been living** in this area for a long time.)*

- If the reference is to an event that was closed and completed at some indefinite point in the past, the **simple form** is used:

> A: *Do you know Great Expectations?*
> B: *I **have read** it, but I don't remember much about it. (**not**: I have been reading it. (✗))*

I've been reading Great Expectations could suggest that the person had not finished it, but would not necessarily mean they were actually reading it at the moment of speaking. However, it could also suggest that this is what had kept the person busy, but that they had, in fact, finished the novel. (I've been reading *Great Expectations*, that's why you haven't seen me all week. I had to write an essay on it.)

"I've got it, too, Omar ... a strange feeling like we've just been going in circles."

Past perfect and adverbs

- In Unit 2 we stressed how past perfect was used for background information (e.g. giving explanations, adding further details, etc.). Some time expressions occur with either **past simple or past perfect**, and it is usually the choice of whether the information is considered to be 'background' or 'foreground' that determines the choice, **not** the fact that something happened before something else. Words in this category include *after*, *before*, *beforehand*, *until*, *when*, and *as soon as*:

  *She came through for a coffee **after she'd finished** cooking. (After she finished cooking* would also have been correct, but with greater emphasis on the second clause than the version with past perfect.)

  *It ended up with her having to go back on the Saturday so that my son could come as **soon as she'd gone**. (As soon as she went* would also be correct, but with a different, more immediate emphasis.)

- Note that the construction *after having* + past participle is rare, especially in informal spoken language. The *after +-ing* construction is much more common, even in writing:

  *He suffered unemployment without relief after being means-tested, starved **after becoming** impoverished, then got a job in a bleach works.* (written)

Past perfect versus simple past

- Sometimes, there can be an important difference between **past simple** and **past perfect**, and **past perfect** may be necessary to resolve possible misunderstanding or ambiguity:

  *They all left the room when **she recited** her poem.* (This suggests they all left when she started reciting.)

  *They all left the room when **she'd recited** her poem.* (This suggests they left after she'd finished reciting.)

- **Past simple** can often suggest a more immediate cause and effect link between two events, compared with **past perfect**:

  *When **he opened** his desk **he discovered** a dead bird.* (Stresses the immediate result, more than *When he had opened his desk*.)

  *When **he'd opened** his third present, **he looked** at the roller skates and smiled.* (There is not such an immediate or direct relationship; the roller skates may not have been in the third present.)

Past perfect in other contexts

- The *reporting verbs* of speech and thought which are often used with **past perfect** include verbs of perception:

  *I **noticed he had hurt** his leg.*
  *He **saw that she had been able** to cure herself.*

Past perfect in conditionals

- **Past perfect** must be used when there is past reference in a hypothetical conditional clause with *if*:

  > *I'd have been killed **if I'd been caught** down there.*
  > *Well, even **if you'd come** home tonight you'd have been upset anyway.*

Future perfect

The future perfect form (*shall/will/'ll have* + past participle) is used to talk about things which will already be completed before or by a particular point in the future:

> *Yesterday and tomorrow altogether I **will have spent** £100 on train fares.* (When tomorrow is over, that will be the total.)
> *It's at the beginning of August, so **I'll have** probably just about **finished** in Berlin **by that time**.* (When the beginning of August comes, I will no longer be working in Berlin.)

Choosing between continuous and simple forms

Present continuous and polite/indirect forms

Some of the uses of **present continuous** with verbs not normally associated with it are connected with indirectness and politeness:

> ***I'm not wanting** to force that idea, but would it be an idea if all Europeans learnt one second European language, do you think?* (indirectness)
> *A full investigation is now being made of the situation. Is that right?*
> ***I'm wondering** what that might be?* (This is more formal/indirect/polite than *I wonder*.)

Present continuous for regular actions/events

If the sentence contains an **adverbial expressing habits or regular events**, or if there is some other indication of repeated events, it does not necessarily mean that present simple must be used. If the emphasis is on an ongoing process, or what is happening at a given, specific time, **present continuous** may be more appropriate:

> *Their numbers build up on the River Exe over autumn until by mid-winter some 6000 birds **are regularly using** the roost*.*
> *They're **winning every other** game. They're not drawing any games.*

Present continuous and physical states

When we refer to physical feelings experienced at the time of speaking, we can often use **present continuous** *or* **present simple**, without any major difference in meaning:

> *My back **hurts**.* **or:** *My back's **hurting**.*
> *Can I sit down? **I feel** a bit dizzy.* **or:** *Can I sit down? **I'm feeling** a bit dizzy.*

---

*A *roost* is a place where birds can nest and breed young.

Present continuous and narratives

Present continuous is often used in stories, alternating with past tenses, especially in spoken story-telling, to describe dramatic or important moments and climaxes:

> *I stayed until four o'clock in the morning watching these awful films, and **I'm looking at** myself thinking 'Oh, no, no!'*

Present continuous and prior arrangements

- **Present continuous** is often used with future reference to indicate things that are arranged or decided:

  > A: ***You're coming*** *on Friday, yeah?*
  > B: *If I can, yeah.*

- Present continuous is not used for future events over which there is no control:

  > *It's **going to rain** tomorrow, according to the weather forecast.* (**not:** ~~It's raining tomorrow~~ (✗))

- **Present continuous** suggests arrangements have already been made:

  > ***I'm having*** *a chat with her next week.* (We've arranged to do that.)
  > *I'm **going to have** a chat with her next week.* (unclear whether it is arranged, or just the speaker's intention)

Present simple and fixed schedules

- **Present simple** can be used to talk about fixed events in the future, particularly referring to timetabled and scheduled events:

  > *The next flight **doesn't leave** till 20.25.*
  > *Their training **starts** the end of September, so it should be quite interesting.*

- It can also be used to refer to expected events in the future:

  > A: *So when **do we do** a firmer estimate on this? (When shall we do this?)*
  > B: *Now.*
  > C: *Okay.*

- Be careful; present simple is not used for making promises and offers:

  > *That looks heavy. **I'll carry** it for you.*(**not:** ~~I carry it for you.~~ (✗))
  > *I promise **I'll look** at it tonight.* (**not:** ~~I promise I look at it tonight.~~ (✗))

Be going to versus *will*

- In Unit 4, we discussed one of the differences between *be going to* and *will*. We noted that if you say 'I'm going to drive', the person you are speaking to has little choice in the matter, but if you say 'I'll drive', the other person can respond to the suggestion or offer. This means that there are situations where it is important not to sound too decisive and assertive, and choosing *be going to* instead of *will* may have an undesired effect.

For example if you are in a restaurant and you are paying for yourself, it would be quite appropriate to say, while looking at the menu:

> *I'm going to have the chicken.*

This might be inappropriate if someone else is paying for you, in which case it would be better to say:

> *I think I'll have the chicken.*

- You will often see *going to* spelt as *gonna* in written dialogues, to indicate the way it is usually pronounced in informal speech:

> *Hopefully she's gonna be back by then.*

Be going to and present continuous

- *Be going to* and the **present continuous** can both be used to refer to the future, but the present continuous suggests a more pre-determined or fixed arrangement, while *Be going to* is more a statement of an intention or a prediction based on present evidence:

> *When are you going to ring me?* (asking the other person what his/her intention is)
> *When are you ringing me?* (I know we've arranged to talk on the phone; please remind me when we have agreed to do it.)

> *When are you heading off again, Bill?* (The speaker already knows Bill is going on another trip, and wants to know when it is fixed for. *Be going to* would be less definite here and might be understood as asking Bill whether he intended to make another trip.)

- When referring to states in the future, rather than events, **be going to** is used, since state verbs are not normally used with the continuous form:

> *Any idea when the car's going to be ready?* (**not**: *Any idea when the car's being ready?* (✗))
> *You're going to need more than that.* (**not**: *You're needing more than that.* (✗))
> *I'm going to have to go to bed soon.* (**not**: *I'm having to go to bed soon.* (✗))

- Both forms are used for orders and prohibitions:

> [to a toddler who picks up a knife] *No, you're not going to play with that!* (could also have been *No you're not playing with that!*)

Be going to and continuous infinitive

Be going to can occur with a **continuous infinitive** form. In this way it is possible to make a statement about future events, based on present evidence, that will be in progress at a given time in the future:

> *I think we're going to be seeing George Brumfit later in the conference.*
> *We're going to be struggling to find enough vases for all these flowers.*

Alternatives to *be + to*

In Unit 5 we noted that *be to* was a rather formal way of stating what was destined to happen in the future, or for issuing orders and instructions. It is rare in everyday conversation. If we are reporting in informal speech something that we read, or which was said to us in an informal context, there are various ways of translating *be to* into informal language:

Supposed to

*Actually, she's **supposed to phone** me this afternoon.* (preferred, in informal conversation, to: *She is to phone me this afternoon.*)

Be going to

*Don't forget, if they **are** actually **going to** build a chemical site, that's when you have to have your meetings.* (preferred, in informal conversation, to: *If they are actually to build a chemical site, ...*)

Present continuous

[The speakers are talking about a local restaurant.]
A: ***It's closing down** is it?*
B: *Well, yeah, to be refurbished.*

 (preferred, in informal conversation, to: *It is to close down, is it?*)

Future continuous with *will / shall / 'll*

- The **future continuous** form (*will/shall/'ll* + *be* + *-ing*) is used to talk about what will be in progress at a specific point in the future:

    *What do you think **you'll be doing** in five years' time?*

- It is also used for things in the future that normally happen, or can be expected to happen:

    *How **will you be celebrating** Christmas?* (The expectation is that you normally celebrate Christmas in some way.)

    Compare a student who says to a lecturer 'Will you be doing phonetics again next year?' (Can we expect that the lectures will be repeated, as often happens?), with 'Will you do phonetics again next year?', which could be a request for the lecturer to repeat the lectures next year.

- The form is also sometimes used in polite and formal contexts to refer to **future events**:

    *I **shall be writing** to you **in the near future** to confirm these arrangements.*
    *Our new sales centre **will be opening on 5 December**, so do come along.*

- We can also use this form to make predictions about what is happening *at the moment*:

    *Don't ring him **now**. **They'll be having** their dinner.*

Choosing between modal verbs

Can and verbs of senses

- One of the uses of *can* to express ability and facts (see Unit 6.1 and 6.3) which is often problematic for learners of English is its frequent occurrence with verbs of sensing (e.g. *see, smell, hear, taste*):

  > [looking through a telescope] *I **can** see a ship!* (*I see a ship* is correct, but sounds rather formal.)
  > ***Can** you smell smoke? I think something's burning.* (preferred to: *Do you smell smoke?*)
  > *What's in this dish? I think I **can** taste garlic, what else is in it?* (preferred to: *I think I taste garlic.*)

- Some mental verbs such as *remember* and *understand* also frequently occur with *can* (and *could* in the past), especially in informal spoken language:

  > *I **can't remember** what she said now, I'll have to ask her again.* (This is more frequent in informal spoken language than, *I don't remember what she said.*)
  > ***Can you understand** what he's saying? I can't.*

- Remember that *afford* (meaning 'have the money to do something') is always used with *can* or *could*:

  > *Only the rich **can afford** the best treatment.*

Could + have

Could have often expresses a reproach or criticism:

> *You **could have** told me you were bringing a friend. I thought it was going to be just you and me.*

Could and suggestions

Could is also used to make suggestions:

> *Maybe we **could** go down there in the afternoon.*

Could do with is a very useful expression:

> *We **could do with** a new fridge.* (This is a less strong version of: *We need a new fridge.*)

Will and repeated events/facts

- *Will* is often used to express a frequent, regular or repeated event:

  > *Sometimes my friend Janet **will come** over and **we'll have** a takeaway meal.* (Janet comes frequently)

- If *will* is stressed in such contexts, it can express irritation on the part of the speaker:

    *Oh! She **will** slam that door! Why can't she shut it quietly, like everyone else?*

- *Will* can express things that are always true, things that everyone knows:

    *Any dog **will** bite, given the right or wrong circumstances.*

- *Will* can also be used to state facts with verbs like *find, see, note, notice* etc., especially in instructions and explanations:

    *On the reverse of this letter **you will find** details of our forthcoming events.*
    *You **will notice** that the tips of the plants become brown.*

Will in promises or offers

- *Will* can be used to express **promises** or **legal undertakings**:

    [holiday company brochure] *Your representative **will advise** you whether the tap water in your resort is safe to drink.*
    [information leaflet about fitness classes] *Whatever your level of fitness this class **will give** you a good workout every week.*

    A: *We do need to talk about it again.*
    B: *Okay. I'll **ring** you tomorrow. (**not**: I ~~ring you tomorrow.~~ (✗))*

- It is also very commonly used to make offers:

    *Hey! That's heavy. I'll **help** you. (**not**: ~~I help you.~~ (✗))*

Would and repeated past events

- One important use of *would* is to talk about events which regularly happened in the past:

    *If we made a noise, they **would bang** on the ceiling with a broom handle, then Mum, in her turn, **would bang back**. (Every time we made a noise, they banged.)*

- However, this use of *would* is only possible if the past time frame has already been established, for example, by a phrase such as *When I was a child*, or *Years ago*. It is not possible to begin with *would* if the past time is not already established. If there is no past time clearly established, *used to* is used instead:

    [driving past a house]
    A: *I **used to** play with a boy who lived there! (**not**: I ~~would play~~ with a boy who lived there!)*
    B: *Really?*
    A: *Yes, we lived round the corner when I was a kid, and I'**d go** there every Saturday.*

Would and 'future in the past'

- *Would* is also used for the 'future in the past', when a speaker or writer projects forward in time from a point in the past:

    *Now it was Monday morning again. Eleanor **would arrive** on tomorrow's flight from New York. She **would be** calm. She **would be** composed and efficient.*

- *Would have (been)* ... is often used to imagine how a situation could have resulted differently from reality:

  > [One popular singer is talking about another one.]
  > *His high voice and my low one blended beautifully. It **would have been lovely** to have done a record together but we were with different companies.*

  > *It was a pity I could not understand her, for I am sure she **would have been** most interesting.*

Would and arrangements/suggestions

- *Would* is a polite form in many common expressions connected with making arrangements, and is slightly less formal than *should* when used with *I* or *we*:

  > *Thank you for your kind invitation. I **would be delighted** to attend.* (more formal: *I should be delighted to attend.*)
  > *It **would be nice to** meet up at some point soon. Are you free next week at all?*
  > *I **would be interested in** making an appointment for a later date.*

- *Would* can also be used as a softener, to make something less direct:

  > *I **would suggest** adding some books to the list.* (This is less direct than *I suggest adding some.*)
  > *I **would hope** that she doesn't take this personally.*

Would that

Would that is a rather formal way of wishing that reality was different from how it is. It is followed by a **past tense** form:

> *Would that all our leaders **had** the courage that she has.* (informal: *I wish all our leaders had the courage ...*)

May/might versus *can/could*

- *May/might* and *can/could* are often very close in meaning, but express different degrees of probability (see below).

- *Can* expresses facts, and things which have happened and do happen:

  > *For newcomers Asia **can** be a confusing place.* (This is a fact.)

- *May* expresses a strong possibility, or something that can be expected to happen:

  > [holiday brochure describing typical problems with water supplies in resorts]
  > *During the high season there **may be** a drop in pressure, and occasionally a breakdown in supply.* (This has happened often, and you should expect it.)

- *Could* is possible in the last example, but would mean that breakdowns are less likely to happen.

- *Might* expresses a more remote possibility:

  > *We **might** win the lottery this week, who knows?*

Might

- *Might* is often an alternative to *may* or *could* (but not *can*, which expresses known facts). *Might* expresses a less likely possibility than *may* or *could*. (See also above):

  He **might (may /could)** be a useful person to make contact with at some stage.

- *Could* is generally not used before *be able*. *May* or *might* is preferred (depending on the strength of the possibility):

  He **might be able to** introduce you to people. (**not**: ~~He could be able to introduce you~~ (**✗**))

- *Might* and *may* are used more often than *could* when an option is being given, especially with verbs such as *prefer, want, wish*:

  You **might prefer** to talk to a female counsellor. (**not**: ~~You could prefer to talk~~ (**✗**))

- *Could* is preferred when ability is being stressed. *May* and *might* are preferred when possibility is stressed:

  I **could** go tomorrow. I have a day off. (I am able to go; there are no obstacles.)
  I **might/may** go tomorrow. It depends on the weather. (There is a possibility I will go.)

- *Might* or *could* are used for criticism or reproach (see Unit 8, **A2**) but not *may*:

  You **might/could** have told me you were going away for the weekend. (I wish you had told me.)
  You **may** have told me you were going away for the weekend. (It's possible you told me and I forgot.)

May in formal spoken contexts

- *May* is used in rather formal expressions connected with wishes and curses:

  May you rot in hell! (less formal: *I hope you rot in hell!*)
  [speech at a wedding, addressed to the married couple]
  May you both have all the happiness you deserve. (less formal: *I hope you both have ...*)

- *May* is quite common in other, similar expressions of apology, suggestion, congratulation, etc.:

  May I offer my sincere regret that you and your family were so dissatisfied with the care you received.
  If **I may** take this opportunity to congratulate you both, on behalf of all the staff, congratulations.

May and regulations

May is used in laws, rules and regulations to express what is permitted or forbidden often in a passive structure:

  No animal **may be brought** into the United Kingdom without a valid import licence.
  Due to the short timescale, places **may be reserved** by telephone.

Must and criticisms

Must, when stressed, in question form can often express a reproach or criticism. *Have to* can also be used in this way:

> ***Must** you make so much noise?* (**or**: *Do you **have to** make so much noise?*)

Must versus have to

- *Must* expresses a necessity or command by the speaker, while *have to* expresses an external obligation. Often, the difference between a command and a statement of external obligation is not important, and both *must* and *have to* can be used:

> *You **must** fill in all these details.* (**or**: *You have to fill in all these details.*)

- When it is clear that an external force is creating the necessity, *have to* is used:

> *We don't have a supermarket that sells them near us. We **have to** buy them in Kettering.* (**not**: ~~*We must buy them in Kettering.*~~ (✗))

- Since *must* has no infinitive and no other tense forms, *have to* is used to express obligations and necessities in past tense and in complex structures with modal verbs:

> *We'll **have to** have a special party for your birthday in the year 2000.*
> *The garage says they'd **have to** take his car in for two days.*
> *In the end I **had to** refuse half of them.*

Must and *have to* can occur together, for example in:

> A: *You **must have to** leave fairly early.* (I suppose you are obliged to leave fairly early.)
> B: *Yes, I do.*

Must not versus do not have to

In the negative, there is a difference in meaning between *must not* and *do not have to*:

> *Because it is gossip it **must not** be considered to be the absolute truth until it is checked in some way.* (It is important that you do not consider it to be the truth.)

Compare:

> *You **do not have to** say anything, but it may harm your defence if you don't mention, when questioned, something which you later rely on in court.* (You are not obliged to say anything.)

Shall in tag questions

Shall is used in tags after ***let's***:

> ***Let's** ring Paul, **shall** we?*

Even though it may not be entirely clear whether *'ll* in the main clause stands for *will* or *shall*, if the speaker is making an offer or a suggestion, the tag is normally with *shall*, not *will*:

> *I'll serve the pasta out here, **shall I**?*
> *We'll go and pay Mary as we go out, **shall we**?*

Shall in formal contexts

- In rather formal styles, and in older varieties of literary English, *shall* often occurs in contexts other than first person singular or plural:

  > *'You **shall** be punished,' said Mrs Marline. 'You **shall** go to your room and stay there without a light when it is dark.'*

  > *He is well, and thinks he **shall** get through the cold season better than we feared.*

  > *They were surrounded by demonstrators chanting 'Fascism **shall** not triumph!'*

- *Shall* is also used in formal, legalistic contexts, where rules and regulations are being quoted:

  > *The application **shall** be received not later than on the 30th day of June in the year following the year to which the application refers.*

Should and hope/think

In Unit 9, **C2**, we looked at some regularly occurring expressions with *should*, including *I should imagine*, and *I should say*. We can add some more to these:

> A: *Maybe we'll have more money then.*
> B: *I **should hope** so.*

> A: *And very expensive too, **I should think**, isn't it?*
> B: *Oh yeah, it is.*

In most of these expressions, *would* can be used instead of *should*, with no change of meaning.

Should have and past participle

Another important use of *should* is in constructions with *have* and the past participle, when giving an opinion on how events would have been in an ideal world:

> [The speaker is regretting giving up work.] *I **should have carried on** working, I think, really.*
> *I **shouldn't have told** you that, should I?* (I did tell you, and I regret it.)

In these cases, *ought (not) to have* can be used, with little difference in meaning, except that *ought* is much less frequent than *should* in spoken language.

Using *should* to form a conditional clause

- In formal contexts, *should* may be used with an inverted subject to mean 'if':

  Should *illness or other circumstances cause a customer to change or cancel their booking an amendment can be made.* (**or**: *if illness or other circumstances causes a customer to change ...*)
  Should *you be considering a move in the near future we would very much like to hear from you.* (**or**: *If you are considering a move ...*)

- *Should* and *if* may occur together in conditional sentences, stressing a remote possibility of something happening:

  And remember, **if you should** *run into difficulties with your payments, please contact us immediately.*

Ought versus *should*

Ought has a meaning very close to *should*, as we noted in Unit 10 **B** Observations, but it is far less frequent than *should* in both spoken and written language, and often carries a stronger feeling of what is morally right in the speaker's/writer's opinion:

She **ought to** *have married someone more like herself.*

Other modal forms and meanings

Need (*not*)

- In its use as a modal verb, *need* has no past tense form. In everyday usage, its present tense form is restricted to the negative form. Affirmatives, and references to time other than the present are normally expressed using *have to* or the main verb *to need*:

  This **needn't be** *kept in the fridge.* (present reference: It is not necessary to keep this in the fridge.)
  This **needs to be** *kept / has to be kept in the fridge.* (present reference: main verb *to need*)
  This **won't have to be** *kept in the fridge.* (future reference: *This won't* **need** *to be kept in the fridge.*
  This **didn't have to/didn't need to** *be kept in the fridge.* (past reference)

- In very formal styles of English, *need* may sometimes occur as a modal verb in interrogative form (e.g. 'Need we be there quite so early?'), but in everyday language, the interrogative is normally formed with *have to* and the main verb *to need*.

Believe

It upset me greatly, as I **didn't believe** *I was being taken seriously.*

The passive form of *believe* is very rare in informal spoken language, but is frequent in written texts:

Mikhail Gorbachev **was believed to be** *under house arrest last night.*

Imagine

*I **imagine** it could be very expensive.* (**or**: *I should think it could be*)

The passive with *imagine* is rare, and only occurs in rather formal written contexts:

*When the last bells rang in a new year, **it was** widely **imagined** that they also tolled the passing of Scottish conservatism.*

Estimate

- *I **estimate** that the work you have requested will take a full two days' design time.*

  Again, the passive is rare except in formal contexts:

  ***It is estimated** that between 1926 and 1977 the company made a total profit of between US$410 and $415 million.*

- The passive voice with these verbs has the effect of attributing the truth of something to some other group of people or to people in general. This type of meaning also occurs with the passive of *think* and *say*, which are also used only in rather formal contexts:

  *There **are thought to be** less than 200 pairs of these beautiful birds in the UK today. During a 1985 visit to Paris she **was said to have bought** a £1,100 pair of earrings.*

Take

Take is often used with a modal meaning of 'be required/necessary/needed', especially in informal contexts:

*I've seen them trying to do it and even with sharp scissors it **takes** some cutting.* (A lot of cutting is needed.)
*It **takes** a good chairman to weigh these situations up.* (A good chairman is needed/necessary.)

Want

- In informal spoken language especially, *want* + the *-ing* form of a verb has a modal meaning of 'needs' or 'is necessary':

  *My hair **wants cutting**.* (more formal: *My hair needs cutting*.)

- *Want* can also have a meaning close to *should* or *ought to* in informal speech:

  *At that age you need a bit of both. You **want** to be looking ahead and you **want** to be improving your skills as well.* (You should be looking ahead and you should be improving your skills.)

Oblige

Oblige is used to talk about strong external forces that make someone do something. It is usually in the passive voice:

[The speaker is commenting on the huge costs of private care for elderly people.]
*You **are** now **obliged** to spend something stupid like, what is it, fifteen hundred quid a week just to keep your parents in a hostel or home.*

Force

Force is even stronger (and sounds less formal) than *oblige* in talking about external obligations. It is also usually in the passive voice:

> *I mean I could work until four in the morning and then get up and have a lazy morning. But with a family you're **forced** to do the opposite of that.*

Mean/entail

- In Unit 10, **B2**, examples with *be meant to* were discussed. *Mean* in the active voice is also used with a modal meaning, expressing necessity. In this case verbs which follow are in the *-ing* form:

  > *The race usually starts at three, so that often **means** leaving the house at two.*
  > (I have to leave at two.)

- A rather more formal version of *mean* in this sense is *entail*. Both *mean* and *entail* can be followed by an *-ing* form of a verb or by a noun:

  > *Marline had been engaged on some charitable work which **entailed** a visit to the Grange.*

Require

Require also has a similar meaning to *entail* and *mean* and follows a similar pattern. It stresses more what is needed rather than what one is obliged to do. It is rather formal:

> *I enjoy my job, which often **requires** giving in-store commentaries and image advice.*

Involve

Involve has a similar meaning and follows the same structural pattern as *entail* and *mean*, but is not quite so strong in its meaning of 'necessity', stressing more what is normally included or expected in something:

> *For this post to work, it will **involve** working in close partnership with senior staff.*

Necessitate

Necessitate also follows the same structural pattern, but is used only in very formal contexts (e.g. academic texts). It stresses the importance and necessity of something:

> *The existence of a united Europe **necessitates** competence in 'trans-national communication'.* (The existence of a united Europe makes competence in 'trans-national communication' necessary.)

Demand

Demand also stresses necessity, but usually only occurs with a noun phrase object:

> *If this is correct then at the very least it **demands** some sort of explanation.*

Suggest

Suggest can be used to mean 'seems to indicate' or 'points towards an interpretation of the truth'. This is in contrast to its most typical meaning of 'make a suggestion/put forward an idea for consideration'. In its modal meaning, it is more frequent in formal written contexts than in informal spoken language:

> Everything **suggests** that he will be racing in Melbourne for the first Grand Prix of 1996.
>
> A police surgeon's preliminary report **suggests** that the murder took place some days before the body was found.

Be sure/likely/bound to

- Some structures with *be + adjective + infinitive* have modal meanings and are quite frequent. These include *be sure to, be bound to, be likely to, be liable to*:

  > I'll put these on the gate tomorrow, 'cos if I put them on now, somebody's **sure to** pull them off. (Somebody will pull them off; I can predict that.)
  >
  > You're **bound to** get seasick, so get some aspirins before you go. (It's certain that you will get seasick ...)
  >
  > I'm **not likely to** exceed the annual maximum. (I will very probably not exceed ...)
  >
  > I think I'll need my guitar because I'm **liable to** damage yours. (There is a strong possibility that I will damage yours.)

- In the examples, *be sure to* and *be bound to* are interchangeable. *Bound to* stresses the certainty more strongly.

- *Likely* (and its opposite *unlikely*) is the only word in this group that can also be used with an impersonal *it* construction and a *that*-clause:

  > It's **not very likely that** she'll meet him. (**or:** She's not very likely to meet him.)

Be prone to

Be prone to also means 'is likely to' or 'has a tendency to', but the *to* in the expression is not an infinitive *to*; it is a preposition, and so must be followed by a noun or a verb in the -*ing* form:

> At my age your gums are receding and you're **more prone to** getting toothache.
> (You are more likely to get toothache.)

Be inclined to

Be inclined to has a modal meaning of 'tend towards', and is often used to make a statement less direct or assertive. It frequently occurs together with other modal expressions, especially in informal conversation:

> I would **be inclined to** get to see her as soon as possible.
>
> I'm sort of **inclined to** think I might as well stay here next year. (Note the combination of modal/softening expressions.)

Be supposed to

Be supposed to is very frequent in everyday spoken language. It has two modal meanings: the first is similar to 'have a commitment to' or 'have an obligation to', and is the more frequent meaning; the second, less frequent meaning, is 'people believe this' or 'this is what people say/claim':

> *I was **supposed to** fill in a form but I didn't.* (I should have filled in a form.)
> *He was **supposed to** have committed this crime and run off through a shopping centre.* (This is what the police/people claimed.)

For sure

For sure is a useful phrase which often occurs in informal spoken language. It is used in a variety of ways to stress the speaker's certainty:

> *We don't want to have to go through that again, **that's for sure**.* (with *that's*)
> *I think this is the nicest, **for sure**.* (as a sentence adverbial)
> *They know **for sure** they're going to get a fine.* (as an adverbial modifying a verb phrase)

For definite and **for certain**

For definite and *for certain* are similar to *for sure*, but are slightly more formal, and are normally only used as adverbials modifying a verb, most typically the verb **to know**:

> *Do you know **for definite/for certain** that she's going to be there?*

Nouns with modal meanings

possibility   impossibility   probability   likelihood   tendency

certainty   uncertainty   obligation

> Examples:
> *The **likelihood** of me getting four out of four is not very high, is it?*
> *Southern audiences have a **tendency** to be more reserved.*
> *The County Council had an **obligation** to look after her in her own home.*

Adjectives with modal meanings

possible   impossible   probable   likely   unlikely   certain

uncertain   definite   sure   unsure   apparent   evident

obvious   obligatory   compulsory   forbidden   prohibited

necessary   unnecessary

> Examples:
> *Of course it's **probable** that the northern dialects of English anyway have some of these forms.* (rather formal spoken language)
>
> A: *Now you said that you were a bit **uncertain** about whether anything would happen at all.*
> B: *Well, I must admit yes.*

*It's already becoming very **apparent** that not only do people want it translated written-wise, but it needs to be on audio cassette, if nothing else, in the various languages.* (rather formal)

Adverbs/adverb phrases with modal meanings

possibly   probably   certainly   surely   definitely   absolutely

undoubtedly   without doubt   necessarily

Examples:
*I'll **definitely** be coming.*
*That is **undoubtedly** true.* (rather formal)
*The best price is not **necessarily** the cheapest.* (almost always used with *not*)

Remember that *surely* does not always mean a hundred per cent certainty. It is often used when someone asserts something that he/she expects others to agree with:

A: *Can I just come in and see you then?*
B: *You **surely** can.*
A: *Thank you very much.*
(very definite, certain)

*Well, **surely** she can make her mind up?* (I expect you to agree with this.)

Choosing and using *if*-constructions

Remember that the future tense is not normally used in the *if*-clause:

***If I get** good results I'll consider going on to do an MA.* (**not**: ~~If I will get~~ *good results …* (✗))

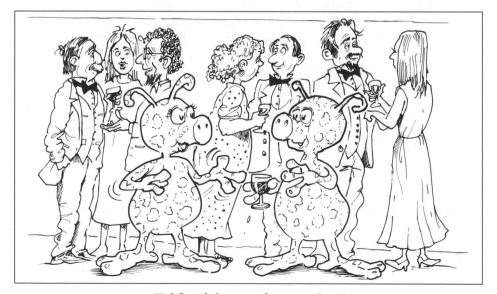

*"I **definitely** know you from somewhere."*

The same applies in past hypothetical sentences. The *if*-clause is in the past, not the conditional:

> *If I brought my CV in, would somebody be able to update it for me?*
> (**not:** ~~*If I would*~~ *bring my CV in ...* (**✗**))

Will/would in the *if*-clause

There are some cases where *will* and *would* may be found in the *if*-clause; this occurs when the *if*-clause is not a hypothetical statement, but refers rather to the **possible result or consequence** of the main clause:

> *If it'll help in any way, I could bring my car.*

If-clauses and requests

Other examples of *will* and *would* in *if*-clauses usually are of the 'polite request/instruction' type (see Unit 11), or when *if* means 'whether or not':

> A: *Shall I put them in a carrier bag for you?*
> B: *Yes please, if you wouldn't mind.*

> *My mum wants to know if you'll take her into town.*

- Note the expression *if I were you*:

  > *I'd just do the warm-up if I were you.*

  In informal spoken language, we often say *if I was you*:

  > *I'd call Roland if I was you.*

- Note that *when* is not a conditional word. It is used to refer to things that will or are more or less certain to happen:

  > *If there are problems, just give me a call.* (conditional: I don't know if there are going to be problems or not. If we said *when* in this case it would mean: I **know** there are going to be problems. Call me the moment they arise.)
  > *He's away at the moment. I'll ask him to give you a ring **when** he gets back.* (not conditional: I **know** he's coming back. At that time, he will ring you.)

Other conditional expressions

What if?

The expression *what if?* is extremely common. It is used to speculate on possible events or situations or courses of action, either referring to the present, the future or the past:

> *What if it had been a person of eighty?* (What would have happened if ...?)
> *What if I come and see you at home on Thursday?* (Would it be a good idea if ...?)

In informal speech, the expression sometimes occurs as *what about if...?*:

What about if *somebody, instead of writing back, had got on the phone to you and explained things over the phone? What would you have felt about that?*

Providing

In Unit 11, **B2**, we looked at a number of conditional expressions including *provided that*. This expression also occurs as *providing*. *Providing* is more frequent in spoken language and *provided that* is more frequent in writing:

It doesn't matter who is punished, ***provided that*** *somebody is punished.* (written)

A: *But presumably you get some sort of senior citizen's fare?*
B: *Yes,* ***providing*** *you've got a railcard.* (spoken)

If at all

If at all is another fixed expression with *if* (see Unit 11, **C2**). It means that the speaker doubts that the preceding statement is true or valid:

Obviously she hadn't slept much last night, ***if at all****.* (It is doubtful whether she slept even a little bit.)

If at all sometimes combines with *possible* to refer to a very remote possibility:

If at all possible *I would get Jeff to have a look but it's not possible at the moment.*

Wh-constructions and fronting devices

Using nouns in place of *wh*-words

In Unit 12, we noted that fronted clauses introduced by *what* were much more frequent than those introduced by *why, where, how*, etc. One reason for this is that the idea of *why, where, who, when,* and *how* is often expressed by another word such as *the person, the place, the way,* etc., while still creating the same kind of emphatic clause:

Now ***the way*** *I look at life is this. A life is precious no matter how long you can prolong it.* (**or:** *How I look at life is this*)
The person *you need to talk to is the manager.* (more common than: *Who you need to talk to is the manager.*)
The place *where I've been is where they train local midwives.* (**or:** *Where I've been is where they ...*)
The reason *it wasn't sorted out earlier was because they were short of staff.* (**or:** *Why it wasn't sorted out earlier was because ...*)
The day *we wanted to travel was a Monday, but it was all booked up.* (more frequent than: *When we wanted to travel was a Monday, ...*)

See also *the thing* below.

Pre-posing and emphasis/focus

What-clauses can be used with *do* to put extra emphasis on the main verb and its complement:

> **What I did** *was I circulated this form to everybody.*
> **What I'll do** *is I'll give you a ring nearer the time.*

A whole event can be emphasised by using *what* with *happen*:

> **What happened** *was I'd arrived so late that I'd missed the tour round the school.*

Pre-posed *it*-clauses

Emphasis can also be created by using an *it*-clause to bring a subject, object complement or adverbial to the front of the clause:

> **It was me** *that did everything.* (subject emphasised: I did everything.)
> *I thought* **it was Mr King** *that you'd been seeing.* (object emphasised: You'd been seeing Mr King.)
> **It was awful** *what happened in Honduras.* (complement emphasised: What happened in Honduras was awful.)
> **It was after that** *that I took the refresher course.* (adverbial emphasised: I took the refresher course after that.)

Fronted clauses with *all*

Clauses introduced by *all* are often fronted for emphasis. The construction emphasises the insufficiency of something, or else that only one thing is necessary:

> **All you wanted** *was a coffee and you ended up eating a big meal.* (**or:** *You just/only wanted a coffee and you ended up ...*)
> **All I got** *was these little scraps of paper with these handwritten notes.* (**or:** *I just got these little scraps of paper ...*)
> **All you need** *is love.* (famous song by the Beatles)

this/that (See also Unit 13.)

> A: *What would you do if you won the lottery on Saturday?*
> B: *What would I do?*
> A: *Yes.*
> B: **This** *is what I thought. If ever I won the lottery I'd help who I wanted to help.* (instead of: *'I thought if ever I won the lottery, I'd ...'*)

> **That's** *what's got to happen, it's got to lock into there when you pull it.* (instead of: It's got to lock into there when you pull it.)

it is/was not until and *It is/was only when*

> **It was only when** *it mentioned that he lived in Cambridge that I knew who it was.* (instead of: *When it mentioned that he lived in Cambridge, I knew who it was.*)
> **It's not until** *we lift the carpet in our bedroom that we'll know what we've got to deal with.* (instead of: *We won't know what we've got to deal with until we lift ...*)

the thing/One thing/Something

> **The thing** *I was struck by was their complacency.* (similar to: *What I was struck by was their complacency.* Compare *I was struck by their complacency.*)
> **One thing** *she's been doing recently is buying white shoes to decorate them for people.* (instead of: *She's been buying white shoes recently ...*)
> **Something** *you might like to look at is the sequence of events in the story.* (instead of: *You might like to look at the sequence ...*)

Forward, present and backward reference with *this* and *that*

- *This* is preferred to *that* when the reference is forward, to something not explained yet:

  > *So* **this** *is what we'll do. Firstly introduce the speakers, then introduce the topics of the debate.* (If the speaker had said *That is what we'll do*, it would suggest that introducing the speakers and topics had already been mentioned.)

  When the reference is to something already talked about, *that* is preferred:

  > A: *Personally I'd find it better to keep the same tutor all the way through.*
  > B: *I'd agree with* **that**.

  (The speaker could have said *I'd agree with this*, but it would sound as if he was taking the statement as a new topic which he was going to expand upon. See Unit 13, **B2**.)

- Both *this* and *that* can refer to the immediate present situation, depending on how the speaker sees things and how closely they associate with them:

  > [The speaker picks up a paper clip.]
  > *Ah,* **this is**/**that's** *what I'm looking for, a really big paper clip!*

- The expression *this is it* is used to agree with someone:

  > A: *But if you knew that before, you wouldn't want to live.*
  > B: *Well,* **this is it**. (You're absolutely right; I agree.)

This/that in responses to the immediate situation

- If we hear a noise or a voice, we normally say *Who's that?* or *What's that?*, rather than *Who's this?* or *What's this?* However, if someone is arriving or coming directly **towards** us but we are not sure who they are, we might say *Who's this?*

- The expression *What's all this?* is used when we come upon a situation which is puzzling or when something is happening that is obviously wrong or problematic.

Passives: *get-* and *have-*constructions

- In Unit 14 we looked at some passive-type constructions with *get*. There are in fact a number of such constructions, each with a different emphasis on the role of the agent and recipient. The table gives examples of these constructions:

Type	Example	Construction
a)	He got killed trying to save some other man.	*get* + past participle
b)	You see, if ever you get yourself locked out ...	*get* + reflexive pronoun + past participle
c)	Rian got his nose pierced and it was so gross.	*get* + object + past participle, agent not mentioned
d)	Right we've got to get you kitted out.	agent + *get* + object-recipient + past participle

- It is worth remembering that *get*-passives in general are common in spoken language but much less frequent in written.

- Type (a) is the typical *get*-passive. It is much more frequent in spoken language than in written, and is most often used to describe negative or unfortunate events, though less often it is used for happy events (e.g. *She got awarded a medal.*). If a *by*-construction is used with it to denote an agent, then it is usually an impersonal one:

    The whole bus got stripped by the Italian police.

- Type (b) suggests the subject him/herself has some responsibility for the event.

- Type (c) is used to indicate that someone else performed the action, but we are not told who. [*Gross* here means 'horrible'.]

- Type (d) treats the object (in this case *you*) as the 'passive' recipient of the action. (*Kitted out* means 'buy you all the clothes you need'.)

Get-passives and adverbials

Because *get*-passives focus so much on the fate of the recipient, adverbials describing time, place or manner are not common with this construction. Adverbials that do commonly occur with the *get*-construction tend to be intensifying or degree adverbs such as **actually, really, nearly**.

*Nothing ever **really** gets followed through.*
*I **nearly** got picked on, but I didn't say yes or no.*

Have + object + past participle

- In Unit 14 we referred to pseudo-passives with *have* as another way of expressing the relationship between the agent and the recipient of an action. *Have* in this construction can express different degrees of involvement of the subject in the action:

*I **had** my car nicked.** (The subject has no involvement, he was simply the victim.)
*I decided to **have** my hair cut short.* (The subject initiated the action, though it
was performed by someone else.)

- Many educated speakers would feel that *get* could be used instead of *have* in the
second example without much difference in meaning, but not in the first. However,
get is sometimes heard in examples such as the first in very colloquial speech.

Get-passive in fixed expressions

Some colloquial fixed expressions for issuing insults use a *get*-passive construction.
They may cause offence to the hearer. They should therefore be understood when
heard, but only used with extreme caution:

A: *It's not the same now we're older and stuff.*
B: ***Get lost!** I'm not old. You're old!* (not too offensive, relatively mild)

*They wanted x number of pounds off me per year and I turned round and told them
basically to **get stuffed**.* (much stronger; very insulting)

Position of adverbs

Auxiliaries in tags and elliptical clauses

In Unit 15 we looked at how adverbs normally occurred after the first auxiliary verb.
However, when auxiliaries are used in tags or in elliptical clauses (especially in spoken
language) the adverb comes before the auxiliary:

A: *It's not the same.*
B: *No **it never is**. (*preferred to*: No it's never.)*

A: *Do you celebrate the New Year too?*
B: *Yeah **we usually do**.*

A: *I hope they'll disappear.*
B: *I think **they probably will**.*

Adverbs with two main verbs

Where there are two main verbs in sequence, adverbs can come after the first verb to
focus the modification of that verb:

*I tried **ever so hard** to get it over to him.*
*I've been going **regularly** to see an osteopath.* (Here *go* is a main verb. Compare Unit
15, **B1**, where *go* is an auxiliary verb in the *be going to* future construction.)

**Nicked is a very informal word meaning stolen.

More than one adverb of the same class in end position

If there is more than one adverb of the same meaning-class there is usually a choice of order:

Manner

a) *We survived **quite well** without one.*
b) *We survived without one **quite well**.*

Order (a) is more common than (b), with prepositional phrases (especially longer ones) usually following shorter adverbs:

*I just wanted to live my life **quietly, independently** and **with the minimum of disruption.***

Place

a) *You'll see the station **just round the corner next to the library**.*
b) *You'll see the station **next to the library just round the corner**.*

Order (a), with the more specific position second, is more common than (b).

Time

a) *I'll see you **at six o'clock on Wednesday**.*
b) *I'll see you **on Wednesday at six o'clock**.*

Order (a), where the more specific time is first, tends to occur more often than (b).

Place and time adverbs together in end position

As we noted in Unit 15, manner adverbs tend to come before place and time. Place and time themselves can often be interchanged (though order (a) below is more normal):

a) We were working **in the garden** *most of the morning*. (**place** + *time*)
b) We were working *most of the morning* **in the garden**.(*time* + **place**)

In all the above cases informal spoken language is more flexible than formal written language with regard to the order.

Adverbs in end position and direct speech

In literary style sometimes the reporting verb and subject are inverted. In these cases the adverb comes in end position, not after the verb:

'*Cut it off short*' said the father **rashly**. (**not**: ... '~~said rashly~~ the father.' (✗))

Linking adverbs

Some linking adverbs are particularly associated with either written or spoken language. For example *on the contrary* is very rare in informal conversation. In written

English it is more common and usually occurs in front (or much less frequently in mid) position:

> He had no private understanding with Mr X. **On the contrary**, he knew very little of him.

On the other hand occurs frequently in both spoken and written English. Do not confuse it with *on the contrary*. *On the contrary* means 'A is not true; B is.' *On the other hand* means 'Both A and B are true, and both must be taken into account':

> On the one hand he seems to be the ideal English gentleman, always proffering a gallant helping hand ... **On the other hand**, he has a large tattoo on one arm.

The concessive adverb *then again* (always in front position) is much more frequent in spoken than in written:

> If it had been at the bottom of a councillor's street then I don't think it would ever have been built. But **then again** that goes on all the time.

Other linking adverbs more common in written than spoken include *accordingly*, *moreover*, *furthermore*, *duly*, *therefore*, *as a consequence* and *in the event*.

Linking adverbs are much less often found in end position, but they do occur there in more formal spoken and written styles:

> There had been twelve cases when it was published. There were at least 60 by a few years later, *however*.
> Comparisons may be unavoidable. They are odious* *nevertheless*.

Viewpoint adverbs

- Adverbs of evaluation and personal perspective are very often found in front position:

  > **Quite honestly**, I think we need more representation. (In my honest opinion)
  > **In fairness**, he did say that he'd tried and spoken to local people. (To be fair to him)

- Adverbs that indicate or restrict the **topic** in some way normally come in front position:

  > Also, **culturally**, if you can speak the language you tend to be better off. (with regard to culture)
  > **Politically**, it may be worth your while pretending you don't know. (As far as the political aspects are concerned ...)

- Viewpoint adverbs can be used in end position for emphasis:

  > We were entitled to use the material, quite **frankly**. (to be frank with you.)
  > I could hardly wait for the news, **personally**.

* *Odious* means unpleasant.

- Topic adverbs may be found in end position both in spoken and written:

   *A trade ban may be less objectionable **politically**.* (from a political point of view)
   *How did it affect you **in terms of everyday life**?* (as far as your everyday life is
   concerned)

Inversion after adverbs

- Adverbs of negative meaning (including negative frequency) which are normally
  found in mid position cause the subject and verb to be inverted if moved to front
  position. This normally occurs only in very formal and literary styles:

   Never could she understand *how he cared.*
   Not only is it a remarkable book *it is also a highly successful one.*

- Other adverbs of this type include *hardly, on no account, on no occasion, under no
  circumstances, rarely, scarcely, seldom* and *little* (in clauses such as *Little did I realise
  that ...*).

Emphasis with adverbs and auxiliary verbs

- Instead of coming after the first auxiliary verb, mid-position adverbs can be placed
  before it for extra emphasis:

   *I **honestly** don't know.* (compare: *I don't honestly know.*)
   *I **probably** could have said if I'd wanted to see it.*

- This feature occurs particularly when the following auxiliary is stressed. (The
  underlining shows which word is stressed in pronunciation:)

   *She **never** <u>did</u> get on with Robert.*
   *I **never** <u>have</u> worked out which is which.*

Adverbs after the second auxiliary verb

Mid-position adverbs can sometimes occur **after** a second or third auxiliary verb
(instead of the more normal position of after the first one). This is common in spoken
language:

   *I think she would've **probably** married him.*
   *They might've **actually** had to alter it I don't know.*
   *It could've been **easily** mistaken for a new one.*

Split infinitives (putting an adverb between *to* and the infinitive)

Many language purists (people who believe rules should be always followed one
hundred per cent) believe that split infinitives (e.g. *I want **to carefully check**
everything*) are wrong or bad style. In fact in spoken English they are very common,
even among highly educated speakers:

   *It's very common **to actually not like** the Birmingham accent, isn't it?*
   *People tend **to automatically laugh** at it.*

Articles

Most uses of the definite article are covered by the meanings focused on in Units 16 and 17, but some uses of the definite article are difficult to predict, and should be learnt together with the nouns they are used with.

Names of geographical/topographical features

- The English names of rivers always have *the* before them:

  the *Thames* (or *the* River Thames)   **the** *Colorado River*   **the** *Nile*

  the *Amazon*   **the** *Yangtsze*   **the** *Danube*

  *I've got photographs of those fishing boats on **the Nile**.*
  *I've been on **the River Seine**, in one of those boats, 'Bateaux Mouches*'.*

- The names of mountains and lakes do not have *the* before them:

  Lake Geneva   *Lake Ontario*   *Mont Blanc*   *Mount Fuji*
  Popocatepetl   *Vesuvius*

  Exceptions are: the Matterhorn, the Eiger.

  *It was the story of **Krakatoa**, the volcano.*

  A: *Is there one event that you can recollect that's given you quite a lot of pleasure?*
  B: *Mm. **Lake Garda** in Italy. It was absolutely beautiful, the scenery and the weather.*

  *With my bad knee, going up and down stairs is like climbing **Mount Everest**.*

- Note that the names of mountain **ranges** do have *the* before them:

  the *Rocky Mountains*   **the** *Alps*   **the** *Himalayas*

- The names of deserts, seas, oceans, groups of islands, major geographical areas and regions usually have *the* before them:

  the *Sahara*   **the** *Mojave Desert*   **the** *Pacific*   **the** *Black Sea*
  the *Prairies*   **the** *Lake District*   **the** *Florida Keys*

  *The programme was about a man that got lost in **the Sahara Desert**.*

  [holiday advertisement] '*In the Saddle*' *offers a 15-day itinerary of riding in **the Mongolian Steppes** with yak herdsmen.*

---

*Bateaux Mouches are a kind of tourist boat that travels on the River Seine, in Paris.

Countries

Names of countries do not normally have *the* before them, except for a small number of countries which should be learnt separately. These often have a word such as *republic*, *kingdom* or *islands* in their name:

> *the* Czech Republic   *the* United Kingdom   *the* United States
> *the* Netherlands

Streets and roads

- When we give an address, we do not normally say *the* with the name of the street or road, except when *the* is already part of its name:

> *I think she was born in Helen Street and then they moved to Nora Street.*
> (**not:** I think she was born in ***the Helen Street*** ... (✗))
> *The address is 75 Trent Road.* (**not:** 75 The Trent Road (✗))
> *King's College is in **the Strand**.* (The name of the road is '*the* Strand'.)

- Road numbers are normally preceded by *the*:

> *We were heading down **the M56**.*
> *Have they finished the roadworks on **the A1** yet?*

Places and buildings in towns and cities

Hotels normally have *the* before them, but other buildings, such as cathedrals, stations, airports, sports grounds, etc. normally do not:

> *the* Holiday Inn   *the* Russell Hotel   *Saint Peter's Cathedral*
> *Grand Central Station   Narita Airport   Shea Stadium*

> *He's working at **the Moat House Hotel**.*
> *I went to many glorious services in **Canterbury Cathedral**.*
> *It was foggy from **Gatwick Airport** all the way to Derby.*

Newspapers and magazines

Newspapers, but not magazines, normally have *the* as part of their name:

> *the* South China Morning Post   *the* New York Times   *the* Independent
> *Hello!   Cosmopolitan*

> *Did you get **the Guardian** today?* (British newspaper)
> *I read about it in **Time** magazine.* (American news magazine)

Weights, measures, times

The indefinite article *a*, not *the* is used when linking one type of measurement to another:

*It would cost you more than **a pound a day** to stay at home and eat.*
(**not:** ~~a pound the day~~ ...)
*I play rugby and so I train **three times a week**.*

It is also possible to say *a pound **per** day* and *three times **per** week*.

Parts of the body

- Do not forget that normally parts of a person's body are referred to with **possessive pronouns** rather than the definite article:

    *I took **my hand** down and it was absolutely covered in blood.*
    (**not:** ~~I took the hand down~~ ...)

- But with prepositional phrases relating to the recipient of an action, *the* is used:

    *He punched him right in **the stomach**.*

- References to body measurements or impersonal references to anatomy often use *the*:

    *She's very big around **the hips**.*
    ***The eye** is a very complex organ.*

Media and entertainment forms

- In general, **television** or **TV** is used without *the* when we refer to the medium itself or programmes:

    *One of the people I hate most on **television** is Brian Morsley.*

    But if we are referring to the TV set itself, then *the* can be used:

    *We turned **the TV** on the morning after the general election to see what had happened.*

- Very informal spoken language is different: *the* is used much more often:

    *We hear it on **the television** and read it in **the newspapers**. Things happen all the time.*

- With **radio**, **cinema**, **theatre**, **web** and **Internet** it is normal to use *the* in most situations:

    *I buy all my airline tickets on **the Internet** these days.*
    *It's got a cinema as well, so people go to **the cinema** there instead of into town.*

- Note *into town*, which has no article. *In/into town* usually refers to the centre of a town, where all the main shops and public buildings are.

- **Television**, **radio**, **cinema** and **theatre** are used without *the* when we refer to them in very general terms as art forms or as professions:

    *A lot of actors prefer **radio** to **television**.*
    With the support of her husband, Gertrude left for London and fulfilled the

*improbable dream of stepping from amateur **theatre** directly into a leading West End role.*

The with identifiable social groups

- All the people in a defined social group can be referred to by using *the* + **adjective**. These include:

  the *blind*   **the** *deaf*   **the** *young*   **the** *elderly*   **the** *homeless*
  the *unemployed*   **the** *sick*

  *They don't charge them under school age, but they charge people who work and they charge **the unemployed**.*
  ***The elderly** are the ones that suffer the most.* (Note the plural verb form: *suffer*.)

  The can also be used with *adjectives* such as *abnormal, paranormal, supernatural, bizarre, unknown, unexpected* and *macabre* to refer to a general state:

  *It was the fear of **the unknown** that stopped me from doing it.*
  *She was not a great believer in **the supernatural**. She had never seen a ghost.*

Exclamations

- The indefinite article *a* is used with countable nouns in the singular in exclamations beginning with *what*:

  What a lovely room! (**not**: ~~What lovely room!~~ (**✗**))

- *A* is not used in exclamations with *what* when the noun is uncountable:

  What awful weather! (**not**: ~~What an awful weather!~~ (**✗**))

Complex noun phrases

Noun modifiers and number

- Noun modifiers remain singular even if they have a plural meaning:

  ***shoe** polish* (polish for shoes)
  ***tooth**paste* (paste to clean your teeth)
  ***car** ferry* (ferry for cars)

  *I used to always put my bike in the **bike shed** at work.* (shed for bicycles)
  *What **shoe size** are you?* (**not**: ~~What shoes size are you?~~ (**✗**))

- This is also true when plural measurements occur as a noun modifier:

  *a **two-litre** bottle* (**not**: ~~a two litres bottle~~ (**✗**))
  *a **five-mile** walk* (a walk of five miles)
  *a **two-hour** lecture* (a lecture of two hours)
  *a **multi-storey** car park* (a car park with several floors/storeys)

  *Exeter is a **seventy-mile round trip** to play a game.*
  *There's usually a **thirty-minute wait**.*

Noun modifiers for established classes of things

For well-established classes of things, noun + noun is often used:

> *I don't know whether I could have coped with a **science lesson** in French at school.*
> (*Science lessons* are a well-established class of things.)

Compare this with:

> *There's a lesson that I've learnt about parenthood.* (a very specific reference,
> **not:** *There's a ~~parenthood lesson~~ I've learnt.* (✗))
> *The **road sign** was missing so we didn't have a clue which way to turn.* (established
> class of objects)
> *It won't be visible until the next **bend in the road**.* (specific reference, **not:**
> *... until the next ~~road bend~~* (✗))

Determiner + noun + *of* + possessive pronoun

Don't forget that we say *a cousin of mine, some friends of yours,* etc.,
not: *~~a friend of me, a cousin of you~~* (✗) etc.

> *She said she might be **a cousin of mine**.*
> *This **friend of ours** used to tell a story about when he was out in Africa years ago.*

Prepositions

Basic prepositions

In a sample of the Cambridge International Corpus of one million words of spoken
and one million words of written English, these are the top ten most frequent
prepositions. It is therefore worth making sure you know how to use these in all their
main meanings.

| *to* | *of* | *in* | *at* | *on* | *for* | *with* | *from* | *about* | *by* |

to

There are some cases where *to* in a verb phrase is a preposition, not an infinitive *to*, and
must be followed by a noun or *-ing* form of the verb. The verbs include: *get/be used to,
look forward to, object to, get (a)round to, be reduced to* and *be opposed to*:

> *I'm **looking forward to** having my own place.* (**not:** *I'm looking forward
> ~~to have~~ my own place.*)
> *Would you **object to** paying for meals in a hospital?*
> *I just haven't **got round to** contacting him.*

In the case of *prefer*, if alternatives are stated, they are linked by the preposition
to, not infinitive *to*:

> *Would you prefer **writing to telephoning** if you wanted put something across?*
> (**not:** *Would you prefer writing ~~to telephone~~ ...*)

At and in

Remember that the basic distinction between *at* and *in* depends on whether you are referring to a point (*at*), or an extended place or time (*in*). This explains many basic uses of the two prepositions:

> *There's a flight at ten o'clock in the morning.* (Ten o'clock is a point in time; the morning is an extended period of time.)

Compare *at* and *in* in these examples:

Things seen as a point	Things seen as extended
I didn't know if you would be at evening class.	*Here are some worksheets that the teachers use in class.*
I'm afraid Dr Willis has got someone with him at the moment.	*He'll be free at about three. Could you wait here in the meantime?*
I'm wondering when I could come and pick up the calendars and Christmas cards that I ordered from you at the beginning of October.	*Maybe we should aim for a little bit of caution in the beginning, and try and get it right.*
On the ninth we went to our brother's at Birmingham to celebrate my sister's and my birthday. We're twins you know.	*He was born and raised in Birmingham, but he's from Dublin.*

On

With **particular days**, or parts of particular days, *on* is used:

> *We always like to meet for lunch on a Friday.*
> *They love to have their grandparents with them, especially on a birthday.*
> *You can't beat a walk on a fine spring morning.* (Compare a more general reference: *You can't beat a walk in the morning.*)

We can compare references to important days in terms of whether they are seen as points on the calendar, parts of the day in general, or as particular days:

Calendar points, periods, or parts of the day in general	*Particular days*
What are you doing at Christmas?	*The family always come over on Christmas Day.*
The semi-finals are in the morning and the finals in the afternoon.	*We had croissants on the morning of the wedding.*
Unemployment fell in April in all regions and age groups.	*At half-past four on the afternoon of 8th April 1912 the weather was mild and hyacinths bloomed in window boxes.*

For

Do not confuse the use of infinitive with *to* to express means, purpose or intention with *for*, which expresses reason, or how we use something (see also prepositional clauses, below):

> *That would be a good way **to spend** your fiftieth birthday.*
> (**not:** *That would be a good way ~~for spending~~ your fiftieth birthday.* (✗))
> *Thanks **for sorting** that out for us yesterday.* (expressing reason)
> *These books are excellent **for reading** to children.* (how we use something)

From

From often indicates the origin or starting point of something:

> I've had a letter *from* Marjorie Swan.
> I got the train *from* Oxford to Bristol.
> The show ran *from* 1948 to 1971.

"It's from us."

Prepositions and -ing forms

- The form of the verb which follows a **preposition** is always the *-ing* form:

  *Rabbits were responsible **for undermining** the tunnels.*
  *The oldest lad is not very good **at reading**, is he?*
  *She wasn't interested **in putting** it on the market.*

- There may be a **subject** between the **preposition** and the *-ing* form. If this subject is a pronoun, it is normally an object pronoun, except in formal style, where possessives often occur:

  *Auntie mentioned about **him being** in hospital.* (more formal: *about his being in hospital.*)
  *Within a few months of **us doing** the audit, the work had already started.* (more formal: ... *of our doing the audit*)
  *This may result in **your receiving** a dividend to which you are not entitled ...* (less formal: *This may result in you receiving a dividend ...*)

- A number of verbs are followed by *for* + **noun/pronoun** + **infinitive**. These include *wait, ask, long* and *arrange*:

  *We all had to wait **for her to get** home.* (**not**: *We all had to wait for her getting home. (✗)*)
  *We also arranged **for you to be** seen again in three months to review progress.*
  (**not**: *We also arranged for you being seen again ...*)

- Similarly, a number of adjectives are followed by the same construction, including *keen, happy, anxious, ready, eager*:

  *Everything's **ready for** you to see.*
  *I'm **happy for** him to say that.*

Prepositional clauses

Prepositions may introduce an *-ing* clause to create a variety of logical relations:

*You know, you're saving time **by going** on a bike instead of walking.* (*by* + *-ing* as 'by means of'; *instead of* + *-ing* as 'not doing x but doing y')
*I've been injured a number of times myself, **through playing** soccer as a goalkeeper.* (*through* + *-ing* as 'because of, but usually not intentionally')
*I just can't stop thinking how stupid I was **for saying** no.* (**for** + *-ing* as 'because of')
*The university has a few vehicles. But they're not really **for running** around in.* (*for* + *-ing* as denoting the general way of using something or the purpose of using it)
*The Cointreau turned milky **on adding** water to it.* (**on** + *-ing* for describing the immediate consequence of something)

A: *I think, isn't that why shops change their layout every so often?*
B: *Mm.*
A: *So you don't keep going to the same product, you have to look round and **in looking** you might find something different.* (in + -ing expressing one event as necessarily leading to another)

Direct and indirect speech

Punctuation

- A variety of punctuation conventions exist for written reported speech. Direct speech may be marked by single or double inverted commas:

  "Not always," replied Bobby. (This convention is sometimes called '66–99', since the commas look like the two figures.)
  'I want to do it, ' Anna said.

- There is normally a comma at the end of direct speech, unless it is a question or an exclamation.

- There is also a comma at the end of the reporting clause when it comes first. The second inverted comma comes after the final full stop:

  Anna said hastily, 'She doesn't mean to be patronising.'

- A colon can also be used to mark quoted speech or writing, especially in quotations in academic articles, journalism, quoting famous people, etc.:

  He said: "If we want to maintain our global role we must be a leading player in Europe."

- In indirect speech, we do not normally separate the reporting clause from the reported clause by punctuation when the reporting clause is first:

  The lorry driver simply said that it was meat and bone meal from another delivery. (**not:** *The lorry driver simply ~~said, that~~ it was meat and bone meal ...* (✗))
  or: *The lorry driver simply ~~said that~~, it was meat and bone meal ...* (✗))

- When the reporting clause comes second, a comma is used to separate the clauses:

  It had been painted with love, he said.

- Indirect reports of questions do not have question marks:

  So people complained and asked him why we were waiting.

Use of *that*

- *That* is often omitted after the reporting verb, especially in informal language:

  *She said (**that**) she was spending the day in Glasgow with a school friend.*
  *I suggested (**that**) she actually invites a group of people back.*

- When the noun forms of reporting verbs are used, it is normal to include *that* in formal contexts:

  *And what about **the suggestion that** George might get an earlier appointment?*

- However, in informal spoken language, *that* is sometimes omitted after a reporting noun:

  *There's **a hint** the government's going to change its policy on house-building.*

Tense in the reporting clause

Most indirect reporting clause verbs are in past simple or past continuous tense (see Unit 20), but other tenses can also be used.

Present simple and reported speech

If the speech reported is seen as always true or relevant, or likely to be said on any given occasion, **present simple** may be used:

> *He went to a lady doctor in there. He **says** she's very nice.* (He would probably always say that if asked.)

Present continuous

If the speech report represents someone's current position or opinion (which might possibly change), then **present continuous** can be used:

> ***He's saying** it was a head office decision but he did know prior to that.* (That is his current position on the matter.)

Say and *tell* plus objects

- *Say* and *tell* have different rules for the use of indirect objects. When referring to the person addressed, *say* requires *to, tell* does not:

    > *She **said**, 'I really like this little car. It's quite good.'* (**not:** ~~She told~~, *'I really like this little car.'* (✗))
    > *I **said to her**, 'When I'm ready I'll tell you.'* (**not:** ~~I said her~~, *'When I'm ready I'll tell to you.'* (✗))

- In formal written style, *tell* but not *say* is used with an **infinitive**:

    > *The man from Foreign Affairs had **told her to** prepare for the worst.*

- But in informal spoken language, *say* and *tell* may both be used with an **infinitive**:

    > *I phoned up the hospital and they **said to go** down.* (or: *they **told** me **to go** down*)

Word order in indirect speech

- When a *wh-*question is reported indirectly, the word order is normally that of a **statement**, rather than question word order:

    > *So I asked him **what the arrangements were**.* (**not:** *So I asked him ~~what were the arrangements~~.*)

- However, in informal spoken style, question word order is sometimes used:

    > *So I asked him **what were the chances** and he said, 'Not in your lifetime, my dear.'* (instead of: *I asked him what the chances were ...*)

- With *yes/no* questions, *if* and *whether* are used with statement word order:

    > *I haven't really asked you **whether you've had** enough to eat.*
    > *I'm just ringing up to enquire **if there is** any more definite news.*

Verb–subject inversion and speech reporting

In written direct speech reports where the reporting clause is final, the **verb** and **subject** of the reporting clause may be **inverted**. This occurs particularly in literary writing and in journalism. It is very rare in informal spoken language:

> *'And have we found a tenant for that charming room upstairs?'* **asked Mr Perkins**.
> *'He is certainly someone the city wants to remember,'* **said a spokesman** *for the city council.*

Adverb and speech reporting

- Adverbs modifying the speech reporting verb can indicate contextual features of the reported clause. These are common in written literary style but rare in informal spoken language:

> *'I don't know what this country is coming to,' she stated* **firmly**.
> *I was* **politely** *informed that he had left the building.*

Go and *be like* and speech reporting

In very informal spoken language, *go* and *be like* are sometimes used to report direct speech. They are often accompanied by dramatising body-language or a change in the speaker's voice to suggest a dramatic re-creation of the original speech:

> *'Cos I was embarrassed, and when we were out, and I had a dress, she* **went**, *'Look at her legs, she's got hairy legs.'*
> *He keeps coming and trying to kiss me and* **I'm like**, *'Go away! Go away!'*

Tails and heads (post- and pre-posed elements of clauses)

Unit 21 covered almost everything you need to know about tails, but it is also worth noting the typical intonation pattern for them. Typically, the intonation on the tail itself ends in a rising tone (since it is not 'new' information; the important new information is in the main clause, which will have a falling tone or a rising tone, depending on its communicative function). The whole clause-plus-tail is uttered together, typically in one long, sweeping fall–rise tone. If the tail contains an auxiliary verb, it is not normally stressed.

> *You're TOO **SLOW**, YOU are.*

(Too and you have secondary stress: slow has the most stress.)

> *He's ALWAYS **LATE**, DAVID.*

Pronouns

In informal speech, tails sometimes consist of a **pronoun** alone; in these cases, the object pronoun is used, not the subject pronoun:

*I'm hungry, **me**. I don't know about you.* (**not:** ~~*I'm hungry, I.*~~ (✗))
*He's crazy, **him**.*

With the pronoun **it**, *this* or *that* is used in the tail. With **they**, when used with non-human referents, *these* or *those* is used in the tail:

*It's a speciality, **that**.*
*They're lovely potatoes, **these**.*

Interrupted patterns of pre-posed elements

A typical pattern is a fronted subject repeated in the subject pronoun (e.g. 'That lorry, it's making a lot of smoke.'). In this construction, the noun and pronoun do not necessarily have to be adjacent, and adverbial structures and subordinate clauses may come in between:

*Paul, **in this job that he's got now**, **when he goes into the office**, he's never quite sure where he's going to be sent.*

Adverbs and pre-posing

With fronted **time** and **place adverbs** that are the subject of their clause, *that* often functions as the repeated subject:

Next Wednesday, that'd be a good day for me.

A: *Where's the dog?*
B: *On the bed again, that's where he is.*

Referents other than subjects and objects

The referent of a fronted element is most frequently the subject or object, but other items in the clause can also be fronted:

*Well, **the street we go down**, the Royal Café is in that.* (fronted object of **preposition** in a phrase acting as adverbial)

Fronted objects and complements

In Unit 21, we briefly mentioned **fronted objects** without a repeated pronoun, e.g. 'I like David but Jill I find rather odd.' This construction is quite common, especially in spoken language, and enables us to create emphasis and is useful for making contrasts:

[advertisement for computers] *They spend their time with clients. **Computer stuff** they leave to us.* (This contrasts spending time with clients and spending time sorting out computer issues.)
***Huge man** he was.* (fronted complement for emphasis)

Ellipsis

Co-ordinated clauses and ellipsis

The most frequent type of ellipsis where elements can be retrieved from the surrounding text is in co-ordinated clauses. Conjunctions such as *and, or* and *but* may be followed by ellipsis.

The omitted elements in the co-ordinated clause may be subordinators (e.g. *if, that*), relative pronouns, subject pronouns, the infinitive particle *to*, and/or auxiliary verbs:

> *If you cannot attend but can send a substitute, just ring us.* (understood as: *but **if you** can send a substitute ...*)
> *In most circumstances, doctors who are actually visiting patients but fail to observe parking restrictions will not have their cars removed or clamped.* (understood as: *but **who** fail to observe parking restrictions*)
> *I'm going to cut up that bit of lamb and give it to Jill.* (understood as: *and **I'm going to** give it to Jill.*)

Co-ordinated ellipsis with *but* is more frequent in formal, written language than in informal, spoken.

Ellipsis of main verb in co-ordinated clauses

The main verb may be omitted when repeated in co-ordination:

> A: *I trust you.*
> B: *And I you.* (understood as: *And I **trust** you.*)

> [describing cars] *One was electric blue, the other white.* (understood as: *the other **was** white.*)

Emphatic *do* and ellipsis

When the second clause contains an emphatic *do*-form, the rest of the clause may be omitted. (Here underlining indicates the word which is stressed or emphasised.):

> A: *Do you have ambitions?*
> B: *Yes I <u>do</u>. Yes.* (understood as: *Yes I <u>do</u> **have** ambitions.*)

This is different from the substitute *do*, which is normally unstressed:

> A: *Who wants another potato?*
> B: *<u>I</u> do.* (understood as: *'**I want another potato**.' not: ~~I do want~~ another potato.*)

More than one auxiliary verb and ellipsis

More than one auxiliary verb may be repeated in the clause that has ellipsis:

> A: *Would you have written a formal letter of complaint, do you think?*
> B: *I **might have**, I don't know.* (understood as: *I might have **written** a formal letter of complaint.*)

A: *Debbie should have said something, shouldn't she?*
B: *Yes, she **should have**. (understood as: she should have **said** something)*

This is common with passive voice constructions, where the auxiliary *be* is not usually omitted:

A: *Hopefully if she can transfer to Berlin she will.*
B: *Would be great, wouldn't it?*
A: *Yeah, I can't rely on it but I mean I was hoping she **will be**. (understood as: I was hoping she will be transferred.)*

Repeated main verb *be* and ellipsis

In a repeated verb phrase with *be*, the complement may be absent:

[octogenarian[1] talking about being old]
A: *I presume every day it's a bonus, isn't it?*
B: *Mm.*
A: *It could be. (understood as: It could be a **bonus**.)*

A: *Are you hungry Joe?*
B: *Yes I am. (understood as: Yes I am **hungry**.)*

Forward-pointing ellipsis

In most cases, ellipsis in clauses is anaphoric (backward-referring), but it may also be cataphoric (forward-referring), although this is rarer and associated with rather formal styles:

*His 'barrio[2]' **was and is** notorious for its heroin users and dealers.* (understood as: His 'barrio' was **notorious** and is notorious ...)
*If you **can**, do try different methods/techniques to see if you can get more.*
(understood as: 'If you can try different methods/techniques to see if you can get more, do try ...')
*If you want **to**, you can have that.*
(understood as: If you want to **have that**, you can have that.)

Subordinate clauses and ellipsis

Subordinators such as *if, when, whenever, although, while, unless* may be followed by ellipsis of subject and verb:

*Being part of a group means that you can carry each other **whenever necessary**.*
(understood as: you can carry each other whenever **it is** necessary)

---

[1]An *octogenarian* is someone in their eighties.
[2]*Barrio* is a Spanish word meaning local area where a person lives.

[In a shop a customer is buying nuts.]
A: *Can I have a quarter of those please?*
B: *Yes.*
A: *Not too heavy on the Brazils[3] **if possible**.* (understood as: *if **it is** possible.*)

- The main verb may be included while subject and auxiliary verbs are omitted. This usage is restricted to rather formal contexts:

  [person explaining to a doctor how a child came to hurt himself while playing on the bed] *He was okay **while jumping** on the bed, but I didn't know he was going to jump off the bed.* (understood as: *He was okay while **he was** jumping on the bed.*)
  *Nerve agents are lethal **if inhaled** or absorbed through the skin.* (understood as: 'If **they are** inhaled or absorbed ...*)
  *If **using** a stove-top espresso machine, clean after each use.* (understood as: *If **you are** using a stove-top espresso machine ...*)

Noun phrases and ellipsis

- Ellipsis often occurs after quantifying expressions in repeated noun phrases:

  A: *Do you want some of that stuff? I'll get some more.*
  B: *I've got **loads**.* (understood as: *I've got loads **of that stuff**.*)

  A: *But otherwise we don't use salt in any cooking.*
  B: *We don't use **very much at all**.*
  C: *Mm.*
  A: *We use **hardly any**.* (understood as: *We don't use very much salt at all.* and *We use hardly any salt at all.*)

- The **noun headword** may also be omitted rather than repeated:

  [shopkeeper to customer]
  A: *I've got scented **candles** on offer at the moment as well ... There's vanilla, bay berry, holly berry and pine.*
  B: *Right, which one?*
  A: *The bay berry's the pink, the holly berry's the red.* (understood as: *The bay berry's the pink **candles**, the holly berry's the red **candles**.*)

- This also happens with determiners such as *another, the other, this, that, these, those*:

  *We could put three in one class and three in **another**.* (understood as: *three in another **class**.*)
  *Are we going to use the green plates or **these**?* (understood as: *or these **plates**?*)

- This kind of ellipsis does not usually occur with the indefinite article. The substitute *one* is preferred:

  A: *We're going to be struggling to find enough vases for these flowers.*
  B: *Yeah.*
  A: *Well I have **a blue one**.* (not: *Well I have ~~a blue~~.* (✗))

---

[3] *Brazils* means Brazil nuts, here.

Adjectives and ellipsis

After intensifiers and downtoners, a repeated adjective may be omitted:

A: *You think it's a bit touristy?*
B: *Well it is a bit.* (understood as: *Well it is a bit **touristy**.*)

A: *Her brain was tremendously active.*
B: *Yeah, always active, yes.*
C: *Yes.*
B: *Always active. **Very very**.*
C: *That's tremendous.* (understood as: ***Very very active**.*)

Articles and ellipsis

The definite article is often absent from the beginning of some common fixed expressions in informal spoken language:

[commenting on someone's choice of red as the colour for a ball gown] ***Trouble** is she's so pale. If she gets red she's going to look really pale.* (understood as: *The trouble is she's so pale.*)

- Other expressions of this type include (*the*) *problem is*, (*the*) *danger is*, (*the*) *good thing is*.

- *The* is sometimes omitted in fronted and appositional phrases:

   *I mean, **poor bloke**, you felt so sorry for him.* (understood as: *I mean, **the** poor bloke, ...*)
   [woman criticising a female colleague] *Now she's managed to get Eileen as her mentor, though how she's managed that, **stupid woman**!* (understood as: ***The stupid woman!***)

- *You* can also be omitted before vocatives:

   *(**You**) stupid idiot! You've let the dog out!*
   *You found it! (**You**) clever boy!*

- The indefinite article may also be omitted from initial noun phrases (particularly those which have post-modification):

   [comparing two electrical lamps] ***Friend of mine**'s got the cheaper one, but he reckons it's not bright enough.* (understood as: *A friend of mine ...*)
   ***Huge man** he was.*
   (understood as: ***A** huge man he was.*)

- Where two nouns that are always closely associated are co-ordinated, the second may be without an article:

   *You'll need a hammer and **chisel**.* (understood as: *a hammer and a chisel*)
   *The top and **bottom** were both rusty.* (understood as: *The top and the bottom*)

Possessives and ellipsis

- Repeated nouns with possessive *'s* may be omitted:

  *How far is the framework as a framework different from **other people's**?* (understood as: *different from other people's framework?*)

  A: *Have you got my case?*
  B: *That's **Robert's**. (understood as: That's **Robert's** case.)*

- The most frequent example of ellipsis with *'s* is references to people's abode (house/flat):

  *Mum said I can stay at **Allan's** tonight.* (understood as: *at **Allan's** house/flat.)*

Infinitive *to* and ellipsis

- Infinitive *to* may be omitted in co-ordinated clauses:

  [discussion about whether there should be charges for healthcare] *I don't mind having to pay to go to the optician's and **go** to the dentist.* (understood as: *having to pay to go to the optician's and **to go** to the dentist.)*

- Infinitive *to* must normally be retained after verbs such as *love, hate, like, wish, want* when the rest of the clause is omitted:

  *I don't want to do this. **I don't want to**. (**not**: ~~I don't want.~~ (✗))*

  A: *D'you want to see our family album?*
  B: *I'd love to. (**not**: ~~I'd love.~~ (✗))*

- Verbs such as *hope, ask, decide, advise, force* may retain infinitive *to* when there is an understood infinitive verb phrase:

  A: *Is she going to university?*
  B: *Well **she hopes to**: (understood as: Well she hopes to **go to university**.)*

  A: *Why did he do that?*
  B: *'Cos I told him **to**. (understood as: 'Cos I told him to **do that**.)*

  [A woman is talking about whether she would take part in a research project or not.] *A lot of women were going into it ... as I say I decided **not to**.* (understood as: I decided not to **go into it**.)

Prepositions and ellipsis

Prepositions may be omitted when the meaning is obvious in the text:

*When she wakes up **Christmas Day** hopefully she'll think, 'Oh, this is different'.* (understood as: When she wakes up **on** Christmas Day ...)

A: *D'you like York?*
B: *Yes, it's a nice place to live. (understood as: Yes, it's a nice place to live **in**.)*

[someone talking about a flight he used to take]
*It used to go **Mombasa, Nairobi, Athens, London**.*
(understood as: It used to go **from** Mombasa, **to** Nairobi, **to** Athens, **to** London.)

Everyday fixed expressions and ellipsis

- Some everyday fixed expressions in informal spoken language often have ellipsis of initial elements, since these can be assumed to be known by everyone in the conversation.

  *I have nothing to go on, **tell you the truth**.*
  (understood as: **to** tell you the truth)
  *Oh, **good job** I've left a little hole then.*
  (understood as: **It's a** good job ...)

- Other examples include:

  *(**It's a**) good thing ...*
  *(**I had**) better ...*
  *(**There's**) no point in ...*
  *(**It's**) not worth ...*
  *(**It would be**) best if you ...*
  *(**I'll**) see you later/tomorrow/soon ...*
  *(**I'll**) be seeing you ...*
  *(**You**) never know, ...*

Fixed similes and ellipsis

Fixed similes can have ellipsis of the first *as*, whereas true comparatives normally do not:

  [fixed simile]
  *Your dad's **strong as an ox**.*
  (understood as: *Your dad's **as** strong as an ox.*)
  [true comparative]
  *I mean this one next door's **not as good as this house** and it's ninety pounds a week.*
  (**not**: *I mean this one next door's ~~not good~~ as this house.* (✗))

Discourse markers

In addition to the markers listed in the summary in Unit 25, there are other useful markers that are common in everyday language.

Other common markers

Anyway

- *Anyway* is used to bring the conversation back to its main line or thread, after an interruption or diversion on to another topic. It is particularly common in moving from one episode to another in spoken story-telling:

  *... I'm not that stupid. **Anyway**, what I was saying was, when I first typed it up it was like normal spacing and normal character size and I'd done nine pages.* (resuming the narrative after a diversion or interruption)

  *... she went back to her seat and stood up and sort of started again. **Anyway**, when I got off the bus the teacher came to me and he said, 'Thank you for that.'* (moving to a new stage in the narrative)

- It can also signal that you are ready to close the topic or the whole conversation:

  *But **anyway** we'll continue this discussion when we get into the regulations. I must run 'cos I have to teach a lecture.* (signalling closure)

Still

As a discourse marker, *still* has a meaning similar to the more formal *on the other hand* or *nevertheless*:

*I worked in cinemas but I was out of work at 51 because the cinemas closed. But **still**, who isn't out of work today?*

Basically

- *Basically* is very frequent in spoken language, used with the meaning of 'what I'm simply saying is ...':

  *I just **basically** told them the situation.*

  ***Basically** you get to the top of the stairs and there's er just this counter and there should be one member of staff standing there on their own.*

- Discourse markers which are normally only spoken do appear sometimes in written texts. When they do, the text becomes more conversational and informal. So, we find discourse markers such as *anyway* or *still*, or *basically* in personal letters and popular journalism.

  [Extract from a letter between two sisters]
  ***Basically**, I think I still like him but I don't want to get too tied down. **Anyway**, I'll try and ring you on Sunday and we can talk some more. I can also hear all your news then too.*

Key

Unit 1 Present perfect

A

1 See Observations in the unit.

2

used with past simple	used with present perfect	used with either
in the last century	up to now	for three months
during President Kennedy's lifetime	over the last hundred years or so	recently (more likely with present perfect)
three months ago	since three months ago	today
throughout the 17th century	this is the first time I	after the Second World War (more likely with past simple)
	lately	
	since the Vietnam War	
	within the last three months	

B

1 The tenses change according to whether the speaker thinks that the topic is 'live' and relevant to the present situation:

> If he **has** brought the ghost 'down here', they might be haunted that night!
> If they **have** lost the bottle-opener, they have a problem 'now'.

■ Therefore, (iii) is the best rule.

2 See Observations in the unit.

C

1 a) This is still a current problem (i.e. her mum does not yet know!).
   b) The class is over, and it is the end of the day. The teacher has separated these events in her mind from her evening conversation.
   c) The problem is current and they are looking at the camera in the present situation.

2 a) Yes, I've been there. I stayed there a couple of days.
   b) Yeah, I went to one, yeah.
   c) Yeah, we've done that, we started off using recipes, and then we soon discovered it was easier to make it our own way.

Further exercises

1   Have you ever been to Moscow?   I've studied there, actually.

How long have you been at college?   I've been there three weeks.

What did you do in Oxford last year?   I studied there, actually.

How many weeks were you in Paris?   I was there three weeks.

What have you done at college?   I've studied a lot.

2 a) has died; did not give up; enjoyed; was
  b) have returned; were; gave

3 Possible answers:
  a) Have you heard? A woman in Madrid has won $5 million in a lottery. She only bought one ticket, and lost it. But then she found it in a rubbish bin, and claimed the prize.
  b) Have you heard? The President has had a heart attack. He collapsed during a debate in Parliament and was rushed to hospital.
  c) Have you heard? A Canadian woman has become the first person to cross the Pacific Ocean solo on a raft. She had only one small sail and built the raft herself. The journey took six months.

4 a) have done; told
  b) have bought; has taught; have had
  c) bought; sold; looked
  d) heard; haven't heard; worried; have been
  e) noticed; went; had; said; have been getting; has caused
  f) has just come

5 Possible answers:
  a) Ever since I was a child, I have been afraid of spiders.
  b) Lately the weather has been unusually cold.
  c) During the 1980s, the economy in my country expanded.
  d) A: Do you still have your school books from when you were a kid?
    B: No, my parents threw them all out.
  e) Over the last six months, I have been to America twice.
  f) This is the first time I have visited England.

6 (a) have won   (b) threw   (c) was married   (d) wrote   (e) has eaten
   (f) have dug   (g) was

Unit 2 Past perfect

A

1 ■ The woman was very surprised (she says *My mouth dropped open*). She tried to guess who had arranged the visit to the cabin.
  ■ You could expand what the woman said into: *Somebody had told the pilots to invite me.*
  ■ The verbs which are in the past simple tense are: *said, dropped, was, was, took, were, was.*

- The verbs which are in the past perfect tense are: *'d had, had been, 'd said, had (said/told)*.
- The past perfect tense.

2 had only just turned; was; was; did

got; had already had; had put

In the case of **do** either the past simple or the past perfect could be used. There would be a slight difference in meaning: 'The police told me that he did it very often' (i.e. the focus is on the fact that he did it frequently) and, 'The police told me that he had done it very often' (i.e. the focus is on the fact that he had done it several times prior to the accident).

B

1 See Observations in the unit.

2 Apart from (b), you can join all these sentences using *because* or *as*. This is because they are all linked by a relationship of explanation:

> *I wasn't going very fast, because I had only just turned the corner.*

If you choose *as*, the sentence sounds more formal.
In (b) there is no relationship of explanation between the clauses, so we use the past simple in both clauses and join them with *but*.

C

a) *Alan's father <u>had put</u> ...*
This is an example of the past perfect used in a clause giving background information = context (ii).

b) *I thought <u>I'd missed</u> you.*
This is an example of the past perfect used after a reporting/thought verb = context (i).

c) *... some bits were bits of ruins <u>they'd added</u> onto.*
This is an example of the past perfect used to give more information about a noun (*ruins*) = context (iii).

Further exercises

1 a) *John told me **he'd actually died** from his injuries you know.* (Past perfect is in a reporting clause explaining the result of the accident.)
   b) *he was saying that **he'd had** a terrible day that **it'd been** so quiet all day.* (As above, but the focus is more on the events before the trader spoke to Speaker A. Note the adverbial *all day*.)

2 a) went;   arrived;   stayed;   had been (relative clause);   turned;
      had started (reporting thought clause)
   b) stayed;   shared;   had gone (subordinate clause giving an explanation)

3 a) i) She didn't believe that the tax loops had been closed.
      ii) He claimed that they had hired investigators to find the information.
      iii) She revealed that the design for the building had been inspired by rock formations.
      iv) It emerged that the pay settlement had been linked to the previous two years' productivity.

b) i) The baby, which had been ill from birth, became ill again.

   ii) Two accidents, which had not been reported, were on the same corner.

   iii) The tennis champion, who had won three tournaments in successive years, gave an interview.

   iv) She bought a cheap house in the village, which had been divided by a motorway.

c) i) When I phoned you on Saturday, you had already gone out shopping.

   ii) The central defender was sent off towards the end of the match. Earlier, he had been given a yellow card.

   iii) After he had been questioned by police, the boy went home.

   iv) The restaurant was closed by the health inspectors. Last week they had visited it and found it had been breaking food regulations.

Unit 3 Present continuous

A

a) This is an extract from a newspaper article about the state of the internet at the time the newspaper was published.

are using (*use* is possible, but read the notes which follow the answers to (b)).

says (*is saying* is **not** possible, *say* is used in the continuous form generally, only in face-to-face conversations to express opinion).

are finding (*find* is possible because this use of it is similar to *discover*. You cannot use *find* in the continuous form at the moment that something is discovered, e.g. [holding up keys] ~~I am finding my keys~~).

are entering (*enter* is **not** possible because it would have a strong focus on habitual action and here, the writer is showing that this is a new and current activity).

(are) selling (as *are entering*)

b) This is an extract from a woman speaking about her home life.

makes (*is making* is possible)

'm not having (*don't have* is possible)

'm doing

'm doing

'm tidying up

B

1 a) No change was made in this extract. The speaker could use the present simple tense throughout (*people who earn ... and think they don't earn enough*), but they want to emphasise the fact that what they are saying is especially true nowadays.

b) This contains one change. *The raw material is becoming more refined ...* Because the process is always true, and is being described in general terms, there is no connection with the present context. It would be impossible to put *nowadays* at the start of the sentence.

If the writer was reporting on the current state of raw sugar supplies at the time of writing, the continuous form could be used: 'Raw sugar is becoming more expensive'. You could begin (or end) this sentence 'Nowadays', 'At present' or 'Currently'.

c) This contains one change. The adverb *usually* indicates habitual action and so we must use the present simple. However, if we complete the sentence thus: *Usually, I am driving to work at that time*, there is no problem. The expression *at that time* creates a current context for the speaker or writer to point to.

d) This contains one change. The writer used *am writing this essay*. Using the present continuous gives the meaning of 'in the process of' and the writer is doing just that. The process of writing is seen as current and incomplete.

2 a) *you are going too fast*; *If your heart is beating*; *you are exercising too hard*. (You cannot use the present simple in any of these cases.)

b) *If he's cooking* (You could replace this, but the sense would become more general.)

C

1 In each case, the first sentence is a simple declarative clause, the second introduces a subordinate clause with a reporting verb in the present continuous, and the third is a *wh-* clause with a verb in the present continuous.

The effect of placing both the reporting verb, and the *wh-* clause in front of the message is to soften it. Speakers choose these latter two kinds of clause when they are trying to express something negative, or which might be criticised by the listener. Note, however, that if the first verb is strongly emphasised in speaking, the statement can be made **more** emphatic.

2 The speakers/writers use the continuous forms to highlight the current, temporary or unfinished aspect of the event/state.

a) *he is loving it* versus *he loves it*: The continuous form emphasises the temporary nature of the work.

b) *I am thinking about* versus *I think about*: These cannot be used interchangeably. The continuous form means something like 'I am considering', or 'I am trying to decide whether to'. The simple form means that the speaker/writer has the object in mind ('I think about you often').

c) *are wanting to* versus *want to*: The two forms could be used interchangeably, but the speaker wants to emphasise the 'nowness' of the state.

d) *are hoping to* versus *hope to*: as (c).

Further exercises

1 a) ii) is more likely to come from his journal because he is talking about a current, limited event (i.e. what is happening to him) rather than a general truth (e.g. it takes time for international students to get used to British English when they study in the UK).

b) He could use present simple to make a general statement in his journal about all international students: *It takes time for students to become familiar with British English.*

2 a) are living; is getting

b) costs

c) are buying; are suffering

3 a) What I'm saying is he's wrong.

b) What I'm suggesting is we need to discuss this further.

c) What I'm hoping is he'll pay for the meal.

4 a) think; are spending

b) are earning; are still paying; earn

c) is going; am feeling; feel

Unit 4 *Will* or *be going to*?

A

1 If you are informing someone about your plans for the weekend, it would be unlikely that you could use *will*. Sentences which you could use would be e.g.: 'I'm seeing a friend', 'I'm going to a football match.'

- We do not normally use ***will*** + simple form of the verb if we are talking about what we have planned or **already decided** to do.

    A: What are you doing this weekend?
    B: I'm going to do some gardening I think, as long as the weather stays fine. How about you?
    A: Oh, nothing much.

2 a) B: I'm going to have lunch in ten minutes. Thanks anyway.
  b) B: Okay. I'll see you on Saturday.

3 we're going to do; we will have to carry; we're going to do; will be all right; It'll hurt a bit; it will be well

B

1 See Observations in the unit.

2 See Observations in the unit.

C

1 In extract (a) Susan has already decided to start spending the twenty-pound note.
- If she used *will* it would imply that she would only break into it if her friends wanted a drink.
- In extract (b) Helen does not choose *will* because she wants to convey that it is inevitable that the sweets will be eaten!

Further exercises

1 The women use *be going to* to one another when they are informing each other about their choices. When they speak to the waitress they use *will/'ll* because there might be a 'hidden' condition, for example, the food they have chosen may not be available.

2 Katharine Hepburn is going to make another movie.

3 a) The speaker might be drinking too much wine!
  b) The speaker might be asking a friend how much he could sell his car for.
  c) This sounds like a fortune-teller (unless the speaker has already sent a letter).
  d) The speaker is predicting what will happen. Their friend has applied for a job, and the speaker may already work at the same place, or have been interviewed there.

4 a) are going to (reminding)   b) will/'ll (arranging)   c) will/'ll (deciding)
   d) is going to (informing)

Unit 5 *Be + to* forms and other tenses with future reference

A

a) *to sit*; *to challenge*; *to press*; *to be closed*; *set to take charge*
b) *will be asked*; *is expected to*; *is due to*

B

1 a) If Tom<u>'s to go</u> and live with his mother, then so should his sister.
   b) If we<u>'re to get</u> there by five, we'd better drive more quickly.
   c) What<u>'s to happen</u> to all of us, if they move the factory to the north of England?
   d) They'll write if I'm on the shortlist. Otherwise, I<u>'m to assume</u> I haven't got the job.
   ■ All these *be to* forms occur in the context of conditional clauses.
   ■ a) *If Tom goes / is going to go* (~~will go~~ (**✗**))
      b) Future form not possible. See below.
      c) *What will happen ...*
      d) As (b)

Note: In (b) and (d) there is such a strong relationship between the *be to* forms and modal forms
   of obligation that it would be preferable to replace them with *have to* or *must*.

2 *Be + to* in media reports such as newspapers and TV and radio news reports is regularly
   followed by the verb *will*.

C

1 a) <u>*was about to leave*</u>
   b) <u>*it was to take place*</u>
   c) <u>*was to occur*</u>
   d) <u>*I was to play*</u>
   ■ (a)–(d) refer to the future but in each case the past tense is used. When we describe past
      actions in which future actions are referred to we can use *was about to / was to*.
   ■ 'He was about to leave' just means that the event was imminent.
      'I was to play ...' means that the speaker is referring to a fixed schedule of matches
      outside his control.

2 All these sentences refer to events which are going to occur in the near future. In (b) the
   present simple is used because there is a regular timetable for the buses which makes it
   appropriate. In (c) the continuous form suggests that the speaker feels the event is very
   current (see Unit 3).

3 a) Spoken: the use of *just* with *about* makes the expression more colloquial and spoken.
   b) Written: in spoken English we would more usually say *we are flying* or *we're going to fly*.
   c) Written: the use of the passive infinitive with *are to* gives it a more written, formal
      character.

d) Either, however, the passive form makes the sentence rather formal for casual speech. Using *I*, however, makes it more like speech. It could be from a personal letter.

e) Spoken: the continuous form for future reference tends to occur more in speech since it is used for imminent or near future events.

f) Either: however, the combination of the *be to* and the passive makes this more typical of writing.

Further exercises

1 a) What is to happen to us now that the factory has closed?

b) The Foreign Minister is to issue a statement later in the day.

c) What are we to make of all the stories about aliens?

d) The company is to deliver the goods by next month at the latest.

2 (a) + (vi): The school **was** to close.

(b) + (viii): She **was** to be promoted.

(c) + (ii): They **were** on the verge of selling the house.

(d) + (vii): The minister **was** due to speak at the conference.

(e) + (iv): They **were** all set to start work on Tuesday.

(f) + (v): If they **were** to get there by five, they needed to hurry.

(g) + (iii): If Tom **was/were** (*were* is more formal and more hypothetical) to go and live with his sister, then his family should have been (or, if *were* is used, then *should be*) informed.

(h) + (i): The town **was** about to be attacked.

3 a) **You'll be freed** could also be *are to be freed*; **It's going to be** could not really become *is to be* as it suggests someone else has destined you for this, whereas *going to* simply predicts what you will experience.

b) **You'll find**, as with *going to* in (a), above, would not be as suitable as *are to find* here, since this is what you will experience, not what someone/something else has decided or destined for you.

c) **You'll be** could be *are to be* for the same reasons as in (a); **you'll realise** is not as suitable as *are to realise* here for the same reason as in (a) and (b).

4 is/'s getting; is/'s coming down; is/'s coming; is/'s sleeping

5 a) Hostages to be released tomorrow.

b) Strong winds to cause serious damage across the country.

c) Top band to release new summer album.

d) Six ministers to have resigned by weekend.

Unit 6 *Can* and *could*

A

	could	*can*	*can't*
possibility	a) could it have been? c) it could be		
capacity or ability	b) could he tell ...		a) Can't remember
impossibility			e) it can't be
none of the above		d) you can sometimes find	

B

1 a) a bank   b) a computer firm   c) a bank   d) a website agency

2 a) The first *could* expresses ability. You can paraphrase it as follows:
> *To find out what **we would be able to do** for you.*

The second example expresses probability:
> *Maybe, it will change your life.*

When used to express probability, *could* cannot be replaced by *can*:
> *It ~~can~~ change your life.* (✗)

b) It is grammatically possible to replace *could* with *can*, but the meaning is different.
> *We **could** leave it all till later* expresses a hypothetical situation (would be possible to) and is a less strong suggestion than We can leave it all till later (nothing prevents us / we are able to).

c) Yes, but the meaning is different as in (b).
> *There's no way you **could** achieve that* ... (hypothetical situation, would be able to)

3 Only (d) is synonymous with *is able to*.

C

1 a) not possible to prevent yourself from
  b) not possible to prevent yourself from
  c) not able to be certain of
  d) not able to be certain of
  e) not able to come

  ■ Past tense forms:
  a) You *couldn't* help having feelings for someone
  b) You *couldn't* help wondering whether it wasn't the media trying to influence things.
  c) In this sentence the speaker is making a very general statement and changing from *can* to *could* makes it more hypothetical rather than having real past time reference.
  d) This is similar to (c). If the doctor says *I **couldn't** say whether it would happen to you*, it becomes more hypothetical in this context.
  e) I *couldn't* make it last night.

2 Only one possibility is given in each case here but many others are possible.
   a) customer to waiter, **MF**
   b) friend to friend, **LF**
   c) customer to shop assistant, **LF**
   d) passenger in car, **LF**
   e) customer ordering food in a restaurant, **LF**, but *please* makes it slightly more formal.
   f) business colleague making arrangements, **MF**
   g) customer asking for refund, **MF**
   h) friend to friend, **LF**

Further exercises

1 a) (Done as example.)
   b) *could*; time reference: future; meaning: will possibly be able to
   c) *could*; time reference: past; meaning: were able to

2 a) *Can*   b) *can't*

3

expression	following construction
can't help	wondering if I made the right decision
can't tell	if the postmark is Nottingham or Northampton
can't say	who told me
can't make	the party

Unit 7 *Will* and *would*

A

   a) photography, *will come out well*, future
   b) place of work, *won't be there anyway*, future
   c) political views, *won't even vote*, present
   d) in a restaurant, *would you like*, present
   e) city life and country life, *wouldn't come back*, present
   f) life with a new baby, *wouldn't sleep*, past

B

1 a) John: We can get the plates out when we're going to have our dinner but if we get them
        out now we might break them and where [**would**] we be then?
    Lucy: We [**wouldn't**] be able to have our dinner.
    John: We ['**d**] have nothing to eat our dinner off. We ['**d**] have to eat our dinner off the
        floor then, and that [**would**] mean cleaning the floor first.
    Lucy: And that ['**d**] be a terrible thing to have to do!
   b) John: I ['**ll**] get the plates.
    Lucy: Yeah, ok, but I ['**ll**] need to warm them, so don't put them there.

2 a) (iii)   b) (iii)   c) (ii)

C

1 These are possible answers; many others are acceptable.

- Pollution: It wouldn't surprise me if the government started asking industry to pay to clean up its pollution soon.
  Education: I'd say exams are getting harder, not easier.
  Newspapers: Wouldn't it be a good idea if newspapers stopped taking photographs of people to try and embarrass them.
  Transport: I wouldn't say cars were the problem, it's drivers!
  (The most tentative of the constructions is *Wouldn't it be a good idea if*...)
- You can ask people their opinion by saying *Would you say ... ?*, *Would it surprise you if ... ?* or *Would it be a good idea if ... ?*
- You form the past tense with the auxiliary *have*:
  It wouldn't have surprised me ..., I would have said ..., Would it have been a good idea ... and so on.

2 a) So what do you think would happen? (future, hypothetical)
  So what do you think would have happened? (past, hypothetical)
  So what do you think happened? (past, real)
  b) I wouldn't drive a Jeep. (present, 'volition')
  I wouldn't drive the Jeep. (past, 'volition'. The use of the definite article changes the sense to a specific occasion when the speaker refused to drive.)
  c) The baby wouldn't sleep. (past, 'volition')
  The baby wouldn't have slept. (past, hypothetical)
  The baby didn't sleep. (past, real)
  d) The job will be difficult to get. (future, fact)
  The job would be difficult to get. (future, hypothetical: You are not going to apply.)
  The job would have been difficult to get. (past, hypothetical: You did not apply.)

Further exercises

1 a) would; wouldn't   b) would   c) wouldn't   d) would   e) will

2 a) hypothetical situation   b) future action, conditional on something else
  c) prediction   d) volition   e) volition   f) future action   g) prediction

3

expression	*following construction*
I'd say	he was older than he looks.
It wouldn't surprise me	if he was older than he looks.
Wouldn't it be sensible	to just ask him?

Unit 8 *May, might* and *must*

A

1 a) Nick: He might be in the garden. You never know.   YES
b) Nick: He may be in the garden. He often has lunch outside on sunny days.   YES
c) Nick: He must be in the garden. You never know.   NO

- When the speaker says 'He *must* be in the garden', he is very sure. Therefore, 'You never know', which shows doubt, is a contradiction here.

2 a) Fred: Sorry, I probably just forgot.   YES
b) Fred: Yes, I can't remember now who I told and who I didn't.   YES
c) Fred: Did I? How can you be so sure?   NO

- (c) is unlikely since George sounds as if he is not sure that he knows the other person was away.

3 a) John: Hmm, so it's just possible she is.   NO
b) John: Yes, there's no way she can be less than that.   YES
c) John: Oh, it's impossible to say.   NO

- (a) and (c) are not possible here since the speaker is very sure that the person is over 70.

B

1 See Observations in the unit.

2 a) No real difference.
b) *May* expresses a stronger possibility.
c) No real difference.
d) *May* expresses a stronger possibility.

3 a) Type 2   b) Type 4   c) Type 5   d) Type 1   e) Type 3   f) Type 2
g) Type 2   h) Type 4   i) Type 3   j) Type 2   k) Type 5

C

1 All the gaps have *may* in them.

2 Possible sentences:
a) I might have guessed he would be late. He always is.
b) Damage to the walls may arise from dampness.
c) If I may say so, that's an extraordinary jacket. Where did you get it?
d) It's what you might call a 'povel', a mixture of a poem and a novel.
e) I must admit, I wasn't expecting such a big response to our appeal for support.
f) I must say, this is the best restaurant we've ever been to.
g) May I offer my condolences. I heard about your uncle's death. I'm very sorry.

Further exercises

1 a) i) YES   ii) YES   iii) NO
    b) i) YES   ii) NO   iii) YES
    c) i) NO   ii) YES   iii) NO

2 a) must   b) might   c) may   d) must
    e) might/may/must (*May* is a stronger decision than *might*, and *must* is an order to yourself to do something.)
    f) may/might (*May* is more probable than *might*.); *must*
    g) Must   h) might   i) might
    j) May/might (*Might* is much more formal here than *may.*)

3 a) I needn't hurry. The train leaves at 6.30.
    b) I wouldn't/couldn't (**or:** I would never) have guessed that Ivor would end up marrying Nellie.
    c) I may not be in the office tomorrow. I'll ring you and let you know.
    d) Visitors to the zoo must not feed the animals.
    e) She might not be his sister, you never know.

- In (a) and (b) it is not possible to just make the verb negative without changing the meaning.

4

expression	conclusion
I must say/admit, ...	... you were right.
May I offer my ...	... sympathy.
I might have guessed ...	... he would leave before the bill came!
If I may say so, ...	... you're wrong.
It's what you might call ...	... 'restructuring'.

Unit 9 *Shall* and *should*

A

- a) shall   b) should   c) should; shall
- a) You can say *I should be able to get out of this cul-de sac*, but the meaning is different (i.e. hypothetical). Because the rest of the conversation uses the future form *'ll* (*will*), rather than *'d* (*would*), it would sound strange for this speaker to use the more hypothetical form here.
    b) You cannot say *you shall always try your best* because the speaker is using *should* to express obligation. The two forms are not interchangeable in this context.
    c) *Maybe we shall make an arrangement for the week after next* is not possible. *Should* is being used to express advisability here, in which case *shall* is not interchangeable with it. *So that we should be sure to meet* is grammatical, but the meaning is slightly different (i.e. more hypothetical).
- *Shall* is used to refer to future events.

B

1 a) _should be enough_   b) _should be leaving_   c) _we <u>shall</u> probably_   d) _I <u>shall</u> ever_
- _Shall_ is used to talk about individuals' futures.
- _Should_ is often used to talk about facts (or speakers' attitude to facts).

2 Only the _should_ in (a) can be replaced with _shall_. All the others can be replaced with _ought to_.

C

1 a) shall   b) shall

2 a) suggesting/arranging
b) introducing an awkward point
c) guessing/speculating
d) agreeing (strongly)
e) guessing/speculating. This use is often expressed as _I'd say_. The other use (b) above, is never shortened.

Further exercises

1 a) will probably

It is grammatically possible to replace _should_ with _shall_ in this extract, because the pronoun is _we_. However, this makes the modal verb equivalent to _will_ and therefore changes the meaning, making it more definite.

b) ought to (all examples)

In this conversation, it is not possible to replace the first two or the last examples of _should_ with _shall_ because the grammatical subjects (_the family, they_) are not first person. The other two examples (_we should_) could be replaced with _shall_, but it would then sound as if the couple were more definite about the visit.

c) will probably

It is not possible to replace this example of _should_ with _shall_.

2 a) shall   b) shall (_should_ is possible)   c) should; should

3 (possible examples)
I should say, I don't have enough money to pay – could you lend me some?

A: He looks ill.
B: He's been drinking. I should say.

I should imagine he'll be very late – he rang to say he had missed his train.

A: He'll pass his driving test this time, won't he?
B: He certainly should. It's his fifth attempt.

I don't want this meeting to go on too long – shall we say half an hour?

Unit 10 Other modal forms

A

The modal items are underlined.
a) I look forward to Christmas. It <u>seems</u> to be the only time the whole family gets together.
b) There have been burglaries in the neighbourhood, but I <u>reckon</u> we're safe here.
c) There are managers, and the junior staff <u>are meant</u> to report back to them.
d) I'm sorry, it's not my department. You <u>need</u> to contact the person who's responsible.

B

1
a) *Tend* stresses more the frequency or regularity with which the family gets together. *Seem* focuses more on the speaker's opinion, how he/she sees things.
b) *Ought* focuses on the ideal state of things in the speaker's mind. *I reckon* focuses more on the speaker's own judgement or personal opinion.
c) *Be to* is a very formal, authoritative way of expressing a decision, order or rule/regulation. *Are meant to* makes the obligation weaker, and means 'it is the general intention that this should happen'.
d) *Have to* suggests a much stronger obligation than *need to*.

2
a) I *seem to* have lost your letter. I'm sorry.
b) It *seems to* be the case that nobody knew what was happening.

c) She *ought to* be **or** *was meant to* be here answering the phone. I don't know why she isn't. (*ought to* is stronger here)
d) That plastic cover *ought to/was* (**or** *is*) *meant to* keep it dry, but it didn't work.

e) This *ought to* be the last one. Let me just check.
f) You really *ought to* pay more attention to what I tell you.

g) This *has to* be the coldest day of the year; it's absolutely freezing!
h) You *have to* take all your documents. If there's anything missing, they'll just send you away.

i) I *reckon* the best way to get there is to take the bus.
j) This restaurant is *reckoned* to be the best in town.

k) You *need to* explain the situation to Barbara; she'll tell you what to do.
l) This system *needs to* be changed; it just isn't working.

m) We *tend to* like less crowded places when it comes to holidays.
n) I don't recommend this program. It *tends to* be difficult to use if you aren't a computer expert.

o) The lists *are to* be ready by next Tuesday, without fail. Could everyone make a note of that please?
p) It *was to* be the happiest day of his life, but it ended in disaster.

C

1 First group: (a), (d), (e), (g)
All these verbs have the negative *not / 'nt* immediately following the verb.
Second group: (b), (c), (f), (h)
All these verbs contain *be* in their structure.

2

a) It seems

I've let you down.	✓
as if everyone has a cold today.	✓
starting to rain.	✗
to have got burnt on the edges.	✓

b) It needs

that it's repaired.	✗
to be looked at.	✓
painting.	✓

c) It needn't

be so loud.	✓
be looked at.	✓
painting.	✗

d) It tends

that it lasts only a short time.	✗
to break easily.	✓
not to run regularly.	✓

e) It doesn't tend

that it lasts very long.	✗
to last very long.	✓
last very long.	✗

f) It ought

never to have happened.	✓
be changed immediately.	✗
not to surprise anyone.	✓
n't matter too much how we do it.	✓ *
to be forbidden.	✓

g) It didn't ought*

to happen.	✓
happen.	✗
happening.	✗

h) Does it

seem right to you?	✓
tend to happen often?	✓
ought to be sent by airmail?	✗
have to be covered?	✓
meant to work only when the light is on?	✗

---

* Some speakers use this form, but many would reject it as ungrammatical. The form without *to* is only heard where the negative follows *ought*. It is not acceptable in (g).

3 a)

	to be okay.	*okay.*	*that it's okay.*	*as if/as though it's okay.*
It seems	✓	✓	?	✓
It appears	✓	✓	✓	✓
It looks	?	✓	✗	✓
It sounds	✗	✓	✗	✓

b)

	to happen.	*that it will happen.*
It's bound	✓	✗
It's likely	✓	✓
It's liable	✓	✗
It's probable	✗	?

c)

	it's the best way to do it.	*it to be the best way to do it.*
I think	✓	?
I guess	✓	✗
I reckon	✓	✓
I consider	?	✓
I suppose	✓	?

d)

	to be the best method.	*the best method.*
It's thought	✓	?
It's guessed	✗	✗
It's reckoned	✓	✗
It's considered	✓	✓
It's supposed	✓	✗

Further exercises

1 a) tend; have to / ought to   b) seems   c) ought to / have to   d) have to
   e) was meant to / was to   f) are to / have to

2 a) I *tend not* to use salt when I cook. **or:** I *don't tend* to use salt when I cook.
   b) *Oughtn't we* to send those forms off to get our money back? **or:** *Ought we not* **to send**
      those forms off to get our money back? The latter is more formal.
   c) You *don't have to* write your telephone number in the box. **or:** You *needn't* write your
      telephone number in the box. **or:** You *don't need* to write your telephone number in the
      box.
   d) She *seems not to have* noticed it. **or:** She *doesn't seem to have* noticed it.
   e) I *don't reckon* it's worth waiting three weeks.
   f) You *don't need* to fill out a form. **or:** You *needn't* fill out a form.

3

a) It needs

that it's painted.	✗
to be covered with something.	✓
repairing.	✓
be black.	✗

b) It needn't

be eaten today.	✓
cleaning.	✗

c) It tends

that it gets dirty.	✗
to stick to your hands.	✓
not to grow very well in a cold climate.	✓

d) It doesn't tend

that it cooks very easily.	✗
to cook very easily.	✓
cook very easily.	✗

e) It ought

never to have been allowed.	✓
be closed for good.	✗
not to happen that way.	✓
n't make any difference really.	✓ *
to be free	✓

f) It didn't ought

to go like that.	✓
go like that.	✗
going like that.	✗

g) Does it

seem crazy?	✓
tend to work better at night?	✓
ought to be put in a plastic bag?	✗
have to be repainted very often?	✓
meant to include everyone?	✗

* This form of the negative is acceptable to some but not all British speakers.

Unit 11 *If*-constructions

A

1 a) (answers given in unit)
b) *if* + present simple + present continuous of *go* + infinitive with *to*
c) *if* + present simple + imperative
d) *if* + present simple + interrogative present
e) *if* + present simple + modal + verb
f) *if* + negative present simple + modal + verb
g) *if* + negative past simple + *would* + verb

- Only (g) fits the second type of conditional sentence given.

2 John: If it ever [**gets**] off the ground, it [**would be**] a good thing for Derby, if it [**gets**] off.
Sharon: What the park?
John: Yeah.
Interviewer: What do you think of that?
Sharon: Well I don't know. Do you know the latest? I [**was wondering**] if that [**was**] what you meant. The millennium thing?
John: Yeah.

- When we speculate about the future in an *if*-clause, we can use either a present or past tense in the clause. The choice of the present tense makes the possibility sound more certain, the choice of the past tense makes the possibility sound a little more remote. The structure *I wonder if* / *wondered if* / *was wondering if* can be followed by either past or present. In this example, the speaker chooses the present to make the speculation sound more immediate and certain.

3 The text is a recipe. The use of conditionals gives the reader choices and allows the reader decisions. Some recipes are no more than lists of instructions but this recipe is different. It is more sensitive to readers and involves them.

B

1 a) and b) (answers given in unit)   c) B   d) A   e) B
f) A   g) B   h) B

2 a) Unless   b) provided that   c) Supposing that   d) on condition that
e) whether or not   f) whether to   g) Given that

- All the sentences except (f) can be replaced by *if*. (b), (c), (d) and (g) are more formal alternatives to *if* and more likely to occur in written English. (a) introduces a negative condition, so would become, *If they do not change the team, they're going to lose the next match*. (f) cannot be used with *if* because it would precede an infinitive: I do not know if to go. (✗)

3 Neither of the uses of *if* in extracts (a) or (b) introduce conditions.
- Both uses of *if* signal requests or invitations. In such functions the *if*-clause is not normally linked to any other clause.

C

1 a) *if you like* = offering an interpretation
   b) *if you want a drink* = making a suggestion/offer; *if we have this* = making a suggestion; *if you need to cut it open* = making a suggestion
   c) *If you look at this photograph here* = giving reasons/explanations and introducing something; *If you look at this one* = making a suggestion
   d) *If you would like to return your original insurance certificate to us* = making a suggestion

2 Suggested answers:
You will often be able to treat your child's common illnesses at home but, *if in doubt*, call your doctor or health visitor.
Check whether they're in. *If so*, why don't you invite them to join us. *If not*, ask those friends of yours next door.
Ring me before you go, *if possible*.
If anything, her sister is even more beautiful.
The train might be full, but, *if necessary*, you can upgrade your ticket to first-class.
If only we had enough money, we could buy a bigger car.
If ever you see him, tell him he's not to come back.

D

Suggested answers:
a) If you want beautiful smooth skin, try the new gentle soap by Orsin.
b) If you want to escape the big city, then a holiday on the Greek island of Spetses is for you.
c) If you enjoyed Zig-Zag's half-a-million-selling debut album, then you'll want to rush out and buy their latest release.

Further exercises

1 a) If you have lost money, contact the police.
   b) If I went to Germany, I would visit Berlin.
   c) If you don't eat too much, you'll stay slim.
   d) If she liked spaghetti, she must have been Italian.
   e) If David phones, you must take the call.
   f) If the weather had not changed, the holiday would have been miserable.
   g) If I were as tired as you, I should take a holiday.
   h) If I had enough money, I would buy a bigger car.
   i) If you can't sleep, take some sleeping tablets.
   j) If they like wine, I like drinking beer.

2 These are suggested completions:

a) can/could/will   b) shall   c) can/could/will   d) will   e) would   f) is

g) you are lifting heavy objects   h) the shop is closed   i) you visit Moscow

j) you couldn't come   k) I'd known she would react like that

l) we'd heard the weather forecast

3 Suggested answers:

a) spoken/written   b) spoken   c) spoken/idiomatic   d) spoken/idiomatic

e) spoken/idiomatic   f) spoken   g) written   h) spoken

i) spoken/idiomatic   j) spoken   k) spoken/idiomatic

4 The products advertised are:

a) a camera   b) a car   c) an insurance company
d) the Royal Society for the Deaf

- The use of a single sentence gives more impact.
- The conditional creates a possible situation which is normally resolved by the product mentioned in the main clause.

Unit 12 *Wh*-constructions

A

See Observations in unit.

B

1 a) *What matters when you're young is that junk food tastes great ...* (iii)
b) *What you need is a list of addresses, plenty of time, determination and a phone.* (i)
c) *What is most important ... is that human beings should always come before economic profit.* (i)

2 a) *I forgot to bring the candle* was originally, *What I forgot to bring was the candle.*
b) *I have my tea and go straight to bed* was originally, *I have my tea and what I do is go straight to bed.*
c) *It's the lack of support that causes them ill health* was originally, *What causes them ill health is the lack of support.*

C

1 a) *Where I saw myself ...* (The focus is on his different perspective in the past.)
b) *Where you lived,* (This introduces the topic.)
c) *Why I like this structure ...* (Having described the structure, he focuses on his opinion of it.)
d) *How I got involved was ... .* (She focuses on the reason/method she joined the club.)

2 See Observations in unit.

Further exercises

1 *That* in brackets will often be omitted in informal speech. The same applies to *to* in (c) and (d).
a) Why he didn't tell us was (that) he thought we wouldn't believe him.
b) Where I misunderstood her was (that) I thought she was complaining.
c) What you really should have done was (to) write it all down so there could be no dispute.

d) What the government must now do is (to) pass a law forbidding such sales as soon as possible.

e) Why she should have gone without saying goodbye was a mystery to all of us.

2 a) We got lost when/in that we turned left instead of right, just as you come into the village.

b) It is a great mystery why certain animals can sense when people are upset.

c) You ought to really be worried about yourself, not your sister.

d) I wanted to know whether you were interested or not.

e) She got herself in such a mess because she got her foot caught in the hosepipe (or: by getting her foot caught in the hosepipe).

3 a) *Who* I'd really like to get to know is that good-looking cousin of yours.

b) *Where* the government has failed is in the relationship between exports and employment.

c) *How* that cat found its way home from 100 miles away is incredible!

d) *What* you really need more than anything is a good holiday.

e) *Why* all children should be given the chance of further education is that without it nowadays, you're unemployable.

f) *What* George was trying to say was that we should go back to square one.

4 i) B ii) D iii) E iv) A v) C

Unit 13 *It, this, that*

A

1

	Example	Reasons for this or that
a)	in this country	Joan refers to the country where the speakers are at the time of speaking.
b)	in this weather	Bill uses *this* to refer to the weather at the moment of speaking, which everyone can see or knows about.
c)	That was West Bay (×2)	Bill and Margaret use *that* to refer back in time and place to the spot where they got swept by the wind.

Note: There is a contrast between something immediate, here and now (when we usually use *this*) and something distant and/or separated from the speakers in some way (when we usually use *that*). These are basic meanings of *this* and *that* (and their plurals, *these* and *those*).

2 Dorothy uses the basic form *it* to refer to the whole event. Gerry says *How long ago was **that*** because the time and place are separated and distant (as in 1, above). However, he also uses *this* when asking about which car Dorothy was in, *Was **this** in ....* This seems to highlight the situation, making it feel more immediate and important. Note that the choice between *this* and *that* is Gerry's. He can make something distant (*that*), or bring it into sharp focus in the present (*this*).

Dorothy replies *It was in my own car*, and Gerry repeats it in his next comment. When the speakers change from *this* to *it*, they are just continuing their topic, without focusing on anything in particular.

B

1 (a) and (b) = (iii)   (c) and (d) = (iii)   (e) and (f) = (i)

- In extract (e), *that* refers to the process of analysing style, i.e. not just the final word of the first sentence but the whole phrase.

2 *It* is used to continue referring to what the speakers are already talking about in (3), (4) and (5).
It is also used in tags (since tags repeat what we are already talking about. We would not say *That's on this floor, is that?*).
This is used for an important, new topic (1), and for the place where the speakers are (6).
That is used for something just mentioned, but which is not going to be important in the story (2).

C

See Observations section in unit.

Further exercises

1 Words as used by the speaker.

A: She's about eighty-odd. She had somebody knocking at her windows shouting "Fire! fire!" and **it** was just a trick to get her out of the house, you see.

[The speaker is simply continuing his topic. He could have said *this*, which would have made this particular statement more prominent in the story. He could have said *that*, which would have made the statement more marginal, less important.]

B: Mm.
A: And er she was very sensible, the old lady was, she phoned.
B: Good.
A: And how we heard about **this**, it was the following morning,

[Speakers often use *this* to refer to a whole set of important events or ideas: *it* would have been correct, but would have made the events less prominent/important; *that* would have made the events even less important for this moment in the conversation]

the window cleaner came. I told him about **it**.

[Nothing new is being said here, so *it* is clearly the best word to repeat the reference to the events; this or that would have sounded odd here.]

He couldn't clean the windows because the detectives were there. The detectives came. **That's** how we heard about **it**.

[Speakers often use *that* when they are rounding off the story, signalling a summary or conclusion. *It* or *this* would not have been appropriate here. It here simply continues reference to the events as a whole, and it would have been odd to use this or that at this point, since nothing new is being added.]

B: Mm.
A: And that was that.

[This expression means 'that was the end of it, no more happened'.]

A: **That's** about the only incident though.

[Again, the story is finished, and the speaker is signalling that it is completed, not still an important topic; *it* or *this* would have been suitable.]

Well, I had the flu. I finished up with … **that's** got nothing to do with crime.

[*That* is a good choice here because it stresses the irrelevance of mentioning flu in connection with the stories about crime. *This* would have suggested 'flu' was important, and *it* would have suggested that the topic was continuing.]

B: **That's** all right.

[This expression is a common way of responding to an apology or acknowledgement of a mistake, such as A admitting that he has changed the subject without meaning to.]

2 a) Daniel felt his life did not begin the day he was born. **It** began when he first saw Mary in the schoolhouse sixteen years ago.
   b) Daniel took the little package. He unwrapped **it** and then smiled. It's gold sovereigns, Mary. His eyes held wide. 'Sure,' she smiled. '**It's** for us to go to America. You've always wanted to go there. Let's go, Daniel, while we can get out.'
   c) The forest was silent and so were the women. They walked steadily, cat-like. **This** moment had been long-rehearsed. Anna, from when she was a baby, knew **this** secret path into the forest and she approved of it.

3 a) this is it   b) this, that and the other   c) that's that (that's it, also possible, but less emphatic)   d) that's it (that's that also possible, but more emphatic)   e) and that

Some of these have been dealt with in the unit. Here is some information about the others:

- *This is it* is an informal expression that means roughly 'this is the important point, something we should take great note of'.
- *This, that and the other* is an informal expression meaning 'general, unconnected things, no particularly important topic'.
- *And that* is a very informal expression meaning 'and such/similar things'.

Unit 14 Passives and pseudo-passives

A

1

A Correct	B Incorrect or inappropriate
b) Languages are taught in every school in the country.	a) The station was left by the train five minutes ago. (Correction: The train left the station five minutes ago.)
c) My jacket was made in England.	
e) Paper was invented by the Chinese.	d) He was died by his brother. (Correction: He was killed by his brother.)
f) The new road will be completed early next year.	
h) The interview is being televised throughout the world.	g) Two litres are contained by the bottle. (Correction: The bottle contains two litres.)
j) You could see that he was going to be attacked by a large dog.	i) A nice house is had by them. (Correction: They have a nice house.)

Rules about passives:

- A passive cannot be formed using an intransitive verb.[1] ('He died' or 'He was killed by his brother', but not 'He was died by his brother'; 'I arrived in London' not 'London was arrived in by me'.)
- A passive cannot be formed using stative verbs[2] (e.g. verbs such as *fit*, *have*, *suit*, *seem*, *resemble*, or *contain*) which refer to states not actions. ('They have a nice house', but not 'A nice house is had by them'; 'The coat really suits you' not 'You are really suited by the coat'.)
- It is not normally appropriate for the least important piece of information in a message to be placed at the beginning of a sentence. In sentence (a) it is correct to say, therefore, that 'The train left the station five minutes ago'. A passive clause would normally be inappropriate.

2 got pushed forward; we'd got hit; had got sort of pushed in; get his eyes tested.

- All these forms except one are examples of the *get*-passive. *had two recovery vehicles free* is also a passive but not a *get*-passive. The structure is discussed in **B2** and **C3** of the unit.

B

1 a) the house <u>was called</u> Commonwood House
b) The hospital where Maggie in *Little Dorrit* **<u>was treated</u>** for fever
c) As a result of the 25-mile Challenge £200 **<u>was raised</u>** for the Cancer Appeal.
d) Most of the work **<u>was completed</u>** before the start of the nineteenth century. Thus the next chapter will focus on how land <u>was farmed</u> in Northamptonshire and Bedfordshire in the eighteenth century. Changes after 1700 <u>will not</u> **be discussed.**

See Observations in the unit for comments on why the agents are not included.

2 *get* + past participle: a), e) and g)
have + object + past participle: c) and f)
'standard' passive: b) and d)

(a) a conversation about criminal justice (b) a conversation about salaries

(c) a conversation about hospital treatment (d) a conversation about crime

(e) a conversation about business practices (f) a story about an injury

(g) an interview about working as an air stewardess

C

1 See Observations in unit.

2 Most of these examples contain negative verbs.

- The exceptions are: get promoted, and get picked for the team.

---

[1]An intransitive verb is a verb which does not take a direct object. For example, *An hour **elapsed***, or *The actress **blushed** several times during the interview.*
[2]A stative verb is a verb which expresses states of being or processes in which there is no obvious action. See also Glossary p.183.

■ The events people are talking about are often problematic. In most cases the speaker is adversely affected by the action or evaluates the process negatively.

3 a) The *have*-passives, *had three plumbers come in* and *had it cut* involve another person doing something for the speaker. The *get*-passives, *got my head stuck* and *got frozen up* do not involve a person other than the speaker.

   b) The following would probably be marked*.
   ii) (This sounds very formal for this topic.)
   iv) (Again, it would need a very formal context for this to be acceptable.)
   vi) (This sounds as if the person arranged the event!)
   vii)(This sounds as if the event happened without the person asking for it!)

Further exercises

1 The *Mona Lisa* was painted by Leonardo da Vinci.
America was discovered by Christopher Columbus.
The telephone was invented by Alexander Graham Bell.
War and Peace was written by Tolstoy.
Born in the USA is sung by Bruce Springsteen.

2 i) (example done in text)
   ii) + (d) The metal should be heated up to a high temperature.
   iii) + (f) The centre of the old town is being rebuilt.
   iv) + (c) The video recorders are all manufactured in Singapore.
   v) + (e) The other candidate must have been interviewed earlier in the morning.
   vi) + (b) The new supermarket was opened by a pop star.

3 i) (example done in text)
   ii) Dogs should be kept on a lead.
   iii) Cars must not be parked on the grass.
   iv) Diving is not allowed in the swimming area.
   v) English is spoken here.
   vi) Fees can be paid at the entrance.

4 double glazed; lost; trapped; reduced; decreased; reduced; installed; fitted.

   Agents are not normally referred to in scientific writing. More emphasis is placed on impersonal actions and processes.

5 i) (example done in text)
   ii) My house was broken into last night. / My house got broken into last night.
   iii) My driving licence must be renewed by January. / I must get my driving licence renewed by January.
   iv) My car is (was) fixed. / I had my car fixed.
   v) My club fees are always paid by my parents. / I have my club fees paid by my parents.

6 Suggested answers:
   Headline A uses the active voice because IBM is clearly responsible for the action.
   Headline B uses the passive voice because responsibility is not clear.
   Headline C uses the agentless passive because it does not want to make IBM responsible.
   Instead it suggests that the factory workers are responsible for their own dismissal.

Unit 15 Position of adverbs

A

a) (Answer given in the exercise.)
b) At the front of the clause.
c) Between the subject and the verb.
d) Between the subject and the verb, but after the first auxiliary verb.
e) Same as c). *Had* is a main verb here, and *'ve* is an auxiliary.
f) Between subject and verb; *have* is a main verb here.
g) After the verb *be*.
h) Between subject and verb, but after the first auxiliary verb. (*Being* is an auxiliary here. The main verb is *accused.*)
i) See below.

- (i) is wrong because in English, we do not normally put any adverbs between the verb and the direct object.

B

1 a) i)   b) i)   c) ii)

Suggested rules:
Adverbs with the *going to* future. Rule: The normal position for adverbs is between *be* and *going to* (in other words, after the first auxiliary verb, since *going* is an auxiliary in this construction. Compare 'I am going to the cinema,' where *going* is a main verb).
Adverbs with *do/does/did* in questions. Rule: The normal position for adverbs is after the subject (in this case *you*) and before the main verb (in this case *go*).
Adverbs with the *get*-passive form. Rule: The normal position for adverbs is between the subject and *get*. *Get* does not operate like an auxiliary verb in the *get*-passive construction (for example, a question would be formed with *do*, not by inversion: 'Did he get injured?' **not:** 'Got he injured?' (✗))

2 a) Many short adverbs (e.g. *just* (as in sentence (a)), *only, also, even*) are often found in the position between subject and verb.
b) Intensifying (and downtoning) adverbs are often found in this position too (e.g. *actually, certainly, sort of, hardly, definitely.*)
c) Negative adverbs occur in this position too (e.g. *not.*)
d) Adverbs of indefinite frequency occur here too (e.g. *seldom, sometimes, often.*)

- In (e), *honestly* is a **viewpoint** (sometimes called **comment**) adverb. It does not tell us **how** something happened, but what the speaker's viewpoint or perspective is. In (f), *honestly* tells us **how** he dealt with people, and so it is an adverb of manner. Viewpoint adverbs often occur between subject and verb; manner adverbs normally go after.

3 a) manner/time   b) place/time   c) place/time i) True ii) False iii) False
iv) True   d) manner/frequency/time   e) time/reason
f) manner/frequency   g) manner/reason

C

1 Both (a) and (b) have adverbs between the verb and the direct object, which is not normally acceptable in English. However, it does happen in journalistic style, in spoken and written contexts.

■ c) Suggested informal spoken version (i.e. adverb after the direct object):

The US Senate approved a bill on Sunday that would compensate Indian tribes in North Michigan for short-changing their ancestors in a 19th-century land deal.

2 See Observations in unit.

Further exercises

1 a) They're **probably** going to sell up and move out.
(Adverbs normally go between *be* and *going* in the *be going to* future.)
b) I **suddenly** got thrown out of my seat.
(With the *get*-passive, adverbs usually go before get.)
c) The tickets are on sale **twice a week**.
(With expressions of definite frequency, adverbs usually follow the verb and any object or complement.)
d) I **simply** did my duty.
(Short adverbs often go between the subject and the verb. Here *do* is a main verb, not an auxiliary.)
e) I couldn't **honestly** think of any reason to say no.
(Adverbs expressing the speaker's viewpoint usually go between the subject and the verb.)
f) He's **usually** the first to complain.
(Adverbs of indefinite frequency usually go between the subject and the verb (compare (c)).
g) She wouldn't allow it **under any circumstances**.
(Adverbs describing the situation or circumstances in which something happens are like manner adverbs and go after the verb and any object or complement.)
h) Would you **just** sign the bottom, please?
(Short adverb (see (d)) with interrogatives, the adverb is placed after the subject.)
i) We **always** have dinner at 6.30, you know that.
(Adverbs of indefinite frequency usually go between the subject and the verb. Here, *have* is a main verb, not an auxiliary.)
j) She always dealt **honestly** with her clients.
(Here *honestly* is a manner adverb (compare (e)), and goes after the verb.)

2 Position of adverbs in the original text:

In 1943 there were two taxis **on the island; by the early sixties, according to popular memory**, this number had rocketed to three.
Almost more remarkable is another pair of statistics relating to private cars.
In the mid-fifties, remembers **one** eminent Ibicenco, there were 'twenty or thirty' cars **on the whole island;** now Ibiza has the highest number of cars per head **in Europe**.
A handful of ancient buses ploughed their way **into town from the villages**, some of which had only one service a day, necessitating long queues **in village squares in the early hours of the morning**.

Comments:

In four cases, time adverbs are fronted (*in 1943, by the early sixties, in the mid-fifties, now*). This is a historical text, and it is organised around a time frame.

Into town from the villages could have been *from the villages into town*, without any real change in the meaning, since these are adverbs of the same class (place adverbs).
In village squares in the early hours of the morning follows the normal order of place adverb before time adverb.

3 a) Here the adverb comes between the verb and the direct object, which is rare except in journalistic styles.
   b) Here the adverb *never ever* comes before the first auxiliary verb, which puts great emphasis on the adverb.
   c) Here *really* follows the second auxiliary verb, *been*, which is unusual. *Really* especially emphasises the verb *longing* as a result.
   d) The adverb of frequency comes at the beginning of the sentence, which is a very emphatic position for it.
   e) This is a very formal word order, with a longer adverb coming after the first auxiliary verb.

Unit 16 Articles 1: *the*

A

   a) ( ) Tensions between ( ) three middle-aged couples after a blonde stranger arrives are explored in a 1984 Greek film.
   b) A hideous comic-book monster comes to ( ) life and terrifies a creepy house where a student lives. (**The**) monster is scary but (**the**) film is not.
   c) Stella: I've only seen (**the**) midwife once.
      Doctor: Right. Right. Okay. Did she explain to you what ( ) 'case-load midwifery' involves?
      Stella: That I would actually see her right from (**the**) beginning, [Doctor: Mm] when she books me in, to (**the**) end, basically (**the**) delivery. She would hopefully deliver (**the**) baby if I wanted her to deliver it.
      Doctor: Mm.

B

1 See Observations in the unit.

2 See Observations in the unit.

C

1 a) He said his name was Paul McCartney. I knew he wasn't **the** Paul McCartney, but he was a good singer anyway.

   b) Airline official: How many bags are you checking in?
      Passenger: Just **the** one.

   c) Receptionist: So it's just one person then?
      Bill: No, no, it's for **the** two of us.
      Receptionist: Oh, I'm sorry. Right, two persons.

   d) The last time I saw her was three weeks ago. She was in England for one week. She phoned me on **the** Wednesday and we met on **the** Friday.

2 i) (c) People often think that other people's situation is better or more attractive than their own.

ii) (b) When the person in authority is not there, people will relax and/or take advantage!

iii) (a) People who plan ahead and are ready for something are successful in getting what they want.

Unit 17 Articles 2: *a*/*the*/no article

A

1 If the speaker limits something or specifies a particular set, then use *the*, as in (b).

2 If the speaker is referring to one example of a general class of things, then use *a*, as in (a).

3 If the speaker is referring to all and any examples of a general class of things, then use no article, as in (c).

B

1 a) *A/an* can be used with uncountables if the speaker or writer goes on to specify it in some way, often with a relative clause, or if the speaker means 'a type of …/kind of …'

A cheese (that) I like is Camembert.

b) i) *Chocolate* is the substance and *a chocolate* is one sweet.

ii) *Iron* is the metal and *an iron* is a utensil, which originally was made from iron, for smoothing clothes and linen.

iii) *Glass* is the substance and *a glass* is something you can drink from.

a) **a cloth**

b) (no article)

c) (no article)

d) **a paper**

e) **a wood**

f) (no article)

g) (no article)

h) **a chicken**

2 a) *a*   b) *the*   c) no article   d) no article

e) no article (but see Reference notes)   f) no article

C

1 a) i) Trevor: It's not a very big town anyway, it's only **a** hundred thousand people.

ii) Doris: It was full of garlic. David took **one** mouthful and shot out of the room!

iii) Assistant: They take **a** week.
Customer: **One** week, right, thanks very much.

iv) Francis: A hundred grams of flour to **one** egg, yeah, mixed up in the bowl.

b) See Observations in the unit.

2 See Observations in the unit.

Further exercises (Units 16 and 17)

1 a) I'll meet you at **the** university at three o'clock, outside room 26.
b) **The** dog needs to go to **the** vet. Can you take him?
c) When I got up, I noticed **the** car windscreen was covered in ice.

2 a) restaurant   b) job   c) cookery book/recipe/gadget
d) film/novel/play   e) accident/disaster/catastrophe/tragedy/event

3 a) I think ordinary people in Vietnam must have suffered terribly during (**the**) years of their war with America.
b) I feel very sorry for ( ) people who have to live in ( ) cities which they absolutely hate because they have no choice.
c) (**The**) role of ( ) computers in ( ) society will only be truly understood when ( ) historians look back on (**the**) end of the twentieth century.
d) ( ) Humans can never really understand what ( ) animals think and feel, or whether they experience ( ) pain and ( ) suffering in the same way that ( ) people do.
e) ( ) Children of ( ) single-parent families often suffer ( ) discrimination in ( ) countries where ( ) marriage is still considered essential.

4 'All ___ good books are alike in that they are truer than if they had really happened.'
'**A** worker is **the** slave of the capitalist society; **a** female worker is **the** slave of a slave.'
'**The** happiest women, like **the** happiest nations, have no history.'
'___ Non-violence is **the** first article of my faith.'
'___ Success is counted sweetest by those who ne'er succeed.'

5 **the** Internet ✓   e-mail ✗   **the** phone ✓   **the** press ✓
tennis ✗   **the** Olympic Games ✓   **the** crowd ✓   **the** world record ✓
the chef ✓   **the** menu ✓   **the** kitchen   breakfast ✗
the Prime Minister ✓   democracy ✗   **the** economy ✓   **the** state ✓

6 she needs **the** money; in **a** big shopping centre; **an** application form; **the** cinema; one day; on **the** telephone; **the** fact

7 a) Nora: It was a terrible week, wasn't it, d'you remember?
Marco: Yes, we had snow on **the** Monday and floods on **the** Thursday!
b) **The** more you study English, **the** harder it seems to get.

Unit 18 Complex noun phrases

A

1 (a) + (l) or (g)   (b) + (g) or (l)   (c) + (j)   (d) + (h)   (e) + (k)   (f) + (i)

B

1 a) Balamurali Ambati graduated <u>last week</u> from <u>the Mount Sinai School of Medicine in New York</u> at <u>the age of seventeen</u>. Dr Ambati, <u>a native of Vellore</u>, India, moved to

Buffalo, New York with <u>his family</u> when he was three. He was doing <u>calculus</u> at four. At eleven, he graduated from <u>high school</u> and co-authored <u>a research book</u> on AIDS with his <u>older brother Jaya</u>. He plays <u>chess, basketball</u> and <u>ping pong</u> and is just learning to drive.

b) Dar-es-Salaam, as capitals go, is <u>a new and fresh face on the holiday map</u> … <u>The shanties, bazaars and marshalling yards</u> have given way to <u>clean streets</u> and <u>plate-glass facades</u> … <u>Banks and insurance blocks</u> dominate <u>the skyline</u>, for <u>Dar-es-Salaam's monuments</u> are not to <u>the past</u> but to <u>present prosperity</u>.

c) I quite like living in Sheffield, I mean, there's <u>lots of good clubs</u> and <u>the sports facilities</u> are great, like <u>swimming baths</u>, most of them brand new, and there's <u>the Don Valley sports and athletics centre</u> … and you're only <u>twenty minutes away</u> from <u>the Peak District</u>, <u>one of the loveliest parts of England</u>, with <u>all kinds of walking, country pubs</u> and that …

- In all these examples the speakers are describing things. Overall there are more pre- than post-modified nouns.

- In the spoken example (c), the information is structured a little differently around the noun. In the written extracts (a) and (b), the nouns are pre-modified, with all the adjectives being placed in front of the noun. In (c) the adjectives more often come after the noun.

- The spoken example (c) is also different from the written examples (a) and (b) in that the information is built up in 'chunks'. It is interesting to compare written and spoken versions by taking the chunk: *the sports facilities are great … most of them brand new* and rewriting it in a typical written version of the same information: *most of the terrific brand new sports facilities.*

2 a) (given in text)

b) There's just so many things <u>that we've got to tell them about and that they've got to just sit down and listen to</u>.

c) A similar situation occurs in the region <u>of the Nile Basin where farmers are forced to use irrigation techniques in order to subsist.</u>

d) While we were on one of those Breton holidays, she swam so far out that she met the only other person <u>who could swim</u> who turned out to be an Austrian and that was the beginning <u>of our link with Austria</u> and the next day Emily went to Graz <u>where the woman lived</u> and your grandfather and I followed the next summer I think.

- (a) and (b) and (d) are likely to be from spoken contexts since the prepositions are in final position in the post-modifying clauses ('… so much about'/'…tell them about'/'listen to'). In more formal written contexts we might expect e.g. (a) 'That's the bit about which we don't tend to know quite so much'; or (b) '… things about which we've got to tell them and to which they've got to listen.' (c) contains a complex post-modifying clause typical of academic textbooks. The complex post-modifying structures in (a), (b) and (d) are typical of spoken conversational styles. See also Observations on p. 126.

C

1 See Observations and Summary in unit, especially p. 128.

2 In written English apposition is more likely to occur at the beginning of a clause; in spoken English apposition can occur in most positions within a clause but it is more likely to occur at the end of a clause of spoken utterance.

Further exercises

1 a) (given in unit)
Suggested answers:

b) i) The programme for the restoration of the inner cities penalises people.

ii) It penalises people least able to look after themselves.

iii) It penalises occupants of council houses.

iv) It penalises those who have not already received grants for repair.

2 Suggested headlines:

b) HEART FAILURE FOR WORLD'S YOUNGEST TRANSPLANT PATIENT

c) RAIL PAY CLAIM DISPUTE TO BE DECIDED

d) LUXURY HOLIDAY PROMISES BROKEN

e) ENGLAND FOOTBALLERS DETAINED ON NIGHT CLUB CHARGE

3 a) <u>interim share dividend</u>   b) <u>*One Fine Day*</u>   c) <u>Prince Charles</u>

d) <u>such as Sky Two</u>   e) <u>an apprentice welder; real money</u>

4 b) a motor car body repair kit   c) a crime prevention officer

d) a computer virus protection program   e) a car insurance certificate

5 a) The Georgian terraced family house has been imaginatively restored.
It has a fitted kitchen.
The kitchen leads to a spacious patio and vegetable garden.
The vegetable garden is 40 sq. ft.

b) Our home protection policies offer a full guarantee.
Our guarantee gives you your money back after fourteen days.
Our claims action line gives expert advice.

c) The sea is slow and black.
The sea is sloe black.
The sea is crow-black.
Fishing boats bob on the sea.

d) The Psion chairman, David Potter, made a statement.
The statement was bullish.
It sent shares to a new five year peak.
The peak was 374p.

■ Sentence (a) is taken from an estate agent's brochure. Sentence (b) is taken from an advertisement for an insurance company. Sentence (c) is taken from *Under Milk Wood*, a poetic play for voices by the Welsh poet Dylan Thomas. Sentence (d) is taken from the financial section of a major newspaper.

Unit 19 Prepositions

A

- These are all e-mails. (You may have thought that they were all letters, but they are are a little more direct than letters generally are, and two of them refer to previous messages.)
- 2 is formal and 1 is the least formal.

- a) 1 with   2 in   3 about   4 in

  b) 6 for   7 from   8 at   9 on   10 in

  c) 11 from   12 in   13 at   14 of   15 on/in*   16 from   17 to
      18 of   19 with   20 in/during   21 of

*On/in (on is generally preferred for any small island, e.g. 'She lives **in** Japan,' but 'She lives **on** the Isle of Skye').

B

1

Extract	Type A (physical location, time, relations between objects)	Type B (grammatically connected to another word in the clause)
a)	in warm water on edge in pots of moist seed compost into permanent pots on horizontal wires with a high potash food	in diameter (also used with 'circumference', 'radius') in late May (*in* is fixed with months of the year but remember '**at the end of the month**', and '**during the month**')
b)	in cold water in a towel in a spin drier on a towel on a table	
c)		in so much pain in constant pain insist on

- Extract (b) contains only basic uses. This is because the topic is a **physical** description.

2
  a) *with* + [x]
  b) thank [x] for [y]
  c) *at* + place
  d) *from time to time* is a fixed expression. (See **C** for more of these.)
  e) be + absent + *from*   *from* + place   *at present* is a fixed expression meaning *now*;
      on + specific date   *in* + place

C

1 a) i) What **for?**   ii) Where **from?**   iii) Who **to?** / Who **from?**

b)

wh-*question words*	*prepositions*
who ('whom' is also possible, but very formal in modern English. The preposition generally precedes 'whom': 'for whom?')	*for/to/from/with/by/about*
what	*for/in/on/about/from/with/at/by* (prepositions of place or direction (e.g. towards or around) are placed before the *wh-*word)
where	*from/to/(until)* until is used to ask about the place in a sequence of action: A: Replay the video. B: Where until? 'Until where?' would be more common
when	*for/from/at/by/(until)*
why	–
which	– (NB **all** prepositions can be placed before *which* (and *what*) to form a short question: 'to which?', 'in what?')
how	*for* (very colloquial, meaning 'why?')

2 a) from bad to worse   b) from start to finish   c) from time to time

d) in favour of   e) in charge of   f) in danger of

Further exercises

1 a) **from** America; **from** my friend; **in** America; **in** the letter
b) hear **from** you; quite a bit **of** today; **after** a real nightmare **of** a trip
c) rubbish **at** English.
d) part **of** the process; talking **to**

2 a) John: Have you got to call for a growbag tonight?
Ellen: Well I was going to get them tomorrow. Haven't got any money tonight.
John: Eh?
Ellen: I'll go and get them tomorrow.
John: We could go up and get one. I want three er 'Moneymaker' or 'Alicante' tomato plants.
Ellen: Where from?
John: Cutler's have got 'em.
Ellen: Have they? Oh all right then. Well, do you want me to call on the way?
John: Yeah.

b) Andrew: Do you live round here?
   Brian: Yeah I, no I'm here visiting you know for a while.
   Andrew: Where from?
   Brian: Well er originally I was from the south of England, from Somerset originally.
   Andrew: Somerset. That's where they make the er cider.
   Brian: Cider apples. Yeah.

3 a)

expression	meaning
from day to day	on different days
from place to place	in different locations
from strength to strength	improving
from bad to worse	deteriorating
from time to time	occasionally
from start to finish	throughout

b)

expression	meaning
in excess of	more than
in place of	instead of
by way of	as
by means of	with/using
on behalf of	in someone's place

Unit 20 Direct and indirect speech

A

1 See Observations in unit.

2 a) (given in text)
   b) When a *yes/no* question is reported indirectly, we use *if* or *whether*.
   c) When a *wh*-question is reported indirectly, we use the normal word order of a statement, not question word order.
   d) Normally, when a reporting verb interrupts the speech quoted, it is put at the beginning (or sometimes at the end) of the indirect report. Also, discourse markers such as 'you know', 'you see', 'well', etc. are omitted from the indirect report.
   e) *Will* becomes *would*. 'I hope' moves to the beginning of the indirect report, and the question-tag 'won't you?' is omitted.

Note that these rules apply to formal written texts. As we shall see, informal spoken language is much more flexible.

B

a) She then uttered a loud shriek, and exclaimed that he was down.
b) Ivanhoe asked who was down.
c) Rebecca answered that it was the Black Knight.
d) Ivanhoe exclaimed that it was Front-de-Boeuf.
e) Ivanhoe asked who were yielding and who were pushing their way.

f) Rebecca replied that the ladders were thrown down.

g) Mary asked Dulcie what she would like to do that afternoon. Dulcie suggested that they went to bingo.

h) Dulcie asked Mary if the bingo would be starting soon. She couldn't see any chairs and tables. Mary agreed and said that they were in the wrong place.

C

1 In (a) the news Tom is reporting is much more important than Brian's actual words. Using the continuous form takes away the focus from the words themselves. (b) and (c) are exactly the same: the speakers are starting new and important topics, rather than reporting someone's words.

2 Possible original words and direct speech reports:
a) 'Will you do this job?' he/she/they/asked me. (typical formal, written)
He/She/They said, 'Will you do this job?' (typical informal, spoken)
b) 'Will you do some GCSE English next term?' he/she/they asked me. (typical informal, spoken)
He/She/They said, 'Will you do some GCSE English next term?' (typical informal, spoken)
c) 'Will you do it?' he/she/they asked me. (typical formal, written)
He/She/They said, 'Will you do it?' (typical informal, spoken)

3 a) 'Who should I address the letter to?' I asked.
b) 'What are the arrangements?' I asked.
c) 'How do you get there?' I asked.

Further exercises

1 Possible answers:
a) She **asked**, 'What time are you all leaving?'
b) 'Help! Help!' he **shouted/cried**, 'I'm stuck! Pull me out!'
c) 'Is it possible they've disconnected the phone?' she **asked/enquired**.
d) 'I don't believe it!' he **exclaimed**.
e) 'Arggh! It's a rat! Take it away!' he **shrieked/shouted/cried**.

2 Suggested answers:
a) Here, the **actual words** of the original speaker are emphasised, so the past simple would be most natural, not the past continuous.
b) Here, the emphasis is on the news or new topic, not on Fred's actual words, so *Fred was telling me* would sound most natural.
c) With the emphasis on the topic rather than people's actual words, the past continuous is quite natural here for both **say** and **tell**.
d) Joe wants to remind Lisa of his words to her on an earlier occasion, so the most natural form is the past simple.
e) Ali can use *was asking* because he is raising a new topic: Brian uses *told* because he wants to emphasise what he actually said to Jill.

3 a) 'Would you be interested in working for me?' ('Might you' is also possible but would sound more distant and formal.) We could say 'I wonder/wondered/was wondering if/whether you would be interested in working for me?'

b) 'Will you / Would you be prepared to sit on the committee?'

c) 'I was/got rung up by someone trying to sell me car insurance at eight o'clock in the morning.'

d) 'Come and give me a hand! You are useless, you are!'

e) 'The kids are making a lot of noise.'

4 a) 'We shall never increase taxes unless it is absolutely necessary,' the Prime Minister promised/pledged.

b) Film star Gloria Fox said/stated, 'I have not been asked to play Juliet in the new film.'

c) Footballer Joss Konran commented, 'Someone asked me recently why I don't go abroad and earn more money. The answer is I want to play for my own country.'

Note: *said* would be possible in all three reports, and the reporting verbs could come before or after the words reported.

Unit 21 Tails (post-posed elements of clauses)

A

1 a) Max was   b) that   c) I am; chilli sauce is

- Conversation (d) is the most formal. A suggested more informal version is:

  A: It's a very nice road that.
  B: It runs right across the moors, it does.
  A: Then it goes through all those lovely little villages.
  B: Yes, they're beautiful, the villages are.

Note: It would be unusual if tails occurred in every utterance.

2 i) (a) F (b) I   ii) (a) I (b) F   iii) (a) I (b) F   iv) (a) I (b) F

v) (a) I (b) F   vi) (a) F (b) I   vii) (a) I (b) F   viii) (a) I (b) F

B

1 See Observations in unit.

2 Tails come at the end of the clauses they relate back to.
They consist of either a single noun (*spaghetti*), noun phrase (*the ice-cream*), pronoun + verb (*it would*) or verb + noun (*hasn't Maria*).

(See the Observations in the unit for further details. C also deals further with the structural possibilities of tails.)

C

1 Most of the sentences express some kind of attitude/opinion, with the possible exceptions of (a), (f), (h) and (j).

a) It'll surely melt, won't it, <u>the ice-cream</u>?

b) It's a nice garden for growing vegetables <u>that of yours</u>.

c) She's a lovely singer <u>Kay</u>.

d) They do take up a lot of time, I suppose, <u>kids,</u> don't they?

e) It can leave you feeling very weak, <u>it can, though, apparently, shingles</u>.

f) I'm going to have Mississippi mud pie <u>I am</u>.

g) It's really cold <u>this wind</u> isn't it?

h) Look how far that comes out <u>that bit of wood</u>.

i) You wonder if it's ever going to stop <u>this rain</u>.

j) It's normally only made of plastic <u>that sort of stuff</u>.

2 a) (in text)   b) you are   c) I am   d) it would   e) it (this) (that) is

(If *this* or *that* are used, *is* is optional.)   f) they do

g) are computers / computers are / they are   h) it would

i) Carol has / she has   j) you have   k) they do

3 See Observations in unit.

D

a) A: Here's the menu. What do you fancy?

B: It's certainly a nice menu this is.

A: I'm going to have steak and chips I am.

B: I fancy the spaghetti but I always manage to drop it down the front of my shirt, I do.

b) A: I like them. They make a nice couple, David and Jean.

B: Do you reckon they'll get married eventually?

A: David is still lacking in confidence and she's a bit too young is Jean isn't she?

c) A: She'll never lose weight, Sophie won't.

B: She hardly ever eats cakes or chips she doesn't.

A: I should eat less I should. I'm far too flabby I am.

Further exercises

1 a) (done in text)   b) David is   c) Alison does   d) REM are   e) Carl does

f) migraine does   g) Claire is   h) Fortuna is   i) London is

Note: In all examples the tail could take different forms. E.g. in (a) the tail could be
Shadows, Shadows is, or *is Shadows*.

2 Suggested points for adding tails:
*I was really cross with Jeff **I was**.*
*It was really dark **it was**.*
*He'd come after me to apologise **he had**.*

Note: Tails should not be overused, otherwise everything becomes highlighted and
emphasised. A tail could be inserted after most of the sentences in the narrative in **2**
but, if they were, emphasis could not be achieved.

3 a) (done in text)

b) The one with the picture on the front, that was the book I wanted.

c) Walking into that place, it was a strange feeling.

d) Those countries where it's all humid, they're far too hot.

Unit 22 Heads (pre-posed elements of clauses)

A

1 The third lines of the exchange are more informal, interactive and are sensitive to the listener. (In each case the subject noun phrase is followed by a pronoun which refers back to the noun phrase. The head emphasises things for the listener and makes sure the listener can follow what is referred to. In written English heads are not normally used because the reader has more time to read and understand the sentence.)

- A more formal grammatical choice for each third line would be:
  a) A city like London is not very safe at night.
  b) Most places in Ireland are really quite cheap.
  c) The teacher with glasses seems very nice.
  d) All the people in the audience started crying when the dog died.

2 a) Do they live in that house on the corner?
b) Is the girl who drives the Ford his sister?
c) Is that black jacket yours?
d) Did you say the shop by the traffic lights that's open until nine has gone out of business?

B

1 See Observations in the unit.

2 Suggested answers:
a) wife   b) husband   c) boyfriend   d) family   e) he   f) her sister

- All the heads are different from the subjects which follow them, apart from (e).

C

1 The following are fronted:
a) This friend of ours
b) Madge, one of the secretaries at work
c) Brian
d) The chap in Cardiff I bought the car from
e) His cousin in London, her boyfriend

- In each of these cases the fronted items are different from the item being introduced, whereas in **A1** they are the same.
- Speakers often introduce a person into the conversation in this way to link the new character to one already known by the listener.

2 a) that time on the way back from Hong Kong
b) just the milk, the flour and two eggs
c) an old country proverb
d) a man in a pub with a parrot on his shoulder; the parrot

- The speakers focus on the topic in this way to set the scene for the listener (as in (a) and (d)), or provide a 'menu' of items which will be discussed, (b), or the genre, (c) – in this case a proverb.

Further exercises

1 a) (done in text)
    b) (done in text)
    c) The man with the T-shirt
    d) The girl with the brown eyes and dark hair
    e) That big house in front of the park
    f) The boy who drives the VW
    g) The trainers with the red stripe
    h) Pizzas

2 a) Most castles in Spain, they're really impressive.
    b) The English football team, they're always losing.
    c) That laptop computer, it's very reliable.
    d) That boy with the dark, curly hair, is he a friend of yours?
    e) That house with the large garden, do they live there?
    f) The very fast red cabriolet sports car, he owns it.
    g) Montpellier, it's a city with lots of old buildings in the centre.
    h) Supermarkets which sell fresh bread, they're very popular.
    i) The girl with brown hair and glasses, is she his sister?
    j) Most Australian wines, they're not expensive.

3 Possible answers:
    a) **Our new neighbour**, he seems very nice.
    b) **Tokyo**, it's too crowded for me.
    c) **Going for long walks, playing with the kids**, I like that kind of thing on Sundays.

4 a) The files about the yearly results, they are ready. / What are ready are the files about the yearly results.
    b) That software you wanted to see, I've brought it. / What I've brought is that software you wanted to see.
    c) The figures for March, they are terrible. / What are terrible are the figures for March.
    d) Mr Brown, his secretary, her sister from Australia is coming to work here. / Who is coming to work here is Mr Brown's secretary's sister from Australia. (Note: The second version would be very unlikely in speech, because it would be very difficult to understand! It is, however, possible in writing)

Unit 23 Ellipsis 1: at the start of clauses

A

1 a) Jim: And I came over by Mistham. I came by the reservoirs.
       Ken: Oh, you came by Mistham. You came over the top. It is a nice route.
       Jim: The colours are pleasant, aren't they?
       Ken: Yes.
       Jim: That is a nice run.

    b) Matt: Are you late?
       Roman: Yes, I'm really late.
       Matt: What time's the film start?

Roman: It starts at seven-thirty.

Matt: You've got half-an-hour.

Roman: Is there any chance of a lift in your car?

c) A: I didn't know you used boiling water.

B: They reckon it's quicker.

2 See Observations in the unit.

B

1 a) **do you** (want); **Would you** (like)   b) **There was** (nobody at home).

c) **Have you** (seen)   d) **Have you** (heard)

- All these are auxiliary verbs and pronouns, apart from *There was*. When *there* is used in this way, it is known as a dummy subject. It is often omitted in casual conversation.

2 a) *What was it? Renault?* (*a* is ellipted, and later there is the repetition *What was it? A Renault?* when the garage man is pressing for an answer)

b) *I didn't know that* becomes *Didn't know that*.

- In each case the speaker uses ellipsis when they are not expecting the listener to need an explanation, or for the item to be strongly focused on.

3 Ellipsis occurs at the beginning of each sentence. The subject and verb are ellipted; if replaced, they would be: *They/these are* (sentence 1), *They consist of* (sentence 2), *They/The eggs contain* (sentence 3), *They are made of* (sentence 4) and *They are* (sentence 5). The text is a consumer report written in the form of notes rather than as a formal report.

C

1 a) Ann: I like it. I'm very happy there, I must say.

Tom: It makes (It's) a bit of a change from London, I suppose.

b) Phil: Yeah, I think so. It rings a bell.

c) Mary: I sat on a bench there and honestly, I've (I have) never seen so many people.

d) David: It happened right in front of the police station.

e) Cath: It's a bit dangerous there, isn't it?

f) Helen: That (It) sounds good.

g) Jean: Yes, it's been far too cold for him.

2 See Observations in the unit.

Unit 24 Ellipsis 2: later in the clause

A

1 'I'm off,' she said.

'Don't go,' I said.

'I must <u>go</u>,' she said.

'Where <u>are you going</u> to?' I said.

'<u>I'm</u> not <u>going</u> far,' she said.

'Let's talk,' I said.
'There's no time,' she said.
'Is there someone else?' I said.
'I'm afraid so,' she said.
'I thought so,' I said.
'Can you guess who it is?' she said.
'Don't say who it is,' I said.
'I must say who it is,' she said.
'OK,' I said.
'It's your friend,' she said.
'It's my Vauxhall Astra!' I said.
'You knew who it was,' she said.

Note: When the ellipsis involves an auxiliary verb and a main verb, the main verb can be
left out (for example, 'I must' for 'I must go'). The auxiliary verb is not ellipted.
See **B1**.

2 Three possible questions:
Has it got power steering?   Does it take unleaded fuel?   Can it go very fast?

Notice that the answers in the advertisement all involve an auxiliary and a main verb and
that ellipsis occurs when the main verb is left out. We should note that the subject is also
kept with the auxiliary verb.

B

1 a) See Observations in the unit.
b) Answer (b) is the most natural in both cases. Answer (a) is not correct in either case.

2 See Observations in the unit.

C

1 a) informal   b) informal   c) formal
d) incorrect: correct answer *I'd like to.*   e) formal
f) incorrect: correct answer 'Yes, in front of it.'

2 See Observations in the unit.

Further exercises (Units 23 and 24)

1 Here are the dialogues with the crossed-out words removed:
a) A: Seen Roger at all this morning?
B: No, haven't seen him since yesterday.
A: Wonder where he is.
B: Yes, strange he hasn't come.

b) A: Veronica leave a letter for me?
B: Think so. Saw it here somewhere.
A: Doesn't matter. I'll come back later.

c) A: Did you go out with Beryl after all?

B: Yeah, didn't really want to. Just felt I had to really. Sorry I did now.

Note: There is normally no ellipsis of the subject with *will, 'll* and *shall*.

2 Words which have been added are in bold.

a) A: **Do you** know anyone who does translations?

B: **It's** funny you should say that. **I** met a man just the other day. **He said** he was setting up an agency.

A: **They** don't do Chinese to English by any chance, do they?

B: I wouldn't have a clue. **I** could give you his number, if you like. **I've** got it here somewhere.

b) A: **Are** you going to do that exam after all?

B: I suppose so. **The** trouble is, **I** just can't be bothered studying for it.

A: Why should you **study for it**? No-one else seems to be working. Why don't you just do it?

B: I could do I suppose.

3 Words which need to be added are in bold.

a) A: Have you heard from Raj lately?

B: Yeah. I got a letter **the** other day.

A: Really? What **did** he say?

B: He wants me to come to India for a holiday.

A: Great. You going?

B: I'm thinking about it. I'd like **to**, but it costs a fortune.

A: Well, better start saving. Go for it. I would.

4 no time; 'Fraid so; Thought so; I must

5 a) A: Ready yet?

B: Yes, OK.

A: How far is it to the station?

B: About ten minutes.

A: Next to that supermarket, isn't it?

B: Think so.

A: We're going to be late.

B: Doesn't matter.

b) A: Like a coffee?

B: Yes, please.

A: Sugar?

B: Yes. Two, please.

c) A: Like to go out tonight?

B: Love to. Anywhere in mind?

d) A: Think the school's over there on the left.

B: Yes, on the left.

A: Wonder if we'll enjoy the concert.

B: I hope so.

6 i) I hope so   ii) I want to   iii) I asked him to   iv) I'd love to

7 Maria: Why don't you come with us tonight?
Bob: Where to?
Maria: Oh, just for a meal. Come with us.
Bob: Mm, well …
Maria: Wouldn't you like to?
Bob: I want to, I mean, I'd like to … but …
Maria: Why don't you come then? (or: Why not then?)
Bob: No money.
Maria: Spent it all?
Bob: Afraid so.
Maria: What did you buy?
Bob: Oh, nothing special.
Maria: I could lend you some.
Bob: Would you? Thanks.
Maria: No problem. You should have said.
Bob: Yes, maybe I should have.

Unit 25 Discourse markers

A

1 a) first (i)   then (ii)   hopefully (iv)   but (ii)   actually (iv)
b) then (i)   however (iii)   rather (iii)   it follows that (i)
c) good (ii) and (iv)   OK (ii)   so (ii)   right (i)

2 Well, I mean and I mean.

- These are discourse markers which signal that the speaker is preparing to comment. The markers also create a little time and space for the speaker. The listener sees them as a kind of preface and waits for the details.

B

1 a) right (lines 1, 4, 7, 11); so (line 5); you know (lines 5, 10); 'cos (line 6); okay (line 11)

- right (i) and (ii); so (ii); you know (i); 'cos (ii); okay (ii)

Note: *'cos* is a shortened form of *because*. In spoken English *'cos* often marks a justification for a previous statement; in written English *because* links a relationship of cause and effect.

b) well (lines 1 and 8); I mean (lines 1 and 12); you know (lines 1, 2 and 4); I think (lines 1 and 8); I don't know (line 8); but (lines 2 and 5)

- well (ii); I mean (ii); you know (i); I think (i) and (ii); I don't know (i) and (ii); but (ii).

2 [rewritten dialogue]
Gill: It's all under control.
Seamus: It's actioned.
Gill: Um when are you going to start handling reprints? I need some advice about reprints for *Changes*.

Mac: It would take me about three months to get an angle on it but I'm not getting it until June.

Seamus: Linda's coming in in June yeah.

Mac: Until June.

The absence of discourse markers here makes the conversation sound rather cold and impersonal.

- 'There's something I wanted to ask you', is a marker of politeness which also signals that the question which will follow is important.
- Similar discourse markers, which are clauses rather than words or phrases, include:
  'As I was saying/as I say …'
  'The other thing I wanted to ask you was …'
  'Could I just come in here to say …'
  'Going back to what we were saying earlier …'

These discourse markers all signal that a statement which has been made already, or which is about to be made is important. In **B2** the question which follows is signalled as important.

C

1 See Observations in the unit.

2 See Observations in the unit.

Further exercises

1 a) Well   b) Right   c) I mean   d) 'cos

2 Suggested answers:
a) So   b) What's more   c) So   d) But   e) You know what I mean

3 This is from the end of a conversation. It is typical for speakers to use these kinds of markers as they close an interaction. *Anyway* signals that Carol wants to go, and *Right* suggests that she thinks the conversation has finished. *Well you know* might mean that Frances has another point to make, but she responds to Carol's *Right,* with *Okay, then,* showing they can finish. The final *Okay* and *Good* show that they are both comfortable finishing the conversation. The whole exchange would take a couple of seconds.

Index